THE TRUMPET OF GABRIEL

By Michael H. Brown

FAITH PUBLISHING COMPANY
P.O. BOX 237
MILFORD, OHIO 45150

The publisher does not endorse the claims of any purported visionary and recognizes and accepts that the final authority regarding
all claimed apparitions within the Catholic Church rests with the
Holy See of Rome, to whose judgment we willingly submit.

Published by Faith Publishing Company.

For additional copies, bookstores and book distributors should
contact:
Faith Publishing Co.
P.O. Box 237
Milford, OH 45150
513-576-6400

Individuals requesting copies of this book should contact:
The Riehle Foundation
P.O. Box 7
Milford, OH 45150
513-576-0032

Published in the United States.

Cover by: Pete Massari
          Rockford, Illinois

Table of Contents

For Lisa, who endured an extreme schedule
in the first year of marriage.

"After these things I saw another angel coming down from Heaven, having great authority, and the earth was illuminated with his glory. And he cried mightily with a loud voice, saying, 'Babylon the great is fallen, is fallen. . .'"
—The Book of Revelation (KJV 18:1-2)

CHAPTER 1

The World Will
Never Be The Same

In Nepal a large cross-shaped cloud is reported by a Methodist evangelist. It changes from a cloud into a fire and suddenly an image of the Lord appears on a flaming cross. The entire village of Taksen watches it for two hours.

From the former U.S.S.R. come reports of supernatural lights—heavenly luminosity—seen by thousands.

In Africa, Jesus appears in dreams to dozens of non-Christian villagers.

In New York, a Jewish sect prepares for arrival of their messiah and reports similar spiritual phenomena.

In Kibeho, Rwanda, Christ appears to a young pagan on the way home from picking beans. The Lord is surrounded by a bright light. He tells the young farmer to pray from the heart and says that time is short.

In Bosnia-Hercegovina, holy visions hint at the coming war and its hideous atrocities.

In hundreds of American hospital wards, patients see great beings of light during "near-death" experiences. They are given insights into the hereafter—the future both in Heaven and on earth.

In South America, a Canadian bishop is healed of a gaping shoulder wound after he is prayed over by an aristocratic woman who exudes the aroma of roses. Her phenomena are attested to by businessmen, medical doctors, and an army general. It is, she says, the "hour of decision for humanity."

In Tennessee, a series of supernatural lights come to the assistance of a Baptist scuba diver who is trapped in an underwater cave. The diver is likewise given a dramatic "message" for mankind.

From all parts of the world, especially the West, come an avalanche of angel sightings. They appear as spirits of light, fleet and airy, or as spirit helpers in the flesh—mysterious strangers. Some arrive with swords, others with soft-spoken advice. And they are featured everywhere: on night-time radio, on a network special, and in news magazines. They too have a message; indeed, the word "angel" means "messenger."

Across all borders, across all denominations, into every sect, in all socioeconomic ranks, are signs of the supernatural. Some are figments of the subconscious. Some are spiritual deceptions. Some are part of our cultural mythology and illusionary thinking.

But a number possess the ring of truth, and they indicate that God is ready to renew the earth. He is sending His forces. He is intervening! After decades of lust, crime, war, repression, doubt, atheism, division, depravity, drugs, idolatry, and general godlessness—after decades of immersion into materialism and the occult—He is now lifting a finger in a way that will be felt by everyone.

A glorious change is on the horizon. Humankind will soon more fully recognize the supernatural dimension. We will conduct our lives from a different point of view, looking upward, looking for heavenly guidance, instead of relying on our own limited cerebration. God will be worshipped as in ancient times. We will see His hand in natural and societal events. We will pay more attention to harvests, shortages, and weather patterns, just as older and wiser civilizations did. We'll pay more attention to the timing and circumstance of wars and calamities. And we'll understand why certain storms strike at centers of occultism while earthquakes like the one in Los Angeles rattle the pornography industry.

We are in special times. A "high-point event" is about

to occur. God is moving His Hand. He is interceding. Around Israel, Arabs in the occupied territories encounter an astounding array of Christian phenomena, including bilocation and baptism in the Spirit, while across the Mediterranean, in Italy, a group of children playing in a square encounter a struggle between demons and Godly forces. The devils materialize and are defeated! In Indianapolis, a non-denominational charismatic claims to see a manifestation of Christ with beard, which materializes on his bedroom ceiling. In Costa Rica, a woman in distress sees a towering presence of the Archangel Michael. The vision is followed by a miracle. Across America come strange tales of "vanishing hitch-hikers." In Nebraska, a nun is given interpretations of *Revelation* by a radiant, beautiful man who vanishes when she comes out of a store. In Tennessee, a chemist is given passages from Scripture by an old man who then drives off in a truck—and similarly disappears.

Are these reports real?

More to the point, are they good? Are they of God?

That is for your personal discernment. We must all pray about it. We must all ask the Lord. We must always be wary of deception. Lucifer can come, of course, as "an angel of light" (*2 Corinthians* 11:14). Even the most well-intentioned can be deceived. But we do know this: some of the reports have the ring of truth. Spirits from both realms, good and evil, are visibly manifesting. It's a fascinating and dangerous time. It's an age of wonderment. It's a time to prepare for the coming transformation.

For soon, the world will be a different place. We are on the verge of renewal. We are on the brink of yet greater miracles. Signs of the times are everywhere. Our era is ending. Earth will be a better place. It will be more like what God originally intended.

But before that happens, before the glory, certain events will occur to break down our evil and end the high reign of Lucifer. We are approaching the conclusion of a satanic era and during the coming years (between now and 2040 perhaps), we must be ready for the Glory of God as few of us have ever known it. It's a great time to be alive and yet also a trying time. That's why I write for all God's children. There is no more time for Christians to carp at each other. We must find common ground. We must unite. The wolf is at our door. His "angels" are also manifesting. We see them in satanic ritual abuse, claimed UFO abductions, and multiple personality. We see them when a rock musician puts a gun to his head and our movie "stars" turn to witchcraft.

"Demonic activity and Satan worship are on the increase in all parts of the world," says Billy Graham. "The devil is alive and more at work than at any other time. The Bible says that since he realizes his time is short, his activity will increase. Through his demonic influences he does succeed in turning many away from the true faith; but we can still say that his evil activities are countered for the people of God by His ministering spirits, the holy ones of the angelic order. They are vigorous in delivering the heirs of salvation from the stratagems of evil men. They cannot fail."

God's angels are on the scene! They are tall and short, winged or without wings, slender or chunky; eyes of flame. They come not to dazzle but as another sign of the times. That's why we'll be looking at them.

But this is not an "angel book." Other authors have quite capably compiled such accounts. What I seek is to take such accounts and situate them in a larger context. That context involves the Holy Spirit, for angelic phenomena are only part of the larger supernatural intervention. The intervention is occurring across all denominations. The Spirit and His ministering agents are appearing according to our particular acculturation or systems of belief. Around the globe, across the continents, on farms and in the inner cities, the spiritual world is on the move and gaining momentum. Some of the experiences reek of deception, sending us into frenzied prophecy, and some are aberrations of the subconscious, an artifact of fantasy. But a significant measure of the phenomena, in my opinion, may be of a divine origin. The Lord has always been generous with His wonders, and He always warns us through prophecy. *"Surely the Lord God does nothing, unless He reveals His secret to His servants the prophets,"* says *Amos* 3:7. We are constantly told that while we should not be obsessed with the future, nor seek after too many signs (*Matthew* 12:39), neither should we ignore the heavenlies.

And what the heavenlies are saying is that we are in a special period. Great and perhaps awesome events are coming. We are approaching not just the end of a *period* but the end of an *age*. Our era is winding down to a close, and one day soon the world will be different from what it is today. While there may be painful events, even cataclysms, leading up to that change, the end result will be glorious—like the clean air after a summer rain.

I call it "the Purification" and "the Awakening." Soon, God will once more be honored by the masses and in an active fashion. There will be worldwide evangelization. We will feel the Spirit as never before. Those who are afflicted with troublesome marriages, or are chronically lonely, or addicted and obsessed, or suffering from emotional and physical ailments, will receive special help as the Lord manifests in a special way.

From all indications we are on the verge of a major manifestation. Babylon is still rising but soon will fall, this time, we hope, permanently. I'm not speaking about the end of the world, nor about the Final Coming, but of a manifestation that in some unfathomable manner will touch all our lives in the coming decades.

Perhaps it will come almost imperceptibly. Perhaps the change will be gradual. But perhaps it will come as a global event, with a cosmic array.

However it arrives, God will take the place of materialism and the era of mechanical naturalism, the epoch of godless intellectualism, which has been with us since the late 1700s, will finally and gladly end. The Lord is coming to bring us back to our senses. He is coming to heal the wounds inflicted by Satan. That is the essence of the intervention, to break down evil and expand our spiritual perception. Soon, we will no longer view the world in only three dimensions. We will no longer look upon our reality as quite so limited and material. It will be the end of the "earth-is-all" deception, which historically is the essence of witchcraft, secular humanism, and atheism.

It will be the end of the "New Age." It will be the end of the fanatical scientism that has warped our views of reality and caused entire societies to live only for the physical world. In so doing, in lifting our eyes to the spirit world, it will greatly diminish sin. It will spell the end of our rampant pride and sensuality. It will diminish crime. It will spell *finis* for many pornographers and child abusers. It will break down our pretenses and create a renewed Church. It will be good news for preachers and bad news for Hollywood.

Does that all sound like wishful thinking? The cravings of a religious zealot?

If but a fraction of reports are true, then it is not wishful thinking but revelation. It is what the Holy Spirit has arrived to accomplish. It is renewal. It is biblical. It is a getting-back to our faith. It is seeing earth for what it is: a temporary place where we are tested and tested long and hard before we are allowed progression into another dimension called the afterlife.

The change of era will include a period of Warning, which has already begun; the Purification (or judgment) of societies, which hovers in the near future; the Manifestation, a special sense of heavenly presence; and finally the Awakening, which will renew not just the Church but the entire planet.

Already, events are unfolding, events that lead up to the Purification. It remains unclear whether most such events will be earthly or spiritual. We hear such talk everywhere, from Pat Robertson to EWTN. The world will not end. It will *transform*. We are approaching a major change of era. We are also approaching the end of a period *within* that age in which Satan has been exerting extended power. While I believe we are in what may be called "apocalyptic" times, I *don't* believe we are approaching the Final Judgment. I doubt we are ready to encounter an event that will pulverize earth and disperse its fragments.

No, it is not the end, but a new beginning. Satan's power is about to be broken. Soon, the devil's influence, so pervasive right now, will be substantially dissipated. It remains unclear whether these events will take place over a period of months, years, or decades. What *is* clear is that it will be the end of agnostic modernism. It will be the end of depersonalization. It will be the end of societal aloofness, an aloofness that has turned countries such as America into cold and secular wastelands.

It has been the Period of the Spirit of Anti-Christ, and it has been symbolized best by miniature antichrists such as Marx, Hitler, Stalin, Mao, Sanger, and Lenin. This began around the time of the French Revolution, evolving into Communism and scientific atheism. It is now using its last reserve of energy.

But before the age ends—between now and the next several decades—another evil force will arrive. The battle will rage as never before. There will be at least one more "anti-christ" personality, and he may come fairly soon. He will be in league with the demons who have now taken full flight in the air around us. We see these devils in the divorce rate, the abortion rate, and in the rate of theft and homicide. We see them in political corruption, RU-486, and euthanasia. We see them on MTV (with its often macabre rock videos), and we see them in the rise of occult practices, including Satanism. We gauge an extraordinary level of evil in any culture that welcomes the condom but forbids the crucifix.

As evil has risen in our midst, however, so has the presence of heavenly entities. As devils multiply around us, so do the good spirits sent to help and protect us. At the same time there has been an *ascent* of demons from their pit, so too has there been a *descent* of the angels.

They are right now descending. They are right now coming at an hour of great need. They are right now available to all of us, through the great grace of God, and only through Him.

They bring a light that, however subtle, is now splitting the great darkness.

They give us encouragement. They grant us inspiration. They hover in our midst and form circles of protection. They feed us positive thoughts. They console us at times of trial or grief. They come especially at critical moments in history. And that is what we are approaching today: a most critical time.

Our age, and all that constitutes our age, is winding down to an as yet uncertain finale. The denouement may be witnessed within the lifetimes of some of you reading this chapter. While we must be careful interpreting Scripture, we seem currently to be progressing from the first to the second half of *Revelation* 12. The warring angels are here. They are arriving with Michael (*Revelation* 12:7). They are coming to help us turn a cosmic corner. They've come to put to run the omnipresent demons.

They come to save lives. I know this from personal experience, as you will see in the third chapter.

In previous books I spoke about mystical prophecies in these waning days of our era *(The Final Hour)* and about the spiritual warfare attendant to such a change of era *(Prayer of the Warrior).* I would now like to make it a trilogy by placing into perspective the next great stage: descent of the heavenlies. Those of you who have read my previous books will note a number of supernatural accounts that are repeated here. This was done for those from other Christian denominations who are first-time readers. Please also note that I do not endorse the more sensational and pessimistic prophecies. While I remain an optimist—believing mankind will come around and that the future can be yet turned bright—I try to be a realist who includes the bad with the good. To ignore the serious nature of our times is not something I want to be accused of doing. It is precisely the danger we are in that has caused angels to move more noticeably among us.

They are descending in Russia, they are descending in Washington, they are descending in blood-soaked Rwanda and Bosnia—both of which experienced supernatural episodes just before major events began to unfold in those countries. They are witnessed in the dark depths of Zaire and the heights of the Himalayas. They are a sign of our times and they fit with the little warnings that we will investigate: the tremors and earthquakes, the typhoons and tidal surges, the hurricanes and societal upheaval, including war, that serve as heavenly omens and are occurring with quickening frequency.

Right now we are being warned. We are being warned that if we don't turn back to God He will send us trends and events that will break down our modernistic arrogance. He will do this by simply withdrawing His protective and bonding force, leaving us to our own devices—and to hostile forces—until we acknowledge our mistakes. This is known as "chastisement" or "purification." And it isn't gloom and doom. It's never gloom when the Lord is at work breaking down evil.

In a small way it has already begun. How does the Lord warn us? Here are the facts: According to the *Associated Press,* five of the ten costliest disasters in all of U.S. history have occurred since 1989. That figure, which adjusts for inflation, does not include the more recent earthquake in Los Angeles, which caused more than $10 billion damage and, by my reckoning, would mean that six of the top ten disasters have occurred in the past half a dozen years. This is another sign of the times. Six of the top ten since 1989 and four of the top ten since 1992, in a period of just three years! Many religious leaders believe, as evangelist Pat Robertson says, that "the millennium is a transition period, when Jesus Christ comes back to earth to show mankind what it would have been like if sin had never entered the world. It will be a time when Jesus Christ will reign as king, and the Kingdom of God will be established on earth."

While there may be questions about millenniarism, and while experts differ on the "Second Coming" and dispensationalism, I do believe we are on the verge of what I prefer to call a major *manifestation*. There's a way in which every period is special going in some direction, but the special note of our time is that we are in the age of the Holy Spirit. This is a special era with a special intervention of the Paraclete. As Father Michael Scanlan, president of The Franciscan University of Steubenville and a graduate of Harvard Law, says, "I believe all of this is to prepare us for the new evangelization. I think with that as the goal and understanding, we can also absorb in the right way the kind of testing, chastisement, and purification which we're constantly being told through apparitions and through some prophetic leaders of our day is upon us. It depends on how much we repent or change before the climax arrives. There's some kind of high-point event that's going to happen."

Both Father Scanlan and Reverend Robertson would agree that our period of darkness will soon be purged and we will enter a new evangelization. The increased presence

of angels, says Scanlan, is only fitting as a counterbalance
to the upsurge of corruption, malevolence, and depravity.
God is trying to halt our race toward Babylon. As a Christian journalist I believe that many folks, especially charismatics, pentecostalists, old-school Baptists, evangelical
churches, and Marian Catholics, are receiving legitimate
words of knowledge. They are being instructed by the
thousands. So are certain Orthodox and Messianic Jews.
There are private revelations everywhere. Listen to one
such charismatic, Angie Ciccone, of Michigan: "We
prayed and asked the Lord to speak to us, and what He
said was that this night (January 1, 1994) was a very special
night in Heaven and that He was releasing myriads of
angels to the earth and that the whole earth was going to
be surrounded by myriads and myriads of angels. At that
point, right there at midnight, he had opened Heaven up.
I could see them. They were headed for the world, the
earth. He was sending them out to us to help us in the days
ahead. The Lord said He was sending these angels for the
times ahead, which means that we have already entered
into difficult times. We can't see angels—they're spirits—
but if they're coming to help us, they must be coming to
battle the evil spirits. Scripture tells us that we battle
powers and principalities, which are other levels of fallen
angels. So I think they have come to do battle because
Satan has stepped up his tactics in these latter days. It was
confirmed by another person who has been given the gift
of vision. She saw what I spoke—before I spoke it. I believe
angels are present now more than ever before in the history
of the world. There are all sizes. My friend saw Heaven
open up and the Lord ushering angels, pointing to earth
and saying, 'Go.'"

I realize that such experiences are tremendously subjective. God's time is often used in metaphor. But I also know
there is a spiritual realm and it is very active. Science and
the media do not see it because they don't *want* to see it.
To acknowledge the supernatural is to play by God's (as
opposed to *man's*) rules. Many are those who are highly
intellectual—greatly educated in the ways of the world—
and yet blind or illiterate when it comes to the larger realm
of spirituality. They want physical or "scientific" proof

and this is impossible when we are speaking about non-physical or "paraphysical" happenings. You cannot place a spirit under a microscope, nor can you see God from the Palomar Observatory.

Thus, I give mystical reports the benefit of the doubt. I start out as a believing Christian. This is the direct opposite of the media's approach, which is to treat such claims with amusement and cynicism.

Will I make mistakes? Of course I will. I already have. My discernment is not 100 percent, and sometimes there is chaff with the wheat.

But it is time to balance the equation. It is time to give God His due. It is time to heed the majority of Americans—69 percent—who believe in entities such as angels.

For too long we have ignored the supernatural because there is no scientific confirmation. The time has come to give supernaturalism, including revelation, a full airing. The time has come to listen to what our modern prophets in all denominations have to say. As it says in *Revelation* (19:10), *"the testimony of Jesus is the spirit of prophecy."* And the prophecy of our times is that we are entering a new era.

Soon the world as you know it will not be quite the same.

CHAPTER 2

Mysterious Strangers

God is telling us as much through signs and wonders, which should come as no surprise. Since the Garden of Eden, He and His agents have regularly communicated with humans. There has always been an overlap of the natural and supernatural, just as we are seeing today.

While most often the Lord speaks softly, hidden in nature, or whispering to our intuitions, there are heightened times when He speaks with heightened force. The Lord spoke to Adam. He *warned* Adam. He spoke to most of the key biblical figures, such as Noah, Moses, and Abraham. The first five books of the Old Testament, known as the *Pentateuch* (or "Torah"), are filled with heavenly locutions. The voice of God, while majestic and to the point, spans dozens of pages.

So do His marvels. Often these marvels are administered through or accompanied by the pure spirits known as angels. There are more than 300 instances in which the Bible directly or indirectly refers to angels, and the New Testament speaks of "an innumerable company" of them. They came to Abraham as mysterious strangers, and also to Joshua, who saw one near Jericho, an angel that was so humanlike—holding a sword—he thought it might be an enemy soldier.

The entire Bible attests to the supernatural, from the pillars of fire in Moses' time to the flaming wonders which appeared to Ezekiel. During the time of Christ there were also strange clouds and tongues of fire, especially after His Resurrection, when He sent the Holy Spirit. The presence of the Holy Spirit is almost always accompanied by the manifestations of angels. It was an angel who announced the birth of Jesus, and an angel who ministered to Him in the garden. At Christ's tomb angels took on visible appearances, including that of a young man (*Mark* 16:6).

Those wonders, those intersections of the natural with the supernatural, peaked with the greatest of all marvels, the corporeal (or "full-bodied") apparitions of Christ after His Resurrection. This set Christ apart from any previous or subsequent human. Just days after the horrible crucifixion—the tearing and pounding of His Body, the horrendous ridicule and sadism—a mighty earthquake announced the coming of an angel who with superhuman strength moved the stone from Christ's tomb. The angel was as a flash of lightning.

Soon Jesus was reunited with His disciples in Galilee. And during His third appearance, breaking bread with them after a catch of fish, He commissioned them to preach to all nations. When Jesus rose to Heaven—in what looked to human eyes like a cloud—two men dressed in white appeared on the scene. *"Men of Galilee,"* said these mysterious strangers, *"why do you stand here looking up at the skies? This Jesus who has been taken from you will return, just as you saw Him go up into the heavens"* (*Acts* 1:10-11).

The miracles continued through the early stage of the Church, just as Jesus and the angels promised. Certain Christians believe that the apostle James witnessed a supernatural manifestation at Zaragossa, Spain, sometime after A.D. 40, and that Peter experienced a vision or apparition of Christ near Rome, along the Appian Way. We know for a fact that Peter encountered an angel while in prison. The angelic being came in a display of light, shined a heavenly glow into his cell, whispered for Peter to prepare his escape (*"Arise quickly!"*), and helped him depart from the ancient jail (*Acts* 12:7). As Billy Graham said, "The empire of angels is as vast as God's creation. If you believe the Bible, you will believe in their ministry."

Although the charismatic gifts, such as prophecy, visions,

and speaking in tongues, began to fade after the first few centuries, never has the Holy Spirit left us without His presence. In the centuries since, countless saints have claimed to see Christ and His angels. An apparition of Christ is known as a "theophany." Other holy figures have similarly manifested, just as holy figures such as Elijah and Moses showed themselves in apparition during the transfiguration. While we have no idea how many were authentic, we do know that Christ's manifestations did not stop after the Resurrection, nor did mankind's sense that we are surrounded by a spiritual realm, both good and evil. From the apostles to Columbus, from the dynasties of China to the Indians of North America, and then the founders of our very nation, man has believed in the constant presence of spiritual agents. They have been depicted by the greatest artists—Rembrandt, Raphael, Michelangelo—through the centuries.

Let's leave it at this: Down through the ages, from the early Christian brethren to Francis of Assisi (in the Middle Ages), angels and other divine gifts have had their place in universal Christianity. Even George Washington is said to have experienced some sort of divine manifestation, and Lincoln's very countenance was mystical. This was most apparent in 1863 when he declared April 30 a day of "humiliation, fasting, and prayer." Like the cavemen who saw spiritual influences even in their hunting, like the biblical figures who heard the Voice of God not only in locutions and visions, not just in signs and wonders, but also in wars, storms, quakes, or plagues, so too did Lincoln recognize that the Lord is responsible both for the blatant miracles—the healings, the pillars of fire, the multiplication of loaves—and for those infinite hidden miracles which hold together the cosmos.

Yet at the same time, starting with philosophers such as Voltaire in the 1700s, then jumping to Darwin in Lincoln's time and climaxing with the scientific fervor of the twentieth century, man's view of reality shifted from a constant awareness of the supernatural—a sense of God even in a budding tree—to a far more limited view of reality. Now, with a sudden onslaught of science, reality consisted almost exclusively of that which could be readily touched, measured, heard, or seen. In other words, we shrugged off our mystical perception and turned totally toward naturalism, discarding the miracles of both the Old and New Testaments.

It was the beginning of the Modern Era, and suddenly the only "world" became the physical or natural world. Physical cause for physical effect. It was the age of Freud and existentialism. Man was no longer in communion with the supernatural. He didn't need it. He was reliant upon his own "rational" thinking.

This was the "Age of Reason." Technology was in and spirit was out. It was man's logic, not his spirit, which gave us the steamboat, radio transmission, the electric light bulb, airplanes, synthetic chemicals, and of course the automobile—all those things that made life "better" and easier. What mattered was the *physical*. Any force which could not be physically measured, any force which could not be captured or at least detected by the tools and instruments of physical science—those same instruments which had given us TV and cars—was no longer valid or needed.

That meant that the supernatural force, never prone to capture in a test tube, became folklore, relegated to the dustbin of superstition.

And ridiculed.

Who needed God's Light? Who needed angels, the supernatural, or the Holy Spirit?

When man wanted light, he now walked to a switch and turned on the electricity.

CHAPTER 3

A Whispering Voice

While the supernatural has come under attack in every age (even in Christ's own time by the Sadducees), there has probably never been an age in which it has met with such widespread public rejection. Even prayer was thrown out of the public school. Asked *Time* magazine, "Is God Dead?"

It was a question many in my generation, the baby-boom generation, began to ask. It was a question posed quietly, in the deep of night, even by priests and ministers: Did the supernatural really exist? Was there room for the Spirit in an era of electronics? Was religion compatible with technology?

Life seemed meaningless. It was the fluke of evolution and other natural forces. You lived and died and then there was nothing. That's what I got from the new and modern system of education. We were being taught, essentially, that the Bible is ancient literature. It is myth. The real truth lay in existentialism and other materialistic schools of thought.

Yet, there was something in us that wondered if life is more than the visible reality. As a child I had always been known as spiritually sensitive, and yearning for answers. Seeking to fill a spiritual void, I began investigating psychic phenomena. This search began when I was a newspaper reporter and continued while I was an author living

16

in New York City. Some of my story I have told before. Some bears repeating. It came down to this: I felt if the Spirit existed, they should be able to demonstrate it in well-controlled scientific experiments.

I never thought of psychic phenomena as the "occult" or witchcraft. It wasn't like I was hanging around covens. I thought parapsychology was a most worthy new science, and indeed there were dozens—hundreds!—of experiments indicating just such a nonphysical or spiritual dimension. The research was conducted at such esteemed places as Duke University, Maimonides Medical Center, and Stanford Research Institute. I investigated clinical tests in which human subjects seemed able to interact with an electronic device known as the random-event generator. I wrote a story about it for *The Atlantic Monthly*, a high-brow magazine in Boston. The odds against mere chance were 10 billion to one. I reported that subjects were affecting the machine's randomness through some kind of "mental" energy!

Laboratory experiments I accepted, but the New Testament? I had never read it. I was naive. I hadn't been to church for years. I wanted "scientific" evidence. I didn't know Peter from James.

I was naive because I didn't see anything "occult" in psychic phenomena, nor did I see anything wrong with investigating a few haunted houses. And that I did. I remember sleeping overnight at a house in Niagara Falls where strange occurrences were reported. Two other reporters accompanied me. In the middle of the night we heard what sounded like a strange haggish cackling coming from the basement, and when we rushed to the door leading into that cellar I recall seeing a fleeting human shadow, like an old woman, pass the light bulb at the base of the stairs.

At an old stonehouse in Lewiston, New York, a dozen of us stayed late into the night and heard strange clanking sounds. This was in 1975. The house was notoriously haunted. It was once a headquarters for Masons and the haunting seemed connected to the well-known murder of a man named William Morgan. I spoke to a maid who supposedly had seen an apparition of the victim.

In Manhattan, I knew of a house that was plagued with foul odors, a window that mysteriously opened and closed, and eerie footsteps. When I entered the room to see for myself the window *cracked*, though no one was within ten feet of it.

While I realize now how silly and dangerous parapsychology is, my foolishness was the result of a searching process. I wanted objective evidence of the supernatural. I wanted scientific "proof" before I committed myself to any system of belief. I was a victim of fanatical logic, or what I call "scientism." I wasn't interested in the occult so much as I was interested in evidence. I was a product of an educational system that had become mechanical and atheistic. I was the product of a Church that, bowing to modernism, had taken spiritual phenomena—and warnings about the occult—out of Sunday sermons.

I was also the victim of my own faithlessness and stupidity. I knew nothing about the dangers. I certainly heard nothing about it in the normal course of most of my journalism, which had involved everything from exposing toxic wastes to writing about other earthly topics like the Mafia. Much of my work included science, and for a while I was even a contributing editor at *Science Digest.* You didn't talk about spirits with serious science journalists.

The devil? He was only in the movies, or a rare menace, like in *The Exorcist.*

Angels?

They belonged at the top of a Christmas tree.

If psychic phenomena didn't give me enough exposure to evil, then my book on the Mafia certainly filled the quotient. Yet, in a strange way these experiences also helped bring me back to Christianity. Seeing real evil made me realize that there is also real good. I was converted or "born again" in 1983. One of the clinchers was a dream in which several luminous entities who had no wings and yet seemed like angels appeared to me. They stood over my body with healing hands, showing me that Satan existed and was at my door. I actually saw the devil's etched, living, and unutterably awful face. The dream was a three-parter that would wake me up and then continue where it left off, when I fell back asleep. And it scared me to the bottom of my soul. It made me realize I was in spiritual danger. So did other events that happened while I was writing the Mafia book. Soon I was back in the pews and reading the Bible every spare moment. I prayed and prayed. Boy did I pray! Each day I spent hours in prayer. I prayed with non-denominationalists, I prayed with charismatics, I prayed with the dear graying women in the nearest church on East 90th, and I even went up to Harlem (not always a safe journey for a white male) to pray with pentecostalists on 125th Street.

Since this is not an autobiography, nor a book about my conversion, I won't get into too many more details. Suffice it to say I was no longer looking for religion at universities, or in laboratories. Nor was I searching, any longer, for supernatural experiences.

Yet they came. I was flooded with both good and bad phenomena. I had experiences of attack from what I can only describe as evil spirits (apparently not too keen on my new course in life), but also experiences of ineffable consolation from heavenly entities.

I am the first to say that such encounters must be tested. I was fooled once, so why not a second time? But to this day I believe that most of them, the large majority, were both supernatural and from the Holy Spirit. Indeed, my previous brushes with evil granted me all the more sensitivity to the dark side. I knew what evil *felt* like. I knew how demonic forces manifested. I could sense their tingling brown dust. And I have since encountered Christians who claim to experience charismatic or apparitional phenomena which I immediately perceived as demonic deceptions. To me their spiritual "gifts" felt more like the phenomena of psychics or mediums.

But many others were truly in touch with gifts of the Spirit. They glowed in prayer, and as we praised God we felt His healing.

At any rate, after my conversion I experienced a number of situations that seemed to involve angels and the Holy Spirit. There were indications that mankind was at a crucial threshold and that God was pouring forth His own brand of supernatural phenomena to convert recalcitrants like me. I remember lying on my couch reading one Sunday when, resting my eyes, I suddenly saw the clear and towering image of a pure-white angel leaning into my field of vision. I don't know why, but in my spirit I felt I was encountering a high-ranking angel. For some reason I felt it was Gabriel. I can still "see" it. Walking up Third Avenue another afternoon during rush hour—at a particularly trying time in my life—I suddenly stopped in my tracks because an old woman, a mysterious stranger, was standing before me. She was right there in front of me! She said nothing, just smiled and made the sign of the cross. Then she disappeared into the sidewalk crowd, leaving me with an overwhelming sensation of well-being.

A woman of similar description (and giving the same blessing) appeared soon after to a friend of mine in a distant part of New York City.

A while later I had another experience. The year was 1986. In Lewes, England, at a church known for its devotion to the Archangel Michael, I was in prayerful meditation when an old woman in the pew in front of me turned to take my hand in an offering of peace. I felt that same heavenly serenity as I had a short time before with the mysterious stranger in Manhattan. It nearly seemed like the same lady!

I have no idea if these were angels or just folks filled with the Spirit. But of this I am certain: heavenly entities do manifest in the flesh. They do so more than we imagine. In fact, rare is the person who hasn't had an encounter with a mysterious stranger or at least hasn't heard of such an encounter from a relative, friend, or acquaintance.

There was an explosion going on. There *is* an explosion going on. Such reports, as we will see, would soon flow from every part of the country. The major angelic experience of my life occurred during the late morning of September 19, 1988. I had just moved from Manhattan to spend some time at my parents' home in Niagara Falls. I was under contract for a book about the origin of modern man, or what they call paleoanthropology. I didn't know it at the time, but I was at a crossroads in my life, about to drop out of the "secular" world and into the world of religious journalism. I was sprawled on the floor in a bedroom on the second floor, transcribing several tapes I had been given during a recent trip to see a paleoanthropologist named Alan Mann at the University of Pennsylvania. They were taped lectures by Mann and other prominent anthropologists.

My routine was to work during the morning, then take

a nap upstairs around noon, before lunch and resumption of my research. I *always* took a late-morning or early-afternoon snooze, and when I did I slept for about an hour. I intended to do just that—take a nap—when I finished the tape I was working on. The cassettes contained discussions on the origins of modern *homo sapiens*. My book was about a theory claiming that by way of DNA, geneticists had tracked back the first common ancestor of all living humans. They called this theoretical ancestor "Eve." I had just returned from research trips to Berkeley and the University of Hawaii, and was preparing for further research in Israel and Tanzania.

As I transcribed one of those tapes I suddenly heard an inner voice say, "Take your nap downstairs."

It was extremely strange to me. I wasn't one to experience locutions. I was certainly no mystic! I had no idea where it came from. I wasn't thinking of *where* to take my nap, just *when*. I always slept up there in the front bedroom. It made no sense to go downstairs, and so I ignored the "voice" as a simple psychological artifact. Put simply, I thought I was imagining things.

Yet a few minutes later—actually about ten or fifteen minutes later, to the best of my recollection—the voice repeated itself very clearly. "Take your nap downstairs." It was an inner voice, but much different than a normal "thought." It was as loud as an inner "voice" can be without being heard auricularly—through the actual ear.

Now I stopped work for a few minutes and meditated on what I heard—or what I thought I had heard. The first time it was easy to brush off, but I was astonished that it had repeated itself. Four simple and yet unforgettable words: "Take your nap downstairs."

I thought about it for a moment. Should I actually obey it?

No. It made no sense to obey that notion. Why downstairs, on a couch, when I was working upstairs right next to my comfortable bed?

Besides, other family members milled in and out of the house and would disrupt a nap on the first floor.

No, I decided, when I finished the tape, around 11:30 a.m. or noon, I would take my nap in bed, where I usually did.

And a while later, again perhaps ten minutes later, the same voice interrupted me. *Take your nap downstairs.* This time I looked all around. This time I stopped work for a longer period of contemplation.

Was I hearing things?

It was a gentle and yet very firm and strong voice, coming from my right. I can still "feel" it. It made an indelible impression and I chose to take it seriously. After all, it had come three separate times, like my dream.

I decided to take my nap downstairs after I completed the anthropology tape. Diligently I finished making notes on a pad and transcribing relevant quotes. When I was done I flicked off the recorder and padded downstairs through a middle bedroom and past another to find my place on the sofa in the family room, nestled near a bookcase in which my mother keeps a collection of porcelain angels.

It was a beautiful day, the summer granting a farewell gift before the density of autumn. I sifted through some monographs concerning the vegetation of prehistoric Africa (which I needed for description), as well as some background reading material on fossil hunter Richard Leakey, whom I was scheduled to meet in Nairobi. Then I settled on the couch for some reading and sleep.

I dozed off but then the phone rang. When I hung up I tried to fall back into my nap. I couldn't seem to rest, so I got up to run a few errands. It was lunchtime. I don't remember what errand I was going to run. I was probably going out to buy a newspaper at the corner store and grab something to eat. I walked toward the side door and as I passed the stairs I suddenly smelled something very strange. It seemed like burnt plastic.

Then I heard it: a crackling noise. There was a fire on the second floor! As I dashed up the fourteen steps I decided it was an electrical fire and that I'd have to smother it with a blanket.

That turned out to be wishful thinking. By the time I got to the second floor, smoke was filling the upper part of the house. It was one of the middle bedrooms that was on fire—not just on fire, but like a furnace! All I could see were the huge licks of angry orange flame. They seemed as tall as the ceiling and were spreading like a blow torch. They were actually causing a roaring sound, and as I ran down the hall the air was so hot that I actually got a slight "sunburn." It singed my face.

I dashed into my room, grabbed my most important documents, looked for my dog, called the fire department, and scrambled to escape. Within two minutes the smoke had filled the entire upstairs. I couldn't see three feet in front of me. I thought of breaking a window. I was going to jump. But instead I crouched as low as I could and made my way back past the inferno and downstairs. By the time I was outside, waiting for the firemen, windows were exploding from the heat.

It took more than an hour for the firemen to completely extinguish the blaze. There was even a photo in the newspaper the next morning. They had to break through a wall and ax their way through the roof to make sure the fire was all out, and the second-floor was virtually destroyed by smoke. The thickest soot was from chemical furniture coating, and it can be highly toxic. The air was hot enough to melt plastic in the next room and damage all the electronic equipment, including my new computer, which was two rooms away. There was $67,800 in damage.

As I stood in the front yard, watching them battle the inferno, one of the firemen came by and noticed my "sunburn." We started to talk. He reprimanded me for going back to retrieve my documents. He told me the flames had been unusually hot. When I asked what would have happened if I had been napping upstairs, the fireman shook his head. He didn't think I would have made it. "The smoke would have been all over the place."

CHAPTER 4

Flames and Spears

That was only one little event. There was a much larger scenario playing out. Thousands reported similar "angelic" incidents that were more dramatic than my own. They came from every corner of the United States, along with other countries. As in ancient Israel, during times of crisis, God was raising up gifts of the Spirit.

How do our experiences compare with the past?

And what does it all indicate?

Is the current episode unique?

The only way to answer that is to take a brief and tantalizing look at mystical history.

Though we cannot fully judge the extent of holy charisms or "mysticism"—simply because most of it went unrecorded—we can be certain that every epoch has witnessed its share of Christian phenomena. This is in fulfillment of Christ's promise that after His death He would send the Holy Spirit or "Paraclete."

One of the earliest charisms was what is known to many of you as "tongues." That is to say, ecstatic communication with God. On Pentecost, the Spirit arrived like a rush of wind and assumed the visible appearance as tongues of fire that rested on Jesus's friends, mother, and disciples, who began to praise God with loud voices in what sounded like strange, babbling languages. Certain authors refer to

24

the continuation of tongues up to the end of the second century, when it became dormant until the charismatic and pentecostal movements of our own time. This charism was one of many. There were also the appearances of Christ to His disciples; their laying of hands on the sick; and supernatural luminosities—manifestations of light—like that which engulfed and converted Saul (*Acts* 9:3). A most unusual exhibition of the same "light" seems also to have taken place when an evangelist named Thaddaeus traveled to Edessa to heal King Abgar V. The king was suffering from leprosy. Thaddaeus carried with him an image of Jesus known as the "Mandylion," which may have been the Shroud of Turin, folded and with only its face showing. When Thaddaeus entered the king's throne room, the image illuminated, casting forth a healing light. King Abgar was instantly well.

Let's race through a bit of history. Exercising many other mystical gifts, Christ's early followers not only healed and spoke in tongues but also saw visions, cast out demons, and uttered prophecy, including John's great *Revelation* (around A.D. 90) on the island of Patmos. Which was all well and good. But then it seems the charisms began to be abused. Onto the scene came Gnostics who tried to incorporate ancient occult religions into Christian mysticism, contaminating what Christ had left us with their arcane philosophies. They were forerunners of the New Age Movement. There were also the Montanists, who believed the "Last Times," Second Coming, and other biblical predictions were about to unfold. While the Montanists were not as heretical as the Gnostics, and can be lauded for their asceticism, they jumped the prophetic gun and set prophets against the bishops, causing hurtful Church division.

It was partly out of concern for heresy and false revelation that early Christians began to organize a federation of religious communities. This included the appointment of local leaders known as deacons and bishops. Doctrines were written and prayer said in a more routine fashion. As a result, mysticism retreated to more controlled and often obscure settings, such as monasteries and convents. While public outpourings of the Spirit were now far less in evidence, private revelations were still allowed. And some of them proved accurate in their warnings. During the fourth century, Anthony of the Desert correctly prophesied that the time would come when "men will surrender to the spirit of the age. They will say that if they had lived in our day, faith would be simple and easy. But in their day, they will say, things are complex; the Church must be brought up to date and made meaningful to the day's problems. When the Church and the world are one, then those days are at hand, because our Divine Master placed a barrier between His things and the things of the world."

This prediction materialized throughout subsequent centuries, most notably with the French Revolution.

Time and again, through those early centuries, prophecy was joined by angelic experiences, especially appearances of the Archangel Michael. He came to the rescue when dreadful wars and persecutions threatened to destroy Christianity. It was Michael who helped Constantine the Great achieve a brilliant victory over the pagan emperor Maxentius *("I am Michael, the chief of the angelic legions of the Lord of hosts, the protector of the Christian religion, who while you were battling against godless tyrants placed the weapons in your hands"),* and in the early Eastern or Byzantine Church, Michael was looked upon not only as a protector, but also a healer. Legend has it that the great archangel caused a medicinal spring to sprout at Chairotopa and healing water at Colossae. The Christians of Egypt placed the Nile under his protection.

That was the supernatural component. There were also prophecies to be found in nature. As in Old Testament periods, signs of the times could be discerned from the weather, volcanic eruptions, heavenly bodies, war, persecution, plague, lunar or solar portents, and seismology. During the first century A.D. earthquakes from Crete to Judea seemed to presage a new time—just as an earthquake had announced Christ's death. In A.D. 66, Halley's Comet made an ominous appearance, described as like a "sword hanging in the sky" and making many wonder if it foretold the subsequent destruction of Jerusalem. Not long after, Mount Vesuvius erupted as winds of change were sweeping the world, destroying Pompeii, which was worshipping strange gods. The sacking of Rome in the 400s seemed to augur the end of time, and on May 20, 526, a major quake cost 250,000 lives in Antioch, Syria, one of the first major cities of Christian evangelization. Soon after, a migrating Germanic tribe called the Lombards crossed the Alps, seized Milan, and chased away the archbishop. Then they advanced south toward Rome.

It was a final blow for the declining Roman civilization and the beginning of Italy's Dark Ages.

Corruption, plagues, and schism once more threatened the early Christians.

Yet again did Michael come to the rescue. Yet again did he supernaturally display himself. During that same time, in 590, just after he was made pope, Gregory the Great took to the streets in a penitential procession seeking relief from a terrible plague. Heavy floods had led to a disastrous period of famine and illness in Rome. And the Church was suffering through the schism that seemed to have been announced by the Antioch quake. According to legend, as Gregory arrived at the bridge crossing the Tiber, he and his followers heard the song of angels and suddenly Michael appeared as a towering apparition in the sky above a mausoleum near St. Peter's Basilica (where today stands Castel Sant'Angelo). He wore brilliant armor and held a sword which he thrust into his scabbard.

It was a fleeting vision, but soon after, the pestilence ended.

If there was no longer the practice of tongues—at least not on a widespread basis—quieter forms of holy mysticism appeared in the Byzantine Church, which carried forth a tradition of deep interior contemplation. It also continued in monasteries such as the one built by St. Columba in the sixth century. Columba was an Irish prophet with another serious message for the future. "Hearken, hearken to what will happen in the latter days of the world! There will be great wars; unjust laws will be enacted; the Church will be despoiled of her property; people will read and write a great deal; but charity and humility will be laughed to scorn, and the common people will believe in false ideas."

In the course of the next four centuries were many other mystics. There was the monk Ansgar, renowned for his miracles. He lived in Westphalia. There were the wondrous cures of England's Venerable Bede. There were the marvels associated with Richard the King, who died in 720. In the ninth century there was the martyr and virgin Solangia, who lived at Villemont near Bourges. When her hour of prayer approached, it was said that she was attended by a light that shone over her head like a guiding star.

There was also the Abbott Giles to whom an angel appeared with a message for King Charles of France. It was written on a scroll.

By the 11th century we had the vision of Bernard of Clairvaux, whose writings were later studied by Martin Luther. Bernard's experiences were not so dramatic as they were subtle and intimate, as God most often communicates. "I confess in my foolishness that the Word has visited me, springing in me, and this has happened more than once," he wrote. "But although He has frequently entered my soul, He has come in such a way that I have never been sensible of the precise moment of His coming. I have felt Him in me, I remember He has been within me, I have sometimes known a presentiment of His coming into me. By what means He made entrance or departure, I confess I know not to this day. He did not enter through my eyes, for He is not a color, nor through my ears, for He is not a sound, nor through my nostrils, for He mingles not with the air but with the spirit of man, nor again does He appear to enter through the mouth, for He cannot be eaten or sipped on the tongue, nor may He be touched, for He is not tangible."

In the 12th century, a mystic named Hildegard correctly prophesied that one day "the German Empire will be divided."

Then came Francis of Assisi, whose explosion of mystical gifts symbolized a revival. He lived from 1182 to 1226 (in central Italy), and was constantly healing the sick, expelling devils, and encountering the manifestations of angels and other holy figures. One angel took the form of an unusually handsome, peaceful, and joyful young man who helped one of Francis's monks cross a deep river. They also experienced visions of Christ, and in 1224, possibly around the middle of September, Francis was praying on Mount Alverna when a flaming six-winged angel or "seraph" flew swiftly from Heaven and hovered overhead.

Francis was filled with joy and amazement. The seraph, who took on the likeness of a crucified man, had two wings above his head, two covering his body, and two spread out to fly. During the apparition shepherds guiding their flocks noticed a strange fire illuminating the mountain.

Francis's experience with the seraphic vision occurred during a 40-day fast for the feast of the Archangel Michael. The angel was seen as the standard-bearer, *signifier sanctus Michaelis,* whose trumpet would arouse the dead on the Day of Judgment.

So beautiful were the angels, said Bridget of Sweden, that they take human form so as not to overwhelm those who set eyes on them.

Much of the phenomena was Catholic, for this was before the Protestant Reformation. There were hundreds of martyrs and saints associated with miracles. Occasionally the mysticism broke into the open. During the 13th century there were so many prognostications, in fact, that Giovanni di Fidanza of Italy, a doctor of the Church who one day would be known as St. Bonaventure, complained of hearing to "satiety" prophecies dealing with the end of the world.

While the Last Days were not upon denizens of the 1200s, there was a rash of quakes, including one in Asia Minor, where Paul himself had preached and where Christianity experienced one of its very first tastes of division.

Was the Church about to encounter another such splintering?

It was. For around this time occurred the Great Western Schism, in which France split from Rome and there were two popes. The spiritual corruption and unrest—not to mention the incredible devastation caused during the 1300s by the "Black Death" or bubonic plague—unleashed a flood of more prophecy. By the end of the 14th century there were seers on all sides and one of them, a canonized saint, spent the last 21 years of his life announcing that the Last Judgment was at hand and that there was a "great probability in my own mind, but without sufficient certainty to preach it, that Anti-Christ was born nine years ago."

Martin Luther believed much the same. In January, 1532, he wrote, "The Last Day is at hand. My calendar has run out. I know nothing more in my Scriptures." He saw demons on a nearly constant basis, and just days before his death one was outside his window near a rain pipe, lewdly displaying its backside.

In Spain was Teresa of Avila, who reported frequent visions, including that of a cherubim who touched her heart with a flaming gold spear.

In Florence was born Philip Neri, who was converted by a mystical experience and would later be known as "the second apostle of Rome."

But as always, as in our own times, legitimate mysticism was diluted by fanaticism, presumption, and hysteria. At the beginning of the 16th century, a veritable epidemic of political and religious prophecy rocked Italy with hermits swarming all over the countryside commenting on the apocalypse as they announced, from the pulpit, or at public meetings, that revolutions were to occur in both the temporal and spiritual governments. It was an accurate prediction, but many were the other "seers" who diluted such prophecy with far more sensational predictions. So many peasants and young girls fell to prophesying that by 1516 the Vatican had to issue a papal declaration disallowing prophecy during formal services.

Was the spiritual agitation a sign of the times?

There was the return of Halley's Comet in 1531 and a flurry of quakes. One that struck Portugal on January 26, 1531, took 30,000 lives, and another devastated the Shaanxi region of China in November of 1556, causing the deaths of 830,000.

What turmoil! What an indication of coming tumultuous times! Plague had ravaged Europe, and now in the 16th century, peasant wars also had erupted in Germany. The Germans turned to unprovoked savagery! As historians have commented, the uprising was nearly inexplicable; no one could satisfactorily explain these regional disturbances. The peasants plundered castles, killed bailiffs, and raped nuns. Some 132 monasteries were destroyed in Thuringia and Franconia. "Many regions (of Prussia) are inhabited by devils," Martin Luther, who lived during this time, once commented.

It was a precursor to the French Revolution and the Age of Modernism.

CHAPTER 5

Vapors of Darkness

The Revolution began in 1789 and grew more vicious with each passing year. There was desecration of churches. There was blasphemy. There was massacre. There was rage against Christians of all stripes as the "revolutionaries" aimed first at Catholics, but also targeted Protestant brethren. It was known as the Reign of Terror, and while outwardly it posed as a democratic revolution—a peoples' uprising to redistribute the wealth—it was just a disguise for godless humanism. It was what mystics envisioned when, in a flurry of new premonitions, they saw a black vapor curling from the bowels of the earth.

More than two centuries had passed since the incredible peasant uprisings. Now it was France that was in a demonic frenzy, and now besides its simple brutality, the Revolution ushered in the era of "rationalism," modernism, and dechristianization. Its misguided and irreverent precepts, its "liberalism" and focus upon man instead of God, would take hold like a mutant virus.

There was a full assault on Christian dogma and the persecution was physical as well as philosophical. First twenty priests were slaughtered, then three bishops and more than 200 other priests during the late summer of 1793—in a period of but four days. Christ was mocked by rationalists who paraded up the French avenues shouting profanities. Church

31

bells, along with sacred chalices, were seized.

It was precisely what the Communists would one day do in Russia, and like Communism, the French Revolution began to assume characteristics of an anti-religion. Names of saints were replaced with revolutionary heroes, and infants were given unchristian baptismal names. All vestiges of Christianity were removed from the calendars. All reference to the birth of Jesus was discarded. The seven-day week and Christian Sunday were replaced by a ten-day week, a new calendar, notes historian Thomas Bokenkotter, that "was supposed to epitomize the cult of 'reason' and reverence for an idealized 'nature.'"

Thus was the new era pronounced, an era that no longer started with the death of Christ but rather with the start of a new French Republic. Temples of Reason replaced churches and clergy were pressured to resign and get married. Liturgies were satirized and paganized. During a celebration at the Cathedral of Notre Dame an actress was enthroned as the Goddess of Reason.

As in ancient occult religions, the goddess, the princess of pride, was back.

And who was her prince but Satan?

A proud spirit indeed. A foul and vaporous spirit. It was preparing for a great onslaught and it moved with the vengeance and vacuum of a tornado. "The thick vapors which I have seen rising from the earth and obscuring the light of the sun are the false maxims of irreligion and license which are confounding all sound principles and spreading everywhere such darkness as to obscure both faith and reason," said a nun named Jeanne le Royer, who was said to have predicted the Revolution. "The storm began in France and France shall be the first theatre of its ravages after having been its cradle. I saw in the light of the Lord that the faith and our holy religion would become weaker in almost every Christian kingdom. God has permitted that they should be chastised by the wicked in order to awaken them from their apathy. And after the justice of God has been satisfied, He will pour out an abundance of graces on His Church."

Years later the Lord showed another mystic, Father Bernard Maria Clausi, "how beautiful the world will be like after the awful chastisement. The people will be like the Christians of the primitive Church."

Indeed, as Thomas Aquinas had said in the 13th century, demons are checked by good angels and "in like manner Anti-Christ will not do as much harm as he would wish."

One day the Lord would descend from Heaven with a shout (*1 Thessalonians* 4:16), with the voice of the archangel, with the trumpet of God. One day the dark would be broken. One day we would feel the glory!

But for the time being, a judgment seemed to be slowly approaching, grinding, grating its way through each decade of crisis and scientism. Before the triumph of the Church, according to Clausi, "evil will have made such progress that it will look like all the devils of Hell were let loose on earth." It took a while, but the cloud France unleashed would soon circulate to other nations, including America. Perhaps it was part of the symbolism that had supposedly been seen in vision by George Washington in 1777, nearly eight decades before Clausi. The account is as apocryphal as it is fascinating and therefore impossible to ignore: Alone in his quarters one afternoon, went the legend, Washington, an Episcopalian who was known to wander off for long sessions of prayer, encountered a mysterious and irresistible influence in his room, which gradually filled with a luminous atmosphere.

It seemed to be the apparition of a female "entity," showing him visions as in a movie. During the first vision he beheld a second entity, a dark shadowy being, in the air between Europe and America. This being dipped water from the ocean and cast it upon America with his right hand while his left hand went upon Europe. Immediately a cloud rose from these nations and joined in the middle of the Atlantic. Then it moved westward, slowly enveloping America. There were lightnings and sharp groanings of the people. After the angel dipped water and sprinkled it a second time, the dark cloud receded and Washington supposedly cast his eyes upon America, beholding villages, cities, and towns from coast to coast.

The visions seemed to involve three major events or stages in America's evolution. He heard a voice say, "Son of the Republic, the end of the century cometh. Look and learn."

There was a second vision. He saw the dark, shadowy figure turn its face southward, and from Africa an ill-omened
specter approached the United States.

America was at war with itself. It was a divided nation.
It was the Civil War which was soon to come.

The angel in the vision, the shadowy one, placed a trumpet to his mouth and blew three distinct blasts. And taking
water from the ocean, he sprinkled it upon Asia, Europe,
and Africa.

It was the third vision. From each of those places rose
thick black clouds that were soon joined into one, and
throughout the mass was a red light by which hordes of
armed men, moving with the cloud, marched on land and
sailed by sea to the Americas, which was then enveloped
in the cloud. These armies destroyed the towns, villages,
and cities.

But when he saw the shadowy angel a final time, Washington, according to the tale, saw the angel dip water yet again
and sprinkle it upon America. Instantly the dark cloud rolled
back, together with the invading armies, leaving America
victorious.

Had America's first president really foreseen three great
perils that America would face, including the Civil War?
And about that third peril: was it something still to come?

Said a Catholic mystic, Marianne Gaultier, as if in
response: "So long as public prayers are said, nothing shall
happen. But a time will come when public prayers shall
cease. People will say: 'Things will remain as they are.'
It is then that the great calamity shall occur. Before the great
battle, the wicked shall be the masters, and they will do
all the evils in their power, but not so much as they will
desire because they shall not have enough time...Such
extraordinary events shall take place that the most
incredulous shall be forced to say: 'The finger of God is
there.'"

It was the great testing of mankind and when consolations came, they did so in the form of mystical gifts that
accelerated during the French Revolution and picked up
yet more speed into the 1800s. If God seemed, on the one

hand, to be in hiding, there were, on the other hand, unprecedented clues and communications. Slowly, the heavenlies were building momentum. Something began to happen, something more than all the previous mysticism. It was as if God were attempting to both warn us and remind us of His very existence. No mincing of words! Sometime around 1820 to 1821, an Augustinian nun named Anne Katherine Emmerich said she saw a vision of a small, sandy place and heard the Lord say, *"Here is Prussia, the enemy."* Then she was shown a second place, to the north. The Lord said, *"This is Moskva, the land of Moscow, bringing many evils."*

Especially around 1830, prophecy spewed like a mystical volcano. It was an accurate reflection of the times, although it also involved a large measure of overstatement and apocalyptic hyperbole. Just as the first Christians perceived the end of the ages prematurely, at a time of trying persecution, and just as Gregory the Great saw the apocalypse in the sixth century, at a time of invasion, quakes, and plague, and just as the 14th-century mystics pronounced the Anti-Christ around the time of the Black Death, misinterpreting the apocalypse for current woes, so too did 19th-century mystics foresee high drama and perhaps even the Last Days when they were caught in a similar storm.

This much became clear: apocalyptic prediction, if jumping the gun, is a terrific benchmark of societal and spiritual turmoil. Many such prophecies were coming from Catholics, especially in France, but in England J.N. Darby, a Protestant evangelist, established the Plymouth Brethren, who announced the End Times and held prophetic conferences. During one such convocation, or at least sometime in this period, supposedly, a prophetic utterance came from a young and charismatic Scottish woman named Margaret Macdonald who may have been praying in tongues. Her revelation was that mankind would experience what became known as a "rapture" in which God's faithful would be "caught up together to meet the Lord in the air" before the coming tribulations.

It was a new concept in Christendom: that the faithful would be *bodily* taken up by the Lord. After the "rapture" would come great calamities known as the Great Tribulation, which would last seven years. The Anti-Christ would be involved. This tribulation or chastisement would end with the Second Coming and the battle of Armageddon, followed by the 1,000-year reign of bliss known as the millennium. Because the scenario involved an earthly millennium with Christ coming before its start, it was known as "pre-millennialism," and it spread like wildfire.

If less specific with time periods and leaving out the "rapture," so too did Catholics feel a coming chastisement. "God will ordain two punishments," said Blessed Anna Maria Taigi. "One, in the form of wars, revolutions, and other evils, will originate on earth. The other will be sent from Heaven. First, several earthly scourges will come. They are going to be dreadful, but they will be mitigated and shortened by the prayers and penances of many holy souls. There will be great wars in which millions of people will perish through iron. But after these scourges will come the heavenly one, which will be directed solely against the impenitent. This scourge will be far more frightful and terrible; it will be mitigated by nothing, but it will take place and act in its full vigor."

Taigi and other mystics foresaw three days and nights in which earth would be covered by "an intense darkness." The air would be laden with pestilence. There would be innumerable devils. Lightning would penetrate homes, said a later mystic named Marie Julie Jahenny of La Fraudais. The earth would tremble to its foundations. Foaming waves would cover the land. Red clouds like blood would scut across the sky.

"I saw a picture of a dreadful battle," said Sister Emmerich, who died in 1824. "The entire field was covered with vapors. They shot everywhere out of thickets, which were full of soldiers, and out of the air. The place was low-lying territory and in the distance were great cities. I saw [Michael the Archangel] descending with a great multitude of angels and dispersing the combatants. That, however, will happen when everything seems lost. There will be a leader who will invoke Michael and then victory will descend."

CHAPTER 6

The Red Cloud

These were dangerous times. They were also dark times. The "red cloud" was already on the horizon. In 1829 a secret cabal of financiers referred to as "Illuminati" reportedly organized a committee that later financed Karl Marx, whose precepts evolved into the red dragon of Communism. These same Illuminati, a branch of high Masonry, had also played a secret role in the French Revolution. Down with God, screamed the modern philosophers like Nietzsche, while Marx, revealing his real source, wrote a poem that included the line, "See this sword? The prince of darkness sold it to me."

Indeed, great darkness. There was a tremendous rise in demonism, just as the prophets foresaw. Its first goal was total and utter materialism. That meant it had to negate belief in all that was supernatural. Only the material, "rational," and scientific world would be acknowledged. This would accomplish two key objectives. It would cause society to question the existence of God—since there is no God if there is only a natural world—and at the same time, with the same master stroke, this denial of dimensions other than the physical would hide the supernatural work—the work in non-physical spheres—of demons, allowing them free flight in the atmosphere.

Negate belief and replace it with sheer materialism.

No Satan. No God.

If that didn't work, and the masses grew spiritually hungry, then Plan Two came into effect: feed them the *wrong kind* of supernatural belief. Feed the people, satisfy their wretched spiritual needs, with witchcraft, superstition, and occultism.

Thus in the 1800s arose the movement known as Spiritualism, whereby followers went to mediums and communicated with the "dead."

There were seances, table-rappers, and clairvoyants from Victorian England to Upstate New York.

It was the birth of psychic phenomena, which later evolved into the "New Age." Paganism had returned in full force.

As the occultism and materialism grew, however, so did gifts of the Spirit. Was there false and even demonic prophecy? Of course there was. And also exaggeration. But no doubt that God was piercing the darkness with His words and wonders. They had been there throughout the centuries, with hundreds of recognized "saints" and thousands of others experiencing charisms, and there had been the great outpourings of prophecy during the 13th and 14th centuries, but these eruptions, from what I can tell, were less than what was now rising. Renewal of the Spirit! War in the heavenlies! The evangelicalism of Methodists and Catholics, the mysticism of millennialists, was joined by a similar revival among Anglicans. "By the mid-nineteenth century," observes sociologist William Martin, "America had become, more fully than ever before or again, a Christian republic, and the dominant expression of that Christianity was Protestant, Evangelical, and revivalistic."

In many denominations rose too a spirit of prophecy. Once more, there was a stream of apocalyptic prognostications. Highly popular in the U.S. were literal interpretations of *Revelation* and the Book of *Daniel*. While their expectation of the Last Days was a bit hasty, it got the point across: beware of coming times, for they are dangerous. It was a message for both the immediate and long-range future. It was a message, perhaps, for both them and us. Were the Four Horsemen about to ride? The idea of millennialism (which, as I said, posits that after tribulation and the Second Coming, Christ will reign on earth for literally 1,000 years) swept from evangelist to evangelist. Throughout the century, prophetic and millennialist ideas proliferated among both orthodox and unorthodox groups, including Mormons, Jehovah's Witnesses, and the Seventh-Day Adventists, who expected the Second Coming in 1843 or 1844.

However the message may have been misconstrued or embellished, it indicated a great agitation of the spirits. Some of it also showed the Spirit's sudden upsurge. A revival was sweeping America, especially in the non-denominational and often schismatic "holiness" movements. With it came a reactivation—a public reactivation—of charismatic gifts. After more than 1,600 years they were again breaking into the open. Mostly, there was prophecy, and it deserved attention, even if some of it was divisive and overwrought. There was chaff in the wheat but these vibrant Christians were trying to obey Paul, who in *1 Corinthians* 14:1-4 had said, *"Pursue love, and desire spiritual gifts, but especially that you may prophesy. For he who speaks in a tongue does not speak to men but to God, for no one understands him; however, in the spirit he speaks mysteries. But he who prophesies speaks edification and exhortation and comfort to men. He who speaks in a tongue edifies himself, but he who prophesies edifies the church."*

It needed all the edification it could get. Difficult spiritual times were coming. Matters would grow all the worse. This time it wasn't just a period of punctuated distress—it wasn't just a schism, a plague in Europe, or a peasant uprising—but an entirely new era with entirely new and anti-Christian thoughts. No wonder the prophetic imaginings were in overdrive! Just as prophets in the 14th century expressed their distress in apocalyptical terms, so too, as the Era of Modernism took hold, did a new generation of prophets overstate the spiritual impulses they now were receiving—and yet too did they accurately convey the sense of spiritual jeopardy.

It wasn't the end of the world, but such predictions certainly indicated great and precarious change, which one day, during the new era, would lead not to The End but to a serious moment.

There was a worldwide dispute with the forces of dark, and it was going to get worse before it got better. Such was also the essence of a Catholic prophecy from LaSalette, France, which foresaw a time of Anti-Christ. "The demons of the air together with the Anti-Christ will perform great wonders on earth and in the atmosphere, and men will become more and more perverted," said one version of this alleged prophecy. "God will take care of faithful servants and men of good will. The Gospels will be preached everywhere, and all peoples of all nations will get to know the truth."

While there would be all manner of calamities, including "infectious plague," and while evil would infect Christian leaders, as too civil government would assault Christianity, trying to abolish every religious principle in the mad dash to materialism, atheism, and occultism, Christ, in His mercy, would in those times command His angels to the rescue, destroying the fury of satanic forces.

Even a pope, Pius IX, set forth the prophecy that "there will be a great prodigy which will fill the world with awe. But this prodigy will be preceded by the triumph of a revolution during which the Church will go through ordeals that are beyond description." According to Clausi, the chastisement "would come suddenly and be of short duration." In 1884 another pontiff, Leo XIII, experienced a vision in which he saw Satan given the period of a century during which he would be allowed to exercise even more power. (As if fulfilling the prophecy of Sister Emmerich, Pope Leo invoked the aid of the Archangel Michael in a special prayer that was said at the end of Catholic Mass until after the Second Vatican Council in the 1960s).

Thus there was the pope issuing warnings from Rome and the Charles Finneys or J.N. Darbys inspiring revival in the U.S. and Europe. There were evangelists like Dwight Lyman Moody, who stressed again the weightiness of the times, warning that we were rushing headlong toward moral and social disaster; and at the beginning of the 20th century, dynamos such as "the Calliope of Zion," Reverend Billy Sunday, came against those who were hellbound.

Clearly, in all that fervor, the spirit world was heating up. There was prophecy all over the place. And there was more—much more—to come. Most of it was apocalyptic and as such, sounded highly allegorical.

But in it were nuggets of truth.

Angels were battling demons.

There was a war beginning in the heavenlies.

A war that in our own day is nearing a conclusion.

While there have been charismatic gifts throughout the centuries, and upsurges in prophecy, as well as claims from oldtime Christians such as Basil way back in the fourth century that the world was drowning in a flood of evil, much of the historical agitation paled in comparison with what was set loose by the French Revolution. After all, it was the forerunner of Communism. It was an era during which hundreds of millions—more than there were people on earth during the fourth century—would consider God an anachronism.

As for the good side, it too was rising in a unique and perhaps unprecedented fashion, with charismatic gifts more blatant than at any time since the Montanists.

Quiet now since the end of the second century, tongues were soon to make a comeback.

If it was the Era of Modernism, it was also the era of charisms and pentecostalism.

It was time for the Holy Spirit.

God was not leaving us alone.

CHAPTER 7

Light in the Night

"Satan may appear to be winning the war because sometimes he wins important battles, but the final outcome is certain," Bill Graham reminds us. "One day he will be defeated and stripped of his powers eternally. God will shatter the powers of darkness."

Indeed, extraordinary signs were sprouting everywhere. At the same time evil rose, at the same time rationalists scoffed at God, so was there a parallel rise in the Holy Spirit. General William Booth, who founded the Salvation Army in 1878, had a vision of angels surrounded by auras of rainbow-like splendor, and on the rainy night of August 21, 1879, amidst the windswept peat of western Ireland, overlooking Mayo, residents bereft of hope and in the midst of fever and hunger saw the south gable of the old stone church in Knock "suffused and covered with a brilliant golden light, a light that sparkled, making the night as bright as noonday, a changing light that sometimes mounted, lighting the sky above and beyond the gable, and sometimes subsided and got whiter and more brilliant, so that the gable seemed like a wall of snow," recounted Mary Purcell, an Irish writer.

In the glow, in this inexplicable and celestial illumination, at the old Irish church, were several apparitional figures, one of whom resembled St. John the Evangelist. He was near a lamb and held a large open book, which they took to be The Book of Revelation.

It was a living tableau. The figures were clothed in dazzling white raiment. Life-sized and living, yet silent.

Angels fluttered above for more than ninety minutes. There at a church wall in Ireland!

There were at least 14 official witnesses that incredible night in Knock, and more elsewhere. Slowly and without loud fanfare, in the gradual yet unforgettable way in which He works, God was beginning—only just beginning, but clearly initiating—the major supernatural episode of which I spoke in the first chapter. His marvels, though unreported, and thus often obscured, extended from northern Europe all the way to the Iberian Peninsula and then east to those regions which soon would be imprisoned behind the Iron Curtain. On May 12, 1914, in a remote and equally impoverished village in Ukraine called Hrushiw (pronounced *Hro-shoo*), peasants encountered a similar supernormal presence in a wheatfield near a byzantine-style chapel, while the following August, in the middle of one of the first skirmishes of World War One, there were reports, conveyed through military nurses, of British and French soldiers seeing angels on the battlefield, including the Archangel Michael on a white horse. Others said it was Saint George. Whoever it was, it gave the soldiers, who were in retreat, tremendous courage, while on the other side, the Kaiser's soldiers found it impossible to proceed and thought there were thousands of troops in the allied position when in fact there were just two regiments.

It was called the "Angel of Mons." A year after that, in the midst of the same war, with all of Europe in fear, another major angel appeared to four peasant children in Portugal.

They were watching sheep on hilly terrain along a ridge at Cabeco, about 90 miles north of Lisbon, when the youngsters saw what appeared to be a cloud in human form. As it approached it came to a pause over a pine grove. It looked like a statue made of snow or a person wrapped in a sheet, according to one of the eyewitnesses, a broad-faced girl named Lucia dos Santos. That was 1915. The next year the angel reappeared to Lucia and two of her cousins, Jacinta and Francisco. The kids were playing when, without warning, a strong wind began to blow, shaking the pines, which moaned and swayed. That was when they saw a light moving over the trees, east to west, this time coming near enough that they could see the form of a "transparent young man." He was as brilliant as crystal penetrated by the rays of the sun. "Don't be afraid," said the visitor. "I am the Angel of Peace. Pray with me." Kneeling to the ground, the angel prostrated himself until his forehead touched the earth, repeating three times, *"My God, I believe, I adore, I hope, and I love you! I beg pardon of You for those who do not believe, do not adore, do not hope and do not love You."* Upon a later return he identified himself as the "Angel of Portugal."

Clearly, there was a descent of the angels, just as *Matthew* promised in Chapter 13 Verse 41. They did not make the front page of *The New York Times,* but they were as real as anything, and of greater true consequence. The Spirit was beginning to move. His manifestations increased from the early 1900s. He was the great harbinger of things to come. He was the great consoler. In the United States it took the form of tongues, healings, and baptisms in the Holy Spirit, while others noted a surge in apparitions and spiritual promptings. There was an awakening, a revival of charismatic gifts, and the phenomenal rise of tongues that began during 1901 in Topeka, Kansas (at Bethel Bible College) moved into Missouri and Texas, then California and the "city of angels." Soon 26 contemporary church bodies with more than two million members could trace their origin to Los Angeles. In Denver, according to a report in 1905, the entire city fell into worship for two hours at midday, "held captive in a spell under an influence of power that was not of themselves. A power that seems to have made for righteousness. The places of trade were deserted between noon and two this afternoon. All worldly affairs were forgotten. The entire city was given over to meditation of higher things." In Catholic circles the most astonishing charismatic was an Italian priest named Padre Pio who, according to his biographer, the Lutheran minister C. Bernard Ruffin, was associated with thousands of angel stories and had been given a revelation in which he saw a vast field with a great multitude, divided into two groups. On one side were men of the most beautiful countenance—clad in snow-white garments—while on the other side were men of hideous aspect, dressed in black raiment, like dark shadows.

It was a vision of the spiritual war. It was also as it said in *Matthew:* a choosing or separation process. God was giving us miracles to bring us back, to let us see His magnificence, to ward off danger and inform us, to bolster that faith which had been stolen by the modernists. He was urging us through various means—not all pleasant—to choose Heaven. The signs and wonders were accompanied by natural and man-made disasters. They too were "signs of the times," they too indicated a special era in human history, and they too pointed to the dangers of materialism.

While many evangelists declared the End Times upon mankind, and waited for the "imminent" return of Jesus, revving their congregations with talk of Armageddon and the coming millennium, the impulse they were trying to express, the prophetic inspiration they felt in prayer, was not the actual "end," but instead a metaphor for the beginning of sorrows.

It was a prelude to some form of coming tribulation or judgment.

There would be wars and rumors of wars, said Christ (*Matthew* 24:6-8). *"And there will be famines, pestilences, and earthquakes in various places."* By this we could know that we were approaching the beginning of sorrow or what can also be termed as the end of the age. Already a pandemic of influenza was in the process of claiming 20 million lives worldwide, and disasters were striking at regions of occultism and sensuality. Such was the case at the very onset of our century, in September of 1900, when Galveston, Texas, one of America's great party towns, especially in the way of Mardi Gras (one recent costume theme was "Beelzebub and the Devils"), was destroyed by a monumental flood. Seawater inundated the entire island, leaving but the sight of floating debris and surreal flashes of lightning. Between 6,000 and 7,000 of the island's residents were killed and a third of the island scraped of its structures. Afterward, the land was covered with an inch-layer of foul-smelling slime. An article in *National Geographic* described it as "a scene of suffering and devastation hardly paralleled in the history of the world."

Six years after Galveston, a similar catastrophe struck San Francisco, which like Galveston was consumed with finance and partying, with its posh hotels, opium dens, red-lit bordellos, and homosexuals. It was known as "Barbary Coast" or "Babylon on the Bay." Starting at 5:12 a.m. on April 18, 1906, the earth underneath San Francisco shook for 28 horrifying seconds and more than 28,000 structures were destroyed and 478 people were killed. The entire area of Morton Street—where the prostitutes were particularly prevalent—was turned into smoldering ash. About 250,000 people were made homeless.

These American tragedies, unheeded as warnings, were joined by disasters abroad. Across the Pacific, Hong Kong, which was notorious for its narcotics, prostitution, and pagan gods (and as such was San Francisco's sister city in Asia), experienced similar devastation when a typhoon killed 10,000 on September 18, 1906. That was followed by a quake on January 22, 1907, in Jamaica, which was home to marijuana and Obeah, a form of voodoo.

In 1908 there was another catastrophe: 83,000 dead in a quake and tidal wave at Messina, Italy. The tremor was like a harbinger of war, for not two months later, turmoil erupted in the Balkans as Serbia began arming itself, demanding that Austro-Hungarians leave Bosnia-Hercegovina. Within a few short years, the animosities helped trigger World War One. Europe's equilibrium was unhinged on June 28, 1914—just a month after the Hrushiw phenomena—when Archduke Francis Ferdinand, heir to the Austro-Hungarian empire, was assassinated in Bosnia-Hercegovina.

Italy had not yet been dragged into the war, but on January 13, 1915, another quake hit that country. This time it was in the province of Abruzzi. Seventeen villages were leveled, and while there were no injuries in Rome, panic seized inhabitants who rushed into the streets and sought refuge in the churches.

Soon, the Germans ordered total submarine warfare and

their torpedoes would sink the Lusitania. And soon after *that,* Italy went to war with Austria-Hungary and Germany joined Austria against the shaken Italians, whose quake, as it turned out, was but a harbinger of greater sorrows.

CHAPTER 8

Quakes and War

The war was a tremendous signal to all of humanity, embroiling the newly "modern" world as nothing had before, and if events had been signalled by signs in Ukraine and Ireland, as well as by seers such as Anna Maria Taigi, they were also foretold during the supernatural occurrence in Portugal, where besides an angel were also apparitions of Jesus, Mary, and Joseph.

A prophecy was given to the children that while World War I would soon end, a greater war would erupt if mankind did not relinquish its new and godless course.

The young seers were told in 1917 that this second war would be indicated by a strange nightly illumination. *"When you see a night illumined by an unknown light, know that this is the great sign given you by God that He is about to punish the world . . ."*

Wars. Rumors of wars. There would also be signs in the earth. Seven major quakes occurred between 1900 and 1930, and then the same number in just the next ten years, in a single rocking decade, as tremors shook India, Chile, and California. The one in India was a Richter 8.4. The quakes reached a peak just before World War II, and although we can never be sure how earthquakes compare through each decade (because the sensitivity of measurements has increased), they seemed, nonetheless, to be some kind of crude spiritual indicator. So too the floods that struck Communist China. A nearly inconceivable 3,700,000 died along the Huang He River in 1931, as well as 200,000 eight years later in the country's north.

"The furies of Hell rage now," a thirties mystic, Teresa Neumann, said she was told by the Lord. "The chastisement of God is inevitable."

Two years after Neumann's prophecy, on January 26, 1938, an extraordinary display of the aurora borealis or "northern lights" startled all of Europe. Large arcs of light rose in the east and west, described by pilots as a shimmering curtain of fire. Its glow reflected across the snow-clad Alps and caused such an illumination that many in London thought Windsor Castle was on fire. It was the sign promised to Lucia, the Fatima visionary, a decade before.

A week after the aurora borealis, on February 4, 1938, Adolph Hitler promoted himself to military chief in Germany and a month after that marched his Nazis into Austria, setting the stage for real horrors.

In the Soviet Union, as prophesied, Stalin was liquidating not thousands but *millions* in an oppression initiated the very year—1917—of the last major Portuguese phenomena, which had included a prediction of Communist tyranny along with that of the major new war.

"All this and a thousand other disasters must come before the rise of the Man of Sin," said the mystic Jeanne le Royer back around the time of the French uprisings, mentioning "frightful" earthquakes and cities destroyed by "whirlwinds of smoke, fire, sulphur, and tar," while in Rome the pope, Pius XII, felt humanity was in the grip of a supreme crisis. "We believe that the present hour is a dreaded phase of the events foretold by Christ. It seems that darkness is about to fall on the world."

There was warring among nations and also great strife inside China, along with more telltale and prophetic accounts of the supernatural. In Cracow, Poland, a nun named Sister M. Faustina Kowalska was having nearly daily encounters with celestial entities, including the apparition in April of 1938 of a seraph "surrounded by a great light, the divinity and love of God being reflected in him. He wore a golden robe and, over it, a transparent surplice and a transparent stole."

Returning from Mass one day, the Polish mystic also experienced devils. "When I had taken a few steps, a great multitude of demons blocked my way," she said. "They threatened me with terrible tortures, and voices could be heard." Seeing their great hatred, the nun invoked her guardian angel. At once the "bright and radiant figure of my guardian angel appeared," and the evil spirits fled. Another time Sister Kowalska saw a cherub in a little white cloud, guarding a gate that had become dangerous because of revolutionary disturbances outside. The angel's gaze, said the nun, "was like lightning." In 1938, during an alleged locution from the Lord, the nun was told, *"In the Old Covenant I sent prophets wielding thunderbolts to My people. Today I am sending you with My mercy to the people of the whole world. I do not want to punish aching mankind, but I desire to heal it, pressing it to My merciful heart. I use punishment when they themselves force Me to do so; My hand is reluctant to take hold of the sword of justice. Before the Day of Justice I am sending the Day of Mercy."*

And a day of warning. For Sister Kowalska's message was just before Poland was invaded by the Nazis in what we may describe as a chastisement or purification. One prong of the invasion came right through the region of Cracow, officially initiating World War Two. The rest of Europe would also be judged, and then the rest of the world. As foretold at Hrushiw, the Ukrainians and those in surrounding republics lived under unprecedented persecution. Literally millions died, perhaps as many as 4.6 to 10 million during Soviet-induced food shortages in the 1930s. Millions more succumbed in later years through warfare and other forms of persecution. "In terms of absolute data," says one scholar, Lubomyr Hajda of Harvard, "the Ukrainian numbers are probably higher than any other mass atrocity we're familiar with."

Eighty years of persecution! So hungry were Ukrainians in the 1930s that they ate leaves, worms, rodents, and tree bark. When things got really bad they cannibalized each other.

Bodies were piled like cordwood.

Similar horrors occurred in Kuban and North Caucasus.

All told more than 14 million peasants from this region of the Soviet Union died during the years of Communism, along with those millions elsewhere who died fighting Hitler or the forces of Japan and Mao.

CHAPTER 9

The "Vanishing Hitchhiker"

With all this came also a major celestial development: both good and evil spirits seemed to be manifesting in the earthly realm as mysterious strangers and ghostly hitchhikers. Angels and demons, not only showing themselves, but, again as with Abraham (*Genesis* 18:2), taking human form.

According to Dr. Jan Harold Brunvand, author of a book of folklore studies entitled *The Vanishing Hitchhiker,* such stories were in circulation at least as early as 1876, and by the first part of our own century there were accounts as far afield as Illinois, Georgia, and the Russian city of St. Petersburg. It went something like this: the driver of a horse-drawn buggy (later an automobile) was driving down a lonely road one night when he picked up a hitchhiker who got in, seemed pleasant, participated in a bit of small talk, handed out a short but dramatic anecdote or prophecy, and then vanished right there in the back seat, indicating a supernatural encounter.

Most such accounts were third-hand or further removed, which dampened their credibility. Never, it seemed, did the person telling such a story actually know the eyewitnesses, let alone have experienced it for himself or herself. This is one reason the accounts were classified as "folklore."

But they were everywhere, and if only a couple were true, it was an astonishing consideration, indicating some form of intersection between the natural and the supernatural; a materialization of otherworldly forces. Frequently, the hitchhiker was described as someone recently deceased, usually someone who'd died in an accident or otherwise prematurely. Only the location seemed to change, along with gender and age. The hitchhiker could be young or old, male or female. Often the sightings were on a spooky dark night or near a lonely graveyard.

The stories seemed to pick up pace during the 1930s and 1940s. A driver would stop for a hitchhiker only to have the strange passenger disappear in the back seat after a few minutes of unusual and even eerie conversation. According to one version, circulated around 1935 in Berkeley, California, a man was tooling up a road on a rainy night when he saw a female student waiting for a streetcar. He offered the girl a ride since streetcars were no longer running. As they were crossing an intersection another auto came down a steep hill and would have caused a serious collision had not the girl reached over and pulled his emergency brake. The fellow was beside himself. He stared in shock at the other car, which then pulled around and went on its way. When he remembered the girl he looked over and she was gone.

Many of the hitchhikers seemed to be "ghosts." Near where I live, in Delmar, New York, there was a spooky rider who used to jump on young men's horses in the 1890's as they went past a certain woods (or so we are told). It was a mysterious woman who disappeared upon arrival at the destination.

That was the "haunted" aspect. There were also cases that seemed to involve bona fide angels. In 1938, according to author Kelsey Tylor, a young man named Charles A. Galloway, Jr., from Jackson, Mississippi, was trying to jump a ride on a freight train when he came close to death. "Suddenly, the ground beneath him narrowed and he was running alongside a steep ravine," said Tyler. "A few feet ahead he could see that there was no land at all alongside the tracks—only a steep drop-off."

Frantically Charles jumped and because he didn't have quite enough speed he landed only partially in the open boxcar. With nothing to hold onto, he was ready to slip to his death. There was a steep canyon below as the train moved atop a ridge. He was moments away from a gruesome finish—either below in the canyon or beneath the train's clamoring wheels. But after crying for God he opened his eyes and before him was a "fantastic-looking" black man, muscular and in his thirties, who stared intently at Galloway, yanked him to safety, and vanished in the empty boxcar.

Accounts of similar intervention are given us by Joan Wester Anderson in her book *Where Angels Walk*. One involves a woman named Corrie ten Boom in Holland, whose brother, a minister in the Dutch Reformed Church, was sheltering Jewish refugees when Hitler's army moved through Europe in the 1940s. Corrie too, soon helped the horribly persecuted Jews. In 1944, she was arrested along with her sister Betsie and sent to a women's extermination camp at Ravensbrueck. Invoking angels to make her and her smuggled Bible invisible, Corrie was able to walk right by inspectors who stripped and searched the other inmates without a guard so much as looking at her. "Corrie lived for several months at this cruelest of institutions and was subjected to many searches," writes Anderson. "She and Betsie also conducted clandestine worship services and Bible study for inmates of all faiths and nationalities. But there seemed to be an invisible wall of protection around her Bible, for the guards never found it."

Betsie was eventually released under most mysterious circumstances, for all other women prisoners her age were taken to the gas chamber. It was later learned that her release had been the result of a "clerical error," or what others would call a miracle.

There were also accounts of missionary priests aided by angels in Japan during the 1940s. Then, in 1959, a mysterious man who seemed like an engineer, and carried himself in an especially tranquil and dignified manner, appeared to a Baptist minister who was trying to build a replica of Christ's tomb on a hill overlooking the Ohio River. The only problem was that the hill began to give way, threatening collapse. They couldn't figure a way of stopping it. Before vanishing the stranger gave the minister a set of plans for a retaining wall which halted the earth from its seemingly inevitable slide. Henceforth, not a foot of dirt moved. In the early 1960s, a mysterious stranger helped a missionary linguist who was trying to spread New Testaments and hymnals on a remote island of the Philippines—a venture that greatly succeeded—while in the U.S. two angels came to the rescue of a Southern minister whose life was threatened by a political boss named Sam.

The minister had stood up to Sam over some kind of plan and thus the danger: this politico played tougher than most.

"Friends alerted the minister and offered to walk home with him, past a dark woods," says Anderson. "But the minister waved away their concerns. 'The Lord will be with me,' he told them, and he walked home alone in safety. Years passed, and on his deathbed, Sam sent for this minister. 'Reverend, I meant to kill you that night,' he said. 'I was in the woods with a club.'"

When asked why he didn't, this would-be killer replied, "What do you mean—why didn't I? Who were those two big men with you?"

There were no "big men" with the minister.

In 1956, another man of God, this time a Catholic, Monsignor Timothy Ryan of Cape May, New Jersey, was rescued in an entirely different way. "What happened was I was extremely tired from Christmas," he says. "I had taken a ride up to visit family and didn't get too much sleep. I had gone up north of Danbury. Coming back later, down the Garden State Parkway in northern New Jersey around midnight, I was fighting sleep. I was nearly the only one on the highway. I was fighting sleep and without realizing it I was going out for the count. And this big white bird—like a swan—was suddenly over the windshield for a couple of seconds. It was around midnight. It should have crashed into the windshield. It brought me to my senses. I had no doubt then and it remained with me—an angel guardian."

During the 1960s, hitchhikers were being reported all the way down to Brazil. Went one story: A minister was motoring down a road to make a sick call when he spotted a young male on a stretch of uninhabited land. He picked up the man and they began to speak of Jesus. "I believe the Lord's return is getting close," said the minister.

"Well, that may be sooner than you think," the young

man replied in a soft peaceful voice.

When the minister turned to look at him, the young man was naturally gone.

Some seemed like angels. Some seemed to be spirits of the dead. Others seemed like deceptive spirits. This was a major descent of the heavenlies, something truly startling and perhaps significant. In Chicago there were accounts of a "prophesying passenger" who predicted (incorrectly) that a fair in Chicago, the Century of Progress Exposition, would slide off into Lake Michigan, and a cab driver in the same city who reportedly picked up an old nun and listened to her prophecy that the effects of Pearl Harbor would only last four months.

That was in 1941.

In Bluffton, Indiana, Robert Nuddin and his wife, residents of Elmwood, claimed that they were driving to visit her sister in Indianapolis when they saw an old man walking along the road and gave him a ride. "I have no money to pay for your kindness, but I can answer any question you may wish to ask," said the hitchhiker.

When they asked when the world would end, he said, "That's easy. It will end in July."

Mormons in Utah circulated similar myths, identifying the Korean War or tensions between Russia and the United States with disasters prophesied in the Book of Mormon. There were hitchhikers who warned of a coming famine, that Mormons should stock clothes and store staple foods for two years. These hitchhikers were identified with mystical disciples of Christ called "Nephites," who were supposedly granted earthly existence until the Second Coming. If God had something important to say to the Church, taught the Mormons, He would certainly not bypass His chosen leaders but instead spread His message by sending His hitchhikers through the countryside with words of knowledge.

CHAPTER 10

Lying Wonders?

The phenomena continued through the 1960s and again begged the question: Which were good angels and which were lying wonders? Which were the "false prophets" who Jesus warned about in the very same chapter of *Matthew* (24:11) where He also foresaw the beginning of sorrows?

One had to be cautious. Evil spirits are known to masquerade as angels of light or "spirits of the dead," and depending on the epoch or culture, they have also disguised themselves as leprechauns, wood nymphs, nature "fairies," Eastern gods, tribal spirits, elves, and most recently, UFOs or outer spacemen. Indeed, at the very same time as the hitchhiker phenomenon, there was a parallel eruption of unidentified flying objects. And they seemed more *spiritual* than extraterrestrial. I remember the legend of a strange light which hovered over a Tuscarora reservation just outside of Niagara Falls; they seemed to favor cemeteries and Indian burial mounds. Those who witness them, who have a "close encounter" with a UFO, often describe a halo-like effect and begin to experience occult proclivities such as telekinesis, automatic writing, and mind-reading. The most controversial psychic of our time, Uri Geller, claimed he was in touch with an extraterrestrial civilization from the planet "Hoova," and so too were aerial lights associated with an alleged South American psychic known as Arigo.

At some UFO sites a substance resembling cotton fibers or a spider's web—known as "angel hair"—has been found. This is also something that has been associated with spirit seances.

As with rituals of magic, there are those who trace UFOs back to prehistoric times. Strange discs were drawn on cave walls at Altamira in the Santander province of Spain, and they were also reported during the outbreak in mysticism during the 13th century, with accounts of flying objects over Byland Abbey in Yorkshire, witnessed by terrified monks in 1290. During the Revolution in France there were reports of a large flying red globe over Alencon. Other sightings occurred in Ireland.

The modern wave of UFOs, however, started in the 1870s and 1880s, and like the hitchhikers, it too seemed to serve as some kind of indecipherable and possibly sinister barometer. Much of this information comes from an excellent compilation called *The UFO Encyclopedia,* edited by John Spencer. According to Spencer, one of the very first "saucer" sightings in the U.S. was in 1878, around the time hitchhiker stories were first recorded. Then, in May of 1880, a man named Lee Fore Brace saw two enormous luminous "wheels" on each side of the British India Company's steamship *Patna,* which was in the Persian Gulf. It put one in mind of Ezekiel. These rotating "wheels" caused a swishing effect and were perhaps 1,500 feet in diameter. In 1893, an officer on watch aboard another ship, the *Caroline,* cruising in China's North Sea, reported unusual lights that alternately appeared as a mass of luminosity and an irregular line of red globules that emitted smoke and resembled Chinese lanterns. The first reported photograph was by astronomer José A. Y. Bonilla of the Zacatecas Observatory in Mexico, on August 12, 1883—not long before Pope Leo XIII's 1884 vision that demons were being loosed upon the earth. Bonilla saw discs and ovoids crossing the sun, and a little more than a dozen years after that there was a swell of reports in America, where, in keeping with the technology of the day, they were described as "airships."

Matters were greatly elevated in 1947 when a private pilot named Kenneth Arnold, flying on June 24 near Mount Rainier in the Cascade Mountains, spotted a formation of nine objects that seemed to be moving at up to 1,700 miles an hour. They did so in a fashion that reminded Arnold of the way a saucer dish would skip across water. Arnold said his UFOs were shaped like boomerangs, but the description stuck: flying saucers. And indeed many subsequent UFOs were saucer-shaped. All the rage: In August of 1951 another photographer snapped a photo of eerie lights which kept appearing over Lubbock, Texas, in a V-shaped formation.

Over the years many of the reports, of course, have been the product of hoax, swamp gas, weather balloons, the planet Venus (which can shine surprisingly bright), meteorites, satellites, airplane lights, search beams, optical illusions, and over-active imaginations. But others are more difficult to explain, including that of Sergeant Stephen J. Brickner of the U.S. Marine Corps, who saw a formation of 150 UFOs in 1942 over the Solomon Islands. There were also several sightings by the Royal Canadian Air Force in Alberta, Canada, during the 1940s and 1950s, while in the U.S., at this very time, the federal government investigated such unexplainable aerial phenomena through what was known as "Project Grudge" and then "Project Blue Book." The investigation was coordinated by the Air Force, with the scientific advice of Dr. J. Allen Hynek, who later was a consultant for the movie *Close Encounters of the Third Kind.* A former U.S. Navy missile chief, Rear Admiral Delmar Fahrney, has been quoted as saying that "reliable reports indicate there are objects coming into our atmosphere at very high speeds and controlled by thinking intelligences."

If certain cases merit a degree of credence, or at least consideration, there was also a "lunatic fringe" that quickly formed itself into flying-saucer cults. A woman named Marian Keech claimed she was contacted by space beings known as "The Guardians" and her followers waited for a saucer to rescue them before the onset of a flood that was supposed to wipe out Salt Lake City—the Mormon stronghold, and of course where hitchhikers had led to similar prophecies of an apocalypse. Keech's messages were received through automatic writing, in which spirits take control and use one's hands to write messages. It's very similar to occult channeling and as such is looked down upon by Christians as an obvious manifestation of demons. One of the "planets" connected with these UFOs was "Cerus," which sounds a bit like "Sirius," a star that has long been revered by devil worshipers.

Those who followed UFOs were aware of "men in black," mysterious and well-dressed strangers who seemed to pop up after saucer sightings. They drove old cars that were in mint condition, with a strange interior glow, often dark Cadillacs. Reports of them went back to 1953. Most were reported to have a dark complexion, straight hair, and strangely glowing eyes. They wore dark suits, dark hats (sometimes homburgs), dark ties, dark shoes, but white shirts. They seemed cold or otherwise aloof and had a sinister, almost menacing way of speaking—often threatening those they approached—and afterward witnesses were plagued with headaches, memory lapses, nightmares, and foul odors. They conveyed their messages through telepathy.

If that wasn't enough to suggest demonism there was also the famous photograph taken on July 16, 1952, of what looked like four fairly well-defined oval lights over a Coast Guard facility in the very nexus of American witchcraft: Salem, Massachusetts.

In other cases, during the 1950s and 1960s, strange "crop circles"—large symmetrical patterns left mainly in corn fields—began perplexing UFO investigators. Some of them resembled occultic symbols and were near old pagan ritual sites such as Stonehenge.

If there was any doubt that at least *some* UFOs possessed an evil underside, this should have been dispelled by the next major development: the abduction phenomenon. By 1957 there were reports of humans who were kidnapped by "extraterrestrials" and taken aboard their UFOs for sex or medical examinations. One such man was Antonio Villas Boas. He claimed to have had intercourse with a human-like woman who had slanted eyes and the unsettling habit of growling like a dog in passion. This would become a common theme: humans abducted by outer spacemen who engaged in intercourse with them like incubi and succubi, which are sexual demons. Such abductions brought to mind old Celtic legends of "fairies" abducting men and women to their magic circles where their children (or "changelings") were substituted for human ones. It was like the giants in the days of Noah! The most famous "abduction" involved a New Hampshire couple named Barney and Betty Hill, who were returning from a trip to Canada in 1961 when they spotted a strange light near a place called Indian Head. Under hypnosis they seemed to remember that they'd been taken aboard the UFO and that Betty had been "examined" by a needle that the humanoids pressed through her navel.

For a long time Betty was followed by lights in the sky and experienced dreams in which friends and relatives met violent deaths.

Much of it smacked, of course, of sheer lunacy—or demonism. In 1967, near England's Whipsnade Zoo, a boy named Alex Butler reported a "little blue man with a tall hat and a beard."

The man could disappear into a puff of smoke.

In Brazil, two years later, a man fishing near Belo Horizonte claimed he was struck by a blue beam of light and abducted by humanoids into a cylindrical UFO. There he encountered another entity, a dwarf covered in red hair with a face to put you in mind of a gnome or troll.

The entity had pale skin, thick eyebrows, and huge green eyes.

He brawled with the extraterrestrials but was saved by the appearance, in the end, of a Christ-like figure.

CHAPTER 11

Glory of the Celestials

Perhaps it should be no surprise that the onslaught of negativity intensified during the 1960s. In many ways it was the period that would shape subsequent decades. Music turned hard, materialism burgeoned, hearts turned cold, and the pews all but emptied. It was the period in which school prayer was banned, drugs invaded the culture, our youth turned wayward, and illicit sex—soon followed by abortion—broke into the mainstream.

It was, in short, the defining moment of our era.

Men on the moon! Woodstock! A riot at Stonewall!

In 1969, even future President Jimmy Carter reported a UFO, an object the size of the moon that seemed to change colors.

California was the hotspot for those in touch with "flying saucers," but so too did Ann Arbor, Michigan, have its 15 minutes of fame. During 1966 a rash of sightings there made *Life* magazine.

"The coming of the lawless one is according to the working of Satan," says *2 Thessalonians* 2:9, *"with all power, signs, and lying wonders."*

Said the 1846 prophecy from LaSalatte: "Demons of the air together with the Anti-Christ will perform great wonders on earth and in the atmosphere, and men will become more and more perverted."

Along with the flying objects were natural disasters: seven major earthquakes during the 1960's and a graduation of major typhoons, hurricanes, and blizzards. As Nahum the prophet said, *"The Lord is slow to anger, yet great in power, and the Lord never leaves the guilty unpunished. In hurricane and tempest is his path"* (*Nahum* 1:2-3). Where only three such storms were registered during the first decade of our century, there were 12 during the 1950s and then 19 during the turbulent and iconoclastic Sixties. And while only two major floods or tidal waves were listed in the almanac during the 1940s, this mushroomed to six in the 1950s and 16 in the 1960s. On the way also were violence in Ireland and a wrenching famine in Biafra.

Were the wars and natural disasters "signs of the times," or just recording artifacts?

Was it not true that *every* year had its plagues?

Were they clues from on-high or simply the result of heavier population centers and thus an increase in reported damage?

To a certain extent, every generation has its own signs of the times, but something seemed to be happening, something especially intense, something different in the heavenlies. Never mind UFOs; demons were also riding high on societal statistics. According to figures provided by William J. Bennett of the Heritage Foundation, the divorce rate in 1960 was less than 10 per 1,000 women, but by the end of the Sixties it was more like 15. The teen suicide rate went from 3.6 per 100,000 to 5.9 and the number of illegitimate births doubled. Teen pregnancies jumped from 15.3 per 1,000 to 22.4 in 1970.

The figures took a special upward track after 1963—the year they banned school prayer. Immediately there were spiraling rates of drug use, fornication, and sexually transmitted disease. SAT scores dropped, television-viewing rose, and there was a huge escalation in violent crimes: from 288,460 in 1960 to 738,820 by the beginning of the next decade.

America the liberal. America the godless. America, a new edition of the French insurrection, but with the added spice of bloodlust movies and pornography. It was bye bye Miss

American Pie: Revolution was everywhere, a rebellion against God. And that opened the portals of Hell, with yet greater phenomena and more startling crimes. The same year as Carter's UFO we also had an occultist in California named Charles Manson.

On another menacing note, it was also the decade of "cattle mutilations." Actually, the Sixties were only the start; within a short time both cows and horses would be found in Colorado, New Mexico, Montana, Wyoming, Idaho, and Texas. Parts of their carcasses—often their sexual organs— were inexplicably and surgically removed. Some scoffed at the killings while others felt they were the work of satanists who use animal parts in their rituals. Yet others associated the mystery with UFOs. The mutilations would also involve the normally sedate states of Oklahoma and Nebraska, where satanism was set to take a surprising hold. In a few instances crop circles (or at least circularly swirled weeds) were found near the carcasses.

Yet in this upsurge of evil, in the tense energy of darkness and mystery, with the spiritual bats winging their way around, with cults proliferating like fungi, there was a similar rise—really, a *descent,* since they were coming from Heaven—of the angels. Stories of heavenly help—direct and miraculous help—abounded. Angels, in the mode of rescue! One of the most remarkable instances occurred on June 18, 1961, far up a mountain in the Cantabrians. This was in north-central Spain, where four peasant girls in an incredibly backward village known as San Sebastián de Garabandal had stolen apples from a local orchard. They were hiding on a stony, sunken path when it happened. It was about 8:30 p.m. As they ate the apples they heard a violent noise like thunder. Suddenly they were filled with guilt and remorse. "Now that we have taken apples that did not belong to us, the devil will be happy and our poor guardian angels will be sad," commented Conchita Gonzalez, 12. They began to pick up stones, throwing them at a spot where they figured the devil was. That calmed their consciences, and they went back to playing, using small stones for a game of marbles and thinking apologies to their angels.

"Suddenly, there appeared to me a very beautiful figure that shone brilliantly but did not hurt my eyes at all," recalled Conchita. "When the other three girls, Jacinta, Loli, and Mari Cruz, saw me in the state of ecstasy, they thought that I was having a fit, because I kept saying, with my hands clasped, *'Ay! Ay!* (Oh! Oh!)' They were about to call my mother when they found themselves in the same state as I, and cried out together, *'Ay!* Oh! The angel!'"

There was a short silence as they gaped in awe. The angel was wearing a long seamless blue robe and had large pink wings. His eyes were black and his hands fine, with short fingernails. There was a great light about him, but not for long. Soon he disappeared into the thin mountain air.

When the four youngsters went back the next day, they were disappointed that the celestial visitor didn't materialize. He was no longer there, but they heard a distinct voice: "Don't worry. You shall see me again."

And indeed on June 20, back there at the sunken lane (or *calleja*), they were engulfed by a sudden brilliance. "We couldn't see anything but the light," said Conchita. "We were terrified and began to scream."

The angel came with sweetness and yet unimagined power. As C.S. Lewis once said, "In Scripture the visitation of an angel is always alarming; it has to begin by saying, 'Fear not.'" On June 23 the angel appeared again and seemed to have a sign beneath him, a sign containing Roman numerals. He appeared very young, perhaps nine years old. Yet there was something tremendously strong and mature about him. They later identified him as the Archangel Michael, and he was to return with an identical angel as well as the Infant Jesus and His mother Mary. The apparitions continued for more than four years. During that time the children were given glimpses of the future and told that mankind had chosen a dangerous path. As a result, there would come a period during their lifetimes when God would send three major events: a warning, involving some sort of unprecedented occurrence; a great miracle to convert disbelievers, visible there in the Cantabrians; and a purification or punishment, which seemed to involve massive heat and electronic interference, something that would disrupt our technology. Conchita was under the impression that the warning would be "visible all over the world" and would cause people to realize their sins—"a sort of a catastrophe," something like two stars "that crash and make a lot of noise, and a lot of light," but might not cause many deaths. As for the miracle, that would occur on a Thursday evening and would be seen by those at Garabandal. She compared it to rays of light or a "pillar of smoke," something that would be seen but not felt. "It will be the greatest miracle that Jesus has performed for the world," claimed Conchita. These two stages would be followed by tribulation.

Such apparitions were anathema to many Protestants who worried about demonic or psychological counterfeits and also to certain Catholics, especially Church officials, who were familiar with age-old deceptions. Satan, they knew, could dress up any way he wanted to. Back in the 1500s a Franciscan nun in this very same country was found to be the subject of an especially frightening charade: From the age of five the devil appeared to her under the form of different saints, promising, according to theological literature, that if she cooperated he would help to make her famous for her sanctity. It was alleged that the nun, who hailed from Cordova, used Satan's gifts to dazzle witnesses with ecstasies, levitations, and predictions which were often accurate. For 38 years, up to 1543, she succeeded in deceiving some of the best theologians in the country. But at death's door she confessed and her apparitions were formally condemned—as were at least twenty other such "revelations" in the similarly plagued 17th century.

The issue of discernment was also raised with gifts such as tongues. There were good tongues and there were artificial tongues. There was valid prophecy and there was contamination by Satan, who according to Paul in *2 Corinthians* "transforms himself into an angel of light."

Did not Scripture tell us that Satan would specifically come as an angel?

And were there not specific questions about Garabandal itself, such as the confusion which later engulfed these visionaries—who were led to doubt their experiences—and the odd manner of their ecstasies?

Yet the occurrence in Spain was similar in certain regards to what Protestants had also been prophesying, and whatever the case, there was no question, in the 1960s, that mankind was risking God's wrath, especially in the way of occultism. Old Beelzebub was everywhere. The time had come to invoke heavenly legions. It was their charge to pursue evil spirits. And they were. They came both as consoling agents and as warring spirits. They came with more power than Satan. No simple little cherubs! They were here with consolation—great consolation—but also in warning. They came as the largest quake in North America this century, a Richter 8.4, rocked Alaska on Good Friday of 1964.

We needed rocking. We needed the light of Heaven. And praise God, it was coming with abundance. Sweet God! In Zeitun, Egypt, a suburb of Cairo, an estimated million or more onlookers—Coptics, Moslems, Catholics, and Evangelicals—saw magnificent luminosities above a church located near the route Jesus, Mary, and Joseph used after fleeing into Egypt to escape the despot Herod. The lights were seen nearly nightly from 1968 to 1971 and witnesses included not only bishops and preachers but also the nation's former president, Abdul Nasser. It started on April 2, 1968: scintillating, mysterious lights, flashes of light, and flights of what looked like luminous birds. Doves! "They always maintained a definite formation and disappeared suddenly like melted snowflakes," said Francis Johnston, who wrote a book about the happenings. "I was at Zeitun when I saw two 'pigeons' very white, very bright, luminous, radiating light," added Bishop Gregorius, an Orthodox prelate. "They became tiny flakes of clouds and seemed to enter Heaven. They do not flap their wings; they glide. In a flash they appeared; and disappeared in the same way. They do not fly away, but above and around the center dome. They stay quite near and are close to the church when they vanish. Whatever formation they take, they keep. Sometimes as many as seven of them fly in the formation of a cross. They appear and disappear in this formation."

Light. Flashes of light. Sometimes yellow flames in front of the church. Also reddish smoke or incense. The phenomena were photographed. They appeared on television. They filled newspaper columns. They brought together Christians, Moslems, and Jews in common prayer. As it is written, *"And the smoke of the incense, with the prayers of the saints, ascended before God from the angel's hand."* (*Revelation* 8:4).

It was like the supernatural glow in Ireland but on a greater scale. Brilliant blue-white lights and little shooting stars or "meteorites." Among the onlookers was Reverend Dr. Ibrahim Said, head of the Evangelical Church and spokesman for Protestant churches in Egypt. Incense or smoke was witnessed nearly every evening. In *Revelation* an angel stands at the altar and offers incense *"with the prayers of all the saints upon the golden altar which was before the throne"* (8:3) before the trumpets—before the quakes and thunder.

Which raised this question: Were the apparitions intended to ward off the "plagues of Egypt"?

There were no messages from Zeitun but some saw the sky opening like a sanctuary. Lights. Incense. Also an image of the Infant Jesus. An official inquiry on behalf of Egypt's Department of General Information reported the happenings as "an undeniable fact" and on May 5, 1966, a special commission formed by the Orthodox patriarch, Kryollis VI, concluded simply but unforgettably that at a time of desperate need, at a time of apostasy, Almighty God had "allowed the terrestrials to see the glory of the celestials."

CHAPTER 12

Angels On The Turnpike

Thus were the forces of good and evil now manifest. It took a long time to hear about it. These were not events covered by the media. Yet they continued to escalate, as angels and demons continued to square off.

While demons deceived, angels continued their intervention. During the summer of 1969, a 17-year-old Croatian immigrant named Zdenko Singer arrived in Toronto, almost penniless and for all practical purposes without a home. Born in Zagreb to an unmarried woman, Singer had been raised by a kindly grandmother who practiced Christianity despite serious persecution in what was then Yugoslavia. She took Singer from his struggling mother, carrying him onto a train in a wicker basket and returning him only when the boy was 12. It was then that he had joined his mother in Montreal, but after five years of personal difficulties and unhappiness he'd struck out on his own, arriving in Toronto by bus.

"I was working until 3 a.m. every day and education was denied me, so I had no money," says Singer. "It was time for me to move on and do something else. I got my paycheck that last day at the end of July in 1969 and left. I decided not to take anything with me. I didn't have any clothes to speak of. I had a few shirts and little else. About all I took were my swimming trunks, because they had spe-

cial significance to me. They were something I had bought
and had sentimental value to me. And my last paycheck.
I left the money in the bank and took the paycheck. I was
working at the Queen Elizabeth Hotel as a busboy and a
dishwasher. I had about sixty dollars. I got on a bus and
headed for Toronto. I was beyond crying. I had no idea
where I would stay nor what I would do."

He arrived in the middle of the night, at Bay and College
streets in the downtown area, with virtually no luggage.
It was twilight and a hot summer day was dawning. He
walked toward the center of the city and a public square
at city hall, spending the day roaming the downtown and
the first night in a YMCA.

"The next day, Saturday, I was wandering around the
same way," says Singer. "I was probably down to about
$40 and trying to form in my mind what I was going to
do. I was devastated. All I wanted was a place to stay and
a job. I was hurt because I was cleancut even in the hippie
era and dressed as neatly as possible and groomed. But I
felt like a bum. I zig-zagged around the rest of the day.
I ate at little shops, toast and cheddar cheese sandwiches.
I was trying to preserve my money. It was sweltering hot
and all I wanted anyway was cold water.

"That night I spent sitting the whole night in the square.
I dozed in and out of sleep. There were street people in
and out all night. I wandered around a bit myself until morning. The city was quiet, almost dead, starting in early afternoon. Everybody seemed to be drifting toward the square
while everyone else was going home. The streets were emptying. I went back to the square. To this day I could probably bring you to the same bench, and show you the hotdog
stand. There were a lot of families there with their children, and people were strolling around a water fountain
and ice rink that's a pond in the summer. I sat there and
watched all the activity and really didn't know what I wanted
to do but knew I had to do something soon. It was very
crowded, so much so that the cops were there on their horses.

"I was sitting in front of a small building where they sold
hotdogs from a rollup window and watching people mingle
and kids playing. I really didn't want to spend another night
out there in the park. I was focusing on what to do that

evening. I could have gone back to the Y, but I needed to preserve my money. As I was sitting there watching the crowd and thinking, suddenly a couple of men came up straight in front of me and started talking to me. One of them wore a shortsleeve shirt. I'm not good at describing people, but I can still see him as if it were yesterday. I see him clearly. Medium height, balding, just a rim of brown hair, or anyway darker hair, almost like black. Very dark. A little paunchy. Average build. His face was round, not fat; normal nose. I initially thought that this person was an immigrant who spoke fluent English and was probably of Hispanic background, from Spain. He was well-dressed— not a tie, but neat and clean and a good shirt, not something out of Bargain Harold's. Yet neither was it Gucci. He was carrying a dark brown valise. I've often thought since, what was that bag? He was holding it under his right arm. His pants were lighter colored, probably gray, and his shoes I remember well. They weren't typical shoes. They were like mesh shoes.

"The second man I can't describe as closely. Also in a short-sleeve shirt, dark hair too, but a full head of it, same height but skinnier and dressed a little darker—his colors weren't as light. I didn't pay as much attention to him. The first man was the one who approached closest while the second one was to his left and slightly behind. And it was the first man who spoke and did all the talking.

"Suddenly there were these two men just right there in front of me. I had seen them coming but didn't realize they were coming directly for me. Picture this: Here's these two guys who come and stand right in front of me and I'm sitting there minding my own business and they're standing there and I figured they wanted something, that they were provoking me in some way, that they were looking for something. The first man was looking at me. There had been stories I'd heard of what happened in the downtown area and I thought it was my turn. I thought they were men who preyed on young people. There I was in the middle of the big city with two strangers looking at me. Both men looked like they were in their forties.

"The first man was looking straight in my eyes, a serious look but not austere. I could sense that he was caring but not in the sense that he would take all my burden—someone who would give strict directions. Not a dictator but someone with suggestions. He didn't introduce himself. He said right off the bat, 'You're not from this town.'

"I kind of looked at him, even more skeptically. 'Yeah. So?' I almost felt I should get up and walk away. I felt uncomfortable.

"'You don't have to worry,' he said. 'You need a job. You need a place to stay.'"

His voice was authoritative. Then he told Singer where he was going to get a job. "He didn't explain a precise building or name of a company but he named the street, Evans Avenue, and gave me directions on how to get there. He wasn't telling me to follow him or offering me a cup of coffee or offering me a place of shelter, and so he didn't seem like a weirdo—he didn't seem like he was enticing me. Which prompted me to start talking to him. He told me what bus to get on and that I needed money for two bus zones. He described some factories. Then he said, 'I've never been there.' I really found that puzzling. What was I supposed to think? Why was he telling me this? What was in it for him? How did he know I needed a job? How did he even know I was from another country, before I talked to him?

"The other thing he said to me was, 'Look at all these people around here. There are thousands and thousands of people who have a home and are wandering aimlessly. Where do you think they belong? Don't worry. You will have a place to stay.'

"I found that bizarre. I felt there was something deeper, but picture yourself in my position at the time. I didn't need strangers walking up to me—people don't do that in our society—and I was in turmoil. He told me I would have a place to stay. I thought to myself that now he was going to offer me a place to stay. But still, coming from him it didn't seem he had an underhanded purpose. He was just stating facts. You could tell he wasn't trying to lure me away, but I wasn't sure. And then he also said, 'Just go up this way and walk down the road and you'll find something.' He pointed northwest. He said, 'Just go in that direction.' I wasn't scared but starting to fidget, as if to say, 'Leave me alone.' I turned my head for a brief second and when

I turned around they were gone, vanished. They weren't there, and that really puzzled me, because they had no time to meld back into the crowd—a fraction of a second and they simply were no longer anywhere to be seen.''

Singer took the advice and ended up finding a Croatian family who had a room to rent for $15 a week in the section of the city the mysterious men had indicated. He also took the bus they told him to take and found employment in a factory. "That Monday was glorious," he says. "I took a bath, I felt a sense of direction, the first sense of belonging. I bought a couple shirts and basic necessities. I was just starting to shave and needed a razor. On Tuesday I headed to the area mentioned to me by that mysterious man. It was an area where there were industries. I tried one place and couldn't get anyone to speak to, so I left and walked up to the next plant, and it was the same thing, a receptionist in the front hall, and she called the manager and he started talking. I said I was willing to start right away and he hired me on the spot."

It was an ink company that Singer stayed with for the next two decades, working his way up to a managerial position and raising two stellar children who regularly win scholastic and religious awards.

Such stories continued to unfold. So did the mystery. Hitchhikers were still around, indeed more than ever, in fact just south of Canada, on the New York State Thruway. There was said to be a ''beautiful young hippie'' clad in shining white who would enter a car, buckle his belt in the back seat, and talk about religion.

Mainly he seemed to want to know if the driver believed in the Second Coming. When they turned around to answer him, according to a professor who studied it, Lydia M. Fish of the State University College of New York at Buffalo, the hitchhiker had vanished, leaving his seatbelt fastened.

''When they left the thruway they told the toll collector that they had lost a hitchhiker,'' wrote Fish. ''He told them not to worry; at least a dozen cars had come through the gate that day with the same story.''

Fish didn't believe the accounts. No one who actually experienced the hitchhiker seemed to come forth, not in any meaningful way; it seemed like a simple rehashing of ancient tales. The story of a deity or heavenly messenger who travels earth in the guise of a human, she argued, is as old as the Bible and classical mythology. "There is even a Vanishing Hitchhiker story in the New Testament, which is strikingly similar to the modern vision," wrote Fish in a paper published by the Journal of the Hoosier Folklore Society at Indiana University (Volume 9, 1976). "Philip is picked up by an Ethiopian who is driving a chariot. They discuss religious matters and the Ethiopian asks to be baptized. Philip does as he requests and then vanishes" (See *Acts* 8:26-39).

It was true. The Bible is full of supernatural stories. We can go back to *Genesis,* of course, for the very first angelic mention—the cherubim who closed the gate of Paradise— and Noah had regular communication with God. The first highly personalized encounter with an angel happened to the maid named Hagar, who was carrying Abraham's child. The angel told Hagar to go back to her mistress and prophesied that Hagar's descendants would be greatly multiplied. He also told her what to name the child: Ishmael. Another of Abraham's sons, Isaac, was saved by the voice of an angel when his father was about to sacrifice him. Jacob saw angels ascending and descending on a "ladder." Perhaps most relevant is the account of Abraham's nephew, Lot. This biblical figure was sitting in the gate of Sodom when two angels appeared in such human form that he took them home and fed them. (*Genesis* 19:3). They were there to warn Lot and his family to flee the city, which was full of sexual wickedness and idolatry. *"For we will destroy this place, because the outcry against them has grown great before the face of the Lord,"* warned the angels. *"Arise, take your wife and your two daughters who are here, lest you be consumed in the punishment of the city."* That was just before Sodom and Gomorrah were annihilated by fire and brimstone.

No, it wasn't hard to find precedents, and we know that an angel, in this case Gabriel, whose rank is similar to that of Michael, announced Christ's First Coming. But the hitchhiker phenomenon still carried the ring of dubious prophecy. Sometimes he was young and bearded, wearing blue jeans, other times a white-bearded old man. Usually he asked the driver if he believed in Jesus and the Second Coming, but there were also warnings that the day of Judgment was near. In 16 cases that Fish studied the driver stopped and reported the incident, "usually to a toll collector, but occasionally to a gas station attendant or a policeman, and is told that this is not a unique experience."

Two of the drivers in Fish's study thought the hitchhiker was an angel, one thought he was a false prophet, and a third figured it might be the Anti-Christ.

In several cases the hitchhiker identified himself as "Jesus."

These accounts came, as usual, in a very indirect way, after much retelling. In addition to the thruway there were hitchhiker stories from the Pennsylvania, Virginia, and Maryland turnpikes. They also circulated in Ohio and West Virginia. "You better get ready, because He's coming soon," said the mysterious hitchhikers.

Yet no one, it seemed, actually knew a driver who had experienced the hitchhiker first-hand. Wasn't that true? Wasn't it true that you could never actually track down an eyewitness, that it was like the pot of gold at the end of the rainbow—or quicksilver? It always happened to a friend of a friend or a buddy of an acquaintance or a third cousin who sent word through a long-lost aunt, who told it to a nephew known for his farfetched yarns and ghost stories.

Fish collected her information from others and it seemed like a medieval legend replaying in the 1970s. Folklore. It was one thing to hear Singer's story—I interviewed him over the course of ten full days, from morning to evening, without finding a single inconsistency—but other accounts were far more elusive. So many times I heard about hitchhikers, but the story evaporated like acetone.

Wasn't it true that *nobody* really knew someone who had picked up a mysterious stranger himself?

It was not true. There *were* those who claimed to have personally encountered the fleeting, illusory, and phantasmagorical hitchhiker. One I finally tracked down is a retired factory manager, Jack Mattox, from Mattoon, Illinois. He is now 70, a United Pentecostalist with no hint of guile. He told me it happened on the way to a place called Sullivan on the Tuesday before Thanksgiving, which would have been November 20, 1979. "I was on days at that time. It was about 5:30 in the morning. Sullivan is about 16 miles from Mattoon. I was driving along and I got to a little town called Cole Station. There was an old man standing by the side of the road. He had a cane in his hand. He never flagged me down or anything. He was just standing looking at cars coming by, near a road sign just outside of Cole Station. I figured him for a businessman. Very seldom have I stopped for anybody. But all of a sudden I was pulling off to the side of the road."

The "hitchhiker" was humped over, but his face didn't look too old, not to Mattox. He had white hair and also the cane, a chubby face, pretty good-sized man, perhaps 5'11-1/2" and weighing 185 pounds. No beard. Slim nose. Gray suit, older suit, but in pretty good shape, no vest, suit coat and pants and blue shirt with no tie. No hat. Full head of hair. He walked with difficulty, using the cane. "I got out and helped him in the car," said Mattox, "He kind of wobbled a bit."

They proceeded to Sullivan, staring out at the flat farmland: acres of beans and corn. Mattox drove a wine-colored Chevy and worked for a candy manufacturer called Brachs.

There were long moments of silence. Mattox would look in his mirror and the man would still be sitting back there. He was on the passenger side. He said something about the weather, that it was going to be a nice morning. He also asked a question. "You're a Christian, aren't you?"

"Yes, I am," replied Mattox.

"Well, the Lord is coming soon," said the old man. "Spread it around. Tell your family. Tell your church. Tell everybody that the Lord is coming soon."

He said the Church had to get ready, and that's when Mattox felt "the presence of something and when he started talking you could just feel the power of God. You sure could. I was wondering if he was human because of the presence of God. And I kept looking at him in the rearview mirror and he would be looking at me. He had blue eyes. I would guess he was in my car 15 minutes. We got to the edge of Sullivan at a stoplight and I asked him where he wanted out at. I was going to turn left to go to the plant. I asked the question and there was no answer. So I looked to the back seat and he wasn't there. He was gone. As soon as I popped the question to him of where he wanted out, there was nobody back there. I got out of the car and looked and the cane was gone too.

"And so I left, went to the candy factory, went to my office, and got down and was praying. The day manager came around and said, 'What's wrong, Joe?' I told him. And he said, 'Well, you sure entertained an angel.'"

Whatever it was Mattox encountered, I also found a California man, Al Habina of Modesto, a track coach and gym teacher who had a similar experience in the 1970s. Habina was a submarine sailor stationed in New London, Connecticut, at the time, and he was taking a buddy to his parents' home in Cherry Hill, New Jersey.

This time it was two hitchhikers, a young couple, male and female. Al and his friend picked them up near New Haven. They were both very good-looking, she with brown hair, the man with a mustache and casual clothes but very cleancut. They looked to be in their early twenties.

"From where we picked them up I would say they were in the car a good hour," said Habina. "We let them off in New York City. We were just a couple of young sailors and I was bringing my best friend down to my parents' house in Jersey, for some of my mom's cooking, for the weekend. They sat in the back seat and all the way down they were talking about religion and stuff and my best friend and I were just looking at each other."

Did they say Christ was coming soon?

"Well, they said that a couple times, but it was more the fact that they were trying to get us to become Christians. When we went to let them off we got out and went around to the back to get their stuff—she had a jacket—and by the time we got out of the car and opened up the trunk—I mean, this was briefly—they weren't there anymore."

CHAPTER 13

"My Name is Michael"

Habina left immediately. He was blown away. "We got in the car and just said, 'Let's get out of here!'"

More tranquil was the experience in October of 1978 of a highly erudite priest, Father Walter M. Abbott of the Boston area. Abbott was not your typical witness. Known in the echelons of Rome, he had served as general editor for the English editions of the Vatican II documents. His associates were highly discerning and intellectual.

Yet he knew something was happening in the spirit world.

"One very warm Indian Summer day, I walked through Harvard Yard to the bus stop on Massachusetts Avenue and joined the line of five people," Father Abbott recounted to me. "As the bus approached, a young man came from my left to join the line. He seemed to be about 25 years old. He was wearing a gray vest over a white T-shirt, gray slacks, and a white homburg hat. It stood out all the more because it was such a warm day and nobody else in Harvard Square was wearing a hat of any kind.

"The bus turned onto Boylston Street (later to be named John F. Kennedy Street). As we passed a building on our right, I told the young man I had heard that Harvard and MIT had a joint research program going in that building, something about computers, so he began to tell me about them and I began to realize he was perhaps the most brilliant person I had ever met. I asked what he was doing in Cambridge. He replied: 'My father has made it possible for me to spend some time here observing what is going on at Harvard and MIT.'

"When we crossed the river and reached the stop at Commonwealth Avenue where I wanted to get off, I knew he wasn't going any place special, so I invited him to accompany me to my Father Provincial's offices, where I was going to discuss the finances for my sabbatical year with the province treasurer, and to return with me afterwards to Harvard Square.

"When we entered the building, I asked the receptionist if my friend could wait in the lobby, and he took a seat that was provided for him. At that moment a door opened in the far wall of the lobby and Father Provincial came out with his four consultors. He greeted me and invited me downstairs where they were going for a cup of coffee. I said I would come after a word with my friend. 'Bring him, too,' said Father Provincial.

"In the coffee room I met the treasurer and discussed my business with him. My friend was taken into the conversation between Father Provincial and the consultors. When I was ready to go, I took him with me and we returned to Harvard Square. On the sidewalk there, in front of the Würsthaus looking across at the Harvard Co-op, I told him I would return to the Jesuit house where I was staying and I asked him what he was going to do.

"Looking up at the blue sky, he said, 'I will return to my father.' And he stepped off the sidewalk to cross the street. Until that moment, Harvard Square had been filled with traffic, as usual, but at that moment there wasn't a car on the street. I remember thinking that when he reached the other side I would be able to follow him easily in the crowd because of that hat. It was just noontime, and that other side of the street was filled with people. *Halfway across the empty street he disappeared.*

"I stood in astonishment. I suddenly remembered that when I introduced myself to him on the bus he shook hands but said only, 'My name is Michael.'

"Considering his brilliance and his last words, I concluded that I had just spent an hour and a half with an angel. The

Archangel Michael? Hardly likely, I thought. Why would the Chief of the Heavenly Host spend any time with me? It was much more likely that I had met my own guardian angel and that he was one of many who had the name Michael. My mind raced back over the whole conversation with him. The very word 'angel' and the literature about them indicated they brought messages. What message had he given me? I could not think of anything he had told me to do or not to do, nor had he spoken any message to give someone else. I sensed that if I stood there pondering these things with my mouth open, people around me would begin to wonder what was the matter with this priest. I crossed Massachusetts Avenue and walked back through Harvard Square. This visit from Michael must have been intended to remind me of their existence and, more than that, to teach me that I should henceforth give witness to their existence.''

And to their great strength. They had come to help us, he realized. They had come to minister. They had come to ward off the proliferating demons. *"No evil shall befall you, nor shall any plague come near your dwelling; for He shall give His angels charge over you,"* says *Psalms* (91:10-11), and another preacher, Reverend Stewart G. Michel, a missionary in the New Hebrides Islands, learned that first-hand. One night Michel and his wife Jenny were threatened by hostile natives who planned to burn down the mission house—and the Michels with it. According to author Kelsey Tyler, they were upset that the Michels' teachings were negating their time-honored tribal traditions.

The Michels could have given in to the terror, but instead they put their trust in God and spent the night in heartfelt prayer.

Faith, they discovered, is stronger than fear.

The night was June 23, 1973, and there in bed, they could hardly find rest, listening to war cries that increased in nearness and intensity. "Keep praying, Jenny, keep praying," Stewart implored his wife, who fretted in the dark of their thatched-roof bungalow.

There was chanting outside. There were shrill screams.

Still the Michels prayed: "Heavenly Father, You have told us to ask for anything in Your means. Please deliver us from the danger we are in.''

As Tyler tells it, the sounds continued for about an hour and the flicker of flames outside seemed to indicate that the natives were ready to torch the one-room bungalow. But shortly thereafter, the sounds lessened and trailed off, as if they were leaving. The Michels poured thanks upon the Lord, and within six months, the tribe's chief was converted to Christ. When Stewart asked why he hadn't killed them, the chief said they had tried, "but your guards wouldn't let us past.'' He waved his arms dramatically. Stewart explained that only he and his wife had been there. *There were no guards.* But the chief would hear none of it. He insisted that there had been many guards with torches, drawn swords, and gleaming garments.

"Spiritual forces and resources are available to all Christians,'' notes Billy Graham, who tells this same basic story with some variants. "Because our resources are unlimited, Christians will be winners. Millions of angels are at God's command and at our service. The hosts of Heaven stand at attention as we make our way from earth to glory, and Satan's BB guns are no match for God's heavy artillery.''

So important have angels and other forms of the supernatural been throughout our history that we grope to enumerate them. Some Jews believed there are 301,655,722 angels (this calculation was made by cabalists during the 14th century) while Saint Albert the Great came up with a startlingly similar figure of 399,920,004 during the 13th century.

Certain followers of Martin Luther believed the number to be more like 10 *trillion.*

Really, they are countless. I know of a dying man in Grand Rapids, Michigan, who, when he was allowed a vision of the spirit world, saw his house surrounded by angels of many shapes, sizes, and functions. They were on the steps and in the rooms and in the yard. They guarded the windows and doors. Only when we sin or lack faith do chinks appear in the angelic armor; only when we reject the Lord does His saving grace withdraw from our protection.

As a Christian philosopher once said, to deny the angels amounts to ripping every second page out of the Bible. "The angels are the great strangers in this time of 'idolatry of the universe,' '' said Albino Luciani, who became Pope John

Paul I, while writer George Huber added, ''The protective presence of angels at our side is called for by the insidious presence of devils—in addition to that other factor, the wound caused by original sin. Every man, every woman, every child, every adolescent, is continuously being looked after by his or her guardian angel—just as he is also the constant object of the devil's scheming.''

A woman named Carolyn Millard from Lompac, California, told me that in 1975 she met a very unusual woman along a highway, one who seemed otherworldly and gave her advice on what prayer group to attend. Carolyn had been going to one that was starting to limit membership and keep people in their home parishes. ''I had been traveling out to a church every Friday night to attend their charismatic Mass—not knowing that our own church had a prayer group. At that time I thought, 'What am I going to do?' Well there was this lady who was standing on the side of the road and she had run out of gas. I pulled over to see if I could help her. I normally didn't stop for people, but I felt I needed to stop and help her. She had a bumper sticker on the back of her car saying that she was a Christian. As it turned out, we started talking about Jesus and I told her I'd noticed that she had a bumper sticker and she said, 'What church do you go to?' and I said, 'St. Joseph's in Hawthorne.'' And she said, 'Oh, I'm not Catholic but I know that they have a beautiful prayer meeting there.' I said, 'Really. I didn't know that. I've been going to church there every Sunday,' and she said, 'Well call the rectory and find out what day it is, what time it is.' I said, 'Gee, you're an answer to prayer,' and she just smiled. She said, 'You get in touch with them and make sure you go, because I hear it's a *beautiful* prayer group.' She didn't need service. She said someone was going for her gas.''

Around the same time, Carolyn ran into two equally unusual fellows at a gas station. ''It was shortly after I'd come back to the Church. I had stopped dating, trying to clean up my act, and there were two guys there. I remember their eyes. They were like *piercing*. They were at the gas station and I was waiting on my car. These two young men walked up to me and asked me, 'What are you doing?' I said, 'I'm waiting on my car.' They said, 'What are you doing with your life?' I thought it was a really odd kind of question and I said, 'Well, right now, working and trying to put my family together and trying to follow Jesus.' And they both smiled and looked at each other. One said, 'Are you dating much these days?' I thought that was very unusual and I wondered if they were making a pass at me. I looked at them and said, 'No, I've stopped dating because I want to try and put things together,' and they said that was good and they were asking me what I did with my free time and I told them I went to school evenings and prayer group, and they looked at each other and smiled and looked back at me. I couldn't figure why they wanted to know. What really got me were the eyes. They had such gorgeous eyes. I said, 'Well, I need to be on my way,' and they said, 'Okay. On your way.'"

Nowhere was the protection and guidance illustrated more dramatically than in those countries under the yoke of Communism, which during the 1970s continued to spread its insidious errors. I have told this story before but will synopsize it again: the account of a Christian activist named Josyp Jaromyr Terelya, who was placed in a "freeze cell' in Russia's Vladimir Prison.

This was on February 12, 1972. The Communists had had enough of Terelya, who persisted in distributing Christian literature, working alongside Evangelicals and Baptists, who were similarly persecuted. The Communists decided to kill him by venting in the frigid outside air. That way they could blame his death on natural causes instead of trying to get a writ of execution. In a word, it was expedient.

It was the middle of Russia's brutal winter!

Terelya lay on the bare bunk and tried to warm himself. In a short time he felt himself freezing. His eyelids clamped and even the roots of his hair pained him. "My mind was working," he said. "I was aware that I was freezing, and I gathered my strength. I climbed the grate on the cell door to warm my head against the ceiling light bulb. The guard on duty looked through the peephole, saw this, and switched off the light. I sat on my bed and began to freeze. There was an old quilt you could see through and I wrapped myself in it, garnering what little comfort it could

afford me. Too weak, I finally lay down, praying and awaiting my fate. Within another ten minutes my lips wouldn't
move, and my eyelids felt like they too were freezing shut.
My head was splitting, my eyes, my temples, my jaws. I
could still think but I couldn't move my limbs. I was freezing to death.

"It was then that I became aware of an intense flash of
light in the cell, a very powerful light, and heard what
sounded like someone walking. My eyes were clamped. I
couldn't tell who it was. I can't explain what happened—
lying there with my eyes shut, in a state approaching
paralysis—but somehow I became aware that the room was
illuminated. And the cell started to feel warmer. Against
my eyelids I felt the palm of a woman's hand and smelled
the soft pure fragrance of milk."

When Terelya, a Catholic, opened his eyes, there was a
beautiful young woman before him. He took it to be the
Virgin Mary. "You called to me, and I have come," she
said, and then she issued warnings about the world and
events to come.

CHAPTER 14

Return to Babylon

The warnings went right to the heart of the matter, as any heavenly message does. The world had grown cold and perverse. There was not nearly enough recognition of Jesus. God punished nations as he punished Cain, and such a judgment now hung over unbelievers. Terelya saw the vision of a map, and parts of it were burning. Fire erupted all over the Soviet Union, and there was tremendous fear in Moscow. Throughout the countryside, explosions were taking place. Russia was at war with surrounding countries, and somehow China would figure in. He saw their tanks on the Russian side of the border.

If Russia did not accept Christ, there would be a third world war.

"The seal of the devil has been placed on the foreheads of many," he was told during a subsequent vision. *"How many there are who have been crucified on the five-pointed star, the mark of Satan. Lucifer is cunning and clever. He is preparing a great deception for all of God's creation, and especially for the people of God."*

Deception indeed. While no one could decipher them, strange aerial lights continued to haunt the world. On September 29, 1970, a luminous object was photographed over Sarajevo, while three years earlier a UFO had been spotted above Ukraine. There was also a fiery ball over the Tersky Alatan Mountains in Kirghizia, and in Africa, Ugandan Dictator Idi Amin witnessed a UFO over Lake Victoria.

In Arizona, a logger named Travis Walton insisted that on November 5, 1975, he encountered a flying saucer in Sitgraves National Park near a town called Snowflake.

Were UFOs a reflection of earthly occultism? Around the world, from Russia to the U.S., occult practices had opened a window to all sorts of strange and dangerous dimensions. Most blatant were the ufology and psychic phenomena. In many nations there were seminars on meditation, ESP, and mind control; there was astral projection and fortunetelling; and there was a revival of mediumship, soon to be called "channeling." In fact, there were so *many* forms of occultism that at first glance they didn't even seem related to each other. I remember an English fellow named Matthew Manning who could tap into the "spirits" of dead artists and sketch their masterpieces. He was associated with a group of researchers in Toronto who met every week to invoke an energy they called "Philip," which made strange rapping noises. It was also the heyday of Uri Geller, the controversial psychic from Israel. I met Geller when he was living in Manhattan, and as I recall, his phenomena had begun during childhood, after spotting a UFO hovering over his backyard. Soon he could mesmerize classmates with his ability to concentrate on the school clock and cause its hands to move. He also bent spoons by simply rubbing them and sometimes without touching them at all. Although magicians had branded him a fake, certain of his effects could not be explained or duplicated. In 1972, Geller had caused what looked like two impossibly juxtaposed influences: both a freezing effect and incipient melting upon a single platinum surface. It was something even lasers couldn't replicate. The surface indicated that atomic sections had started to melt in a way that would require temperatures of around 1,750 degrees centigrade. Incredibly, it also suggested there had been a near-perfect atomic split. Meanwhile, only a hundredth of an inch from that melted section, the fracture showed another uncanny effect: atoms frozen near absolute zero.

While magicians scoffed at the whole thing, and parapsychologists struggled to understand the mechanics (studying

Uri at such places as Stanford Research Institute), the explanation seemed to reside not in stage magic or ESP, but possibly in spiritual deception. Geller described himself as a "channel" for "higher forces" and claimed the last time these forces were in touch with earth was in ancient Egypt—back when spiritual deception was likewise in the open.

During the 1970s witches were allowed on television and wrote bestsellers about "spirit guides" and astrology. Goddess worship was coming back, the oldest form of witchery. How dark were the 1970s! How darker still would grow the coming decades! Clearly, trouble was on the way. Occultism is an intensely forbidden act, and it comes under the general heading of sorcery, which in the New Testament (*Galatians* 5:19-21) is mentioned in the same breath as fornication, adultery, hatred, murder, and idolatry. Seek mediums and wizards and not the Lord, said Yahweh (*Isaiah* 8:22), and you will be driven into darkness. That's what happened at Nineveh and Babylon, where there were secret societies, shrines to earth divinities, and temples of the "great gods" (including Ishtar, who was portrayed with a serpent). The same idolatry also infested Egypt, but it was Babylon that was known as "the mother of harlots and abominations of the earth." Every woman was required to go to the temple of Aphrodite and give herself sexually to a strange man (in the name of a goddess), while Nineveh, its rival in Assyria, was known as the city of gold and blood. Its people worshipped gods with names such as Assarac, Ashur, and Marduk, which didn't sound a whole lot different than supposed UFO entities who according to contactees had weird names like "Lyra" and "Quazgaa." Indeed, there were those in the 1970s who, making no bones about it, had come to refer to flying saucers as "chariots of the gods." These occult deities were kept alive through the ages by pagans, witches, Masons, satanists, and eventually New Agers. The very bearing of "extraterrestrials" suggested occultism and demonism. In 1974, Betty Andreasson of Ashburnham, Massachusetts, reported small reptile-like aliens in association with a UFO spotted from her kitchen window and humanoids that entered her home *through the walls,* while Walton, in Arizona, described similarly ghoulish entities. The "extraterrestrials" often had gray skin, huge foreheads, and protruding or slanty eyes, like ancient gremlins.

CHAPTER 15

Helping Hands

That was the bad news. The good was that if the air was cluttered with demonic forms, as St. Paul told us it is (*Ephesians* 2:2), and if Babylon was rising again (also the witch of Endor), if it seemed the devil often had the upper hand, and could do most everything, from destroying a family or prayer group to possessing Linda Blair or even controlling world leaders like those in Communism—if Satan seemed like he was nearly God's equal, an adversary threatening His very throne—we had to keep in mind that even in a time of special evil power, in a nefarious century, the devil is nothing next to Christ, who at God's right Hand is *"far above all principality and power and might and dominion, and every name that is named, not only in this age but also in that which is to come"* (*Ephesians* 1:20-21).

Even in the 1970s, there was no reason to act frightened or helpless, *"tossed to and fro and carried about with every wind of doctrine, by the trickery of men, in the cunning craftiness by which they lie in wait to deceive"* (*Ephesians* 4:14). Rather, it was time to stand up and claim victory. Humility, gentleness, and longsuffering granted all the necessary guidance and protection. Through prayer, especially coupled with fasting, was there access to the Holy Spirit and His myriad of angels.

In a time when the struggle gradually draws near, noted Pope John Paul II, "it becomes in a certain sense ever more violent as *Revelation*, the last book of the New Testament, shows in a special emphasis (12:7-9). But it is precisely this book that emphasizes the certainty that is given to us by all of divine revelation, that the struggle *will finish with the definitive victory of the good.*"

In other words, for every weird UFO story, for every tragedy, there were two or more angel stories. Those accounts went largely upspoken—in the age of rationalism, adults didn't *dare* mention such experiences—but that was soon to change. Mainly they involved warnings or consolation. One of the most poignant consolations appeared recently in the magazine *Christianity Today,* which told the story of an aging evangelical who had recently lost his wife of fifty years. "I was in a black hole of despair," the old evangelical related. "I couldn't sleep nights, and one night I was startled to find my bedroom blazing with light, emanating from a human-sized being standing by the foot of my bed. The light radiated from its face, hands, and garments. And then I felt the angel communicating to me. It conveyed a message of personal peace. Calmness overwhelmed me. I fell asleep knowing it was going to be all right."

His nephew, a publishing executive, was nearly startled at the man's bright disposition.

There were also miraculous cures. According to *Time,* in July of 1977 a woman named Ann Cannady learned that she had advanced uterine cancer. She and her husband, Gary, were naturally devastated. "We spent the next eight weeks scared and praying, praying and scared," said Ann. "I kept begging God, saying, 'Please, if I'm going to die, let me die quickly. I don't want Gary to have to face this again.'" Her husband didn't feel he could bear it psychologically. He'd lost his first wife to the same disease.

But three days before Ann was to enter the hospital, the doorbell in their home sounded and Gary went to answer it. When he did he found a tall black man with striking eyes standing on the step. The man stood about 6'5" and introduced himself as "Thomas." Then, out of the blue, with incredible words, he informed Ann that her malignancy was gone.

They debated whether to let "Thomas" in, then decided they should. That gave them a better view of his eyes, which were an extraordinary shade of "deep, deep azure blue." When he entered he quoted *Isaiah* 53:5. (*"And by His stripes we are healed."*)

Ann demanded to know who he was.

"I am Thomas. I am sent by God."

The mysterious visitor then held up his right hand, palm facing Ann, and an incredible heat came from him. Ann's legs gave way and she collapsed to the floor. It was like a white light was coursing through her. "It started at my feet and worked its way up. I knew then, with every part of me—my body, my mind, and my heart—that something supernatural had happened." She slipped into unconsciousness and when she awoke her husband was anxiously pleading for her to speak. Thomas was gone. And everything seemed changed. Despite her weakness, Ann found her way to the phone, called her doctor, and told him she was cured. When she demanded a test before surgery the doctor relented and her test came back clear.

I recounted in *Prayer of the Warrior* how in 1975, while I was researching psychic phenomena, I was at a small non-denominational church in remote Hale Eddy, New York, when suddenly three young people who said they were from New York City knocked on the door. It seemed very odd. New York City is three hours away. Two men and a woman who seemed like "holy rollers." They said they'd awakened that morning and just decided to take a random drive, wherever their hearts led them, which turned out to be this tiny country church where I was observing a woman speaking in tongues as part of my research. After a bit of small talk one of the men turned directly to me and told me I was in danger—which I was. I should have heeded the warning and quit the investigation into parapsychology. It would have saved me much grief! I have no idea if this was a coincidence or angels. I've often wondered. I didn't see them disappear. But there were more substantial accounts from other folks in various places of strange phone calls offering reassurance, or of the image of a white-clad form chasing away bikers who were ready to rob a Bible-reading family on vacation at Big Lake in California. The form was seen in photos that had been taken just before the motorcyclists roared up to the scene. Many of them occurred around the time of my own experience. In 1977, according to Joan Wester Anderson, a rookie cop and his partner in Nutley, New Jersey, were raiding a hideout of dangerous drug addicts. It was a cave. Although they were greatly outnumbered, and the criminals could easily have made a run for it, or even overpowered them, when the two cops made their bold bust the criminals were totally and surprisingly submissive. Later, the cops asked the ringleader why they didn't attack, and in a story highly similar to that of the New Hebrides chieftain, he told the arresting officers that *he had seen the other twenty cops there.*

Of course, there had been no other policemen there.

Such stories, in which angels apparently took tangible form, were all the more remarkable for their frequency. In 1975 there was a hiker in Wisconsin named William Landemann caught on a frozen five-mile-wide lake in a terrifying blizzard near Madison. Blinded by the snow, he was in great danger of falling into a breakwater. But after a frightening time of crawling on the ice and feeling his hands go numb, he heard a foghorn and a man summoned him from a rescue station, guiding him over a speaker system. When Landemann finally made it to the station the man yanked him inside and gave him a cup of gloriously hot coffee. The mysterious rescuer was bearded with crystal-blue eyes, like no color the hiker had ever seen. What made the story poignant, and the subject of a chapter in the fine book, *There's an Angel on Your Shoulder,* was at that time of year the rescue station was closed. In fact, when Landemann went back to it, the building was locked tightly and the front door was nearly covered by a drift of snow that looked like it hadn't been disturbed for weeks. Authorities said there was no one with access to it, and no one knew anything about the strange rescuer. "Although there would never be any way to prove what had happened that stormy afternoon, Landemann had made his mind up," wrote Kelsey Tyler. "From that point on,

Landemann believed he had been helped by an angel who chose to save his life in what was a very special encounter.''

A year later, in Hartland, Michigan, a woman named Shirley Halliday had a terrible intuition that her 13-year-old daughter Janie was in danger. The girl was 1,500 miles away, in Arizona on vacation. As she prayed her morning devotion, Shirley had no doubt that something was very wrong with Janie, who at this precise time was at the top of a ravine in the Painted Desert. It was a breathtaking sight, and Janie decided to step over the guard rail for a better look. That's when she lost her balance.

Frantically the girl tried to grab something but slid faster and faster. It was a certain death. The bottom of the ravine was so deep it was hardly visible. Back home her mother was by this time crying out to the angels, as in *Psalm 91:11-12*.

Suddenly and miraculously, Janie slid to a stop. There were no rock protrusions or clumps of vegetation that had stopped her. It was like an invisible hand ''had reached across her path and caught her,'' according to an account in *Ladies Home Journal*. Both Janie, now 29 and an interior designer, and Shirley ''are still awed by what they believe was a miracle.''

A woman named Keb Burns from Lampasas, Texas, had a similar experience. ''I was 19 or 20 and living in a converted attic above my parents' home,'' she told me. ''The steps had been added as an afterthought and were too steep to be safe. Nevertheless, I bounded up and down them regularly. Late one night during a fit of housecleaning, I gathered up a stack of dishes that had accumulated upstairs to take down to the kitchen. At the very top step my foot caught a slight ripple in the carpet and I tripped, headlong, head-first, downward. My hands were full of dishes so there was not even a chance for me to grab the rail or wall or anything to break my fall. I remember thinking in that split second of realization that I had had it. I don't remember thinking about my angel at the time, but I had always had a devotion to the guardian angels. Futile as it was, my right foot shot out in front of me, but I was in midair. There was nothing to rest on. Sud-

denly I felt on the bottom of my bare foot a *hand,* the
palm, the fingers, the pressure, everything you would feel
if you placed your foot in a human hand. More incredible
still, my weight *rested* on that invisible hand, in midair,
for a second or two! Completely beyond my control, my
foot was gently lowered to the step below it. I still have
a mental snapshot of that moment, of myself *standing,*
for a second or two, in midair.''

In Scarsdale, New York, is a teacher named Adrienne
Montillet who recounted how the parent of one of her
students had once managed to obtain a leave from the
army to attend the funeral of a cousin. ''In his rush to
get to the airport, he had not enough money but stood
in line anyway,'' says Adrienne, retelling the incident.
''A man in a cloak approached him, said he knew that
he was on his way home to the funeral of his cousin,
handed him the money he needed for the flight, told him
to go to the other line which would be faster (it turned
out to be faster), and then disappeared.''

There was help, it seemed, across America. Lori Rose
Cannizzaro of East Aurora, New York, told me: ''My
mother was very sick with cancer (one time) and I had
just spent a long time talking with her in her room while
she was resting in bed. It was night-time and there were
no lights on in the house, only a small nightlight in her
room. As I left her and went into my own room, I closed
my bedroom door and as I closed it I saw a brilliant light
between her doorway and the wall to the hall. In that
light stood a figure in long robes, with arms outstretched,
long hair, and wings. I was astonished and at the same
time felt a wondrous peace. I just knew the angel was
there to bring comfort and peace and let us know everything would be all right.''

If it was nonsense to accept every single claim, it was
equal nonsense to think that every such story was a product of an overactive imagination. Most of those who
reported the phenomena seemed sane, sincere, well-
spoken, and church-going. They were not the type who
fabricated stories. Journalists are trained to be skeptical
but also to hear the ring of truth, and whatever journalistic

instinct I possessed told me there was truth to a lot of these accounts, however incredible or redundant they seemed.

In the index for the King James New Testament alone are 43 references to •angels, and others that are not included in such indexing. In 1950, Pope Pius XII, in the encyclical *Humani Generis,* virtually rebuked those who do not regard angels as personal beings. Added Saint Thomas: "We are like children who stand in need of masters to enlighten and direct us; and God has provided for this, by appointing His angels to be our teachers and guides." And Saint Basil: "We have each an angel at our side, unless, by evil deeds, we drive him from us."

They came to the aid of Isaiah, Ezekiel, and Daniel.

It was an angel who prophesied to Zechariah.

It was an angel who helped Elijah when the prophet was fleeing from Jezebel (*1 Kings* 19:5).

Indeed, the angel provided him with the sustenance of cake baked by coals and a jar of water, like the coffee-bearing rescuer in Wisconsin.

They are here for everyone, and they were all around during the perplexing and precarious 1970s. In the spring of 1973, John P. McNamara, a friend of mine who at the time was a New York City Transit Police officer, and also a volunteer fireman in Westchester County, was at a fireman's parade in Peekskill and attended a party afterwards in a 40-foot tower outside of town where they held their meetings. They had been partying a bit too much, but this was no pink elephant.

"Except for the section where the metal stairs were, the room was enclosed by a walkway with a three-foot-high metal railing going around the other three sides," McNamara recalls. "A person could look right through the metal openings to the concrete sidewalk below. I walked out of the room to get some fresh air. The sun was directly in my eyes and before I knew it I hit the rail with my body, waist-high, and went over. Then it happened. In the blink of an eye, I saw forty feet of concrete coming up to meet me. I saw every scene of my life flash before my eyes. The only words I could say were, 'God help me!' Just then a hand pulled my right arm back to the top of the handrail. I pulled myself back over and stood there clutching the rail with both hands and shaking like a leaf. When I turned around I stood looking at someone who looked like *me*, except his uniform was immaculate. I said, 'Thanks. You saved my life!' He smiled and said, 'It's not your time, John.' Then he walked over to the steps and started going down. I lost sight of him for a second. When I got to the steps, he was gone.''

CHAPTER 16

Descent of the Angels

There were angels who appeared to an inmate in the guise of a guard, or directed a motorist to change lanes, avoiding an accident from the rear, or held the hand of a patient in a hospital ward. There was an angel who came looking like a homeless beggar and cured the child of parents who had been kind to him, giving him food. There were angels who whispered in our ears, or appeared in our dreams, or gave us the subtle taste of spiritual nourishment.

There were angels who appeared to a forlorn missionary on a transatlantic plane, or stayed the hand of an executioner in Africa.

Taking whatever form they desired, angels could assume the appearance of a living person as if that person were in two places at once (known as "bilocation"), or could come in full mystical regalia, as a chubby and twinkling cherub or as an imposing warrior.

Iridescent, but with the soft glow of a pearl.

This luminosity was often described in superlatives, for the light is not an earthly light and truly cannot be compared to anything in the physical realm. Most often angels remain in their invisible state, noticeable only in the soft touch they bequeath, or seen as but a flash in the corner of an eye. A pastor named A. D. Van Hoose once described going into his office and becoming aware of another presence.

When he demanded that whatever was there reveal itself, a chair near his desk suddenly took on a form of white illumination with a tiny dark dot in the center. As the dot grew there was a sensation like something arriving at great speed and the "dot" seemed to explode outward. Suddenly Pastor Van Hoose was looking at the most handsome and vibrant man he had ever seen. The angel was there to offer advice on Van Hoose's ministry.

If the most common manifestation of angels is in the guise of humans (in accordance with *Hebrews* 13:2, which tells us to entertain strangers "for by so doing some have unwittingly entertained angels"), there are also plenty of times they show themselves in their ineffable spiritual form. One of the first modern American angelologists, Betty Malz, described how her own brother Marvin and his wife Sharon witnessed a heavenly spirit during a time of family problems. Marvin was dreaming about God's assurances when the incident occurred. "Whether from the dream or from the power of the Holy Spirit surrounding them, Marvin and Sharon awoke together and were amazed to see the room as bright as if it were midday," Malz wrote in an inspired book called *Angels Watching Over Me,* which treated angels in a biblical way and not like writers who would soon venture into the New Age. "At the side of the bed stood an angel, huge and glowing. The angel leaned over and grasped both of my brother's hands in one of his large hands, saturating his body with the power of God. Marvin told me he felt something like a strange heat, cool and yet white-hot, in his hands and burning in his chest. He felt utterly weak, overwhelmed by the indescribable power in the room. Outwardly he felt paralyzed; inwardly he felt as light as dust dancing in bright sunshine."

Betty also related the story of a young boy named Ryan who had been plagued by nightmares. His parents were praying hard to dispel these dreams and one night Ryan was visited by an angel who looked something like Jesus. He too lit up the room, and no longer did Ryan experience nightmares.

So too are angels our hope against temptation. When we are feeling strong and in good mental shape, it is often because our angels are hovering especially close to us, or even draping themselves over us, causing us to have what others perceive as a nimbus or "glow." According to Malz, a woman she knew who had an alcohol problem was ready to get in her car and go out for a bottle of booze when a bright light appeared between her and the door. A figure formed from the light and transformed into a huge angel clad in white. "He did not speak, but his powerful supportive presence and the look on his face let (the woman) know without a word that she did not need a drink, and that all would be well," says Malz.

Yet they also come to tell us when things are *not* well. They are oracles of God who arrive to "give divine or authoritative decision and messages," according to Graham. As a missionary named Morris Potts once pointed out, the Book of Revelation is just *full* of angels. "It mentions angels all the way through, who in the last days will govern the affairs of men and nations, control the weather and war, fight battles, declare the Gospel of Jesus, and announce His coming back to the earth again. More and more, as we draw closer to that day, angels are helping God's servants reach the ends of the earth with the Gospel."

They come to gather the elect, said Graham. They come at the end of the age "to separate the sheep from the goats, the wheat from the tares, the saved from the lost."

It was an angel who wrote God's impending judgment upon the Babylonian wall.

It was an angel who smote Herod.

It was an angel who David saw *"between the earth and the heaven, having a drawn sword in his hand stretched out over Jerusalem"* (*1 Chronicles* 21:16).

The very presence of angels often indicates danger, and their increasing presence in the 1970s continued to parallel warnings of societal disorder. By 1975 violent crime had shot up to a startling 48.8 per 10,000, which was *three times* the rate of 1960, and the graph curve for juvenile crime looked like Mount Everest. Teen pregnancies shot up to 49.4 per thousand in 1972 and then 78.3 per thousand a mere eight years later. By 1975 about half of black births were to unmarried women, an incredible figure considering that just 15 years before, in 1960, the percentage for blacks was 23 and for all races combined but 5.3 percent. Divorce was more than twice what it had been in 1960 and teens soon underwent abortions at an appalling 43.4 per thousand. The policies of the humanists and rationalists, the liberal "progressives," atheists and agnostics, the intelligentsia and sexual liberators—the Planned-Parenthood types, who sipped tea while kids went to abortion mills (and destroyed a piece of their souls)—really made their mark during the Seventies and were yet to make deeper scars on a society that was quickly and clearly degenerating out of control.

It wasn't going unnoticed by God. His patience was incredible, as infinite as His love, and yet it would not, *could not*, go on forever. Slowly and gradually, with clues here and there, in a very deliberate and yet infinitely powerful fashion, with plenty of forewarning—and much more forewarning to come—God was getting nearer to a point where He had to threaten yet larger warnings. Slow to anger was He, but if it kept up, if the occultism and sensualism, if the humanism, kept up, His great mercy would take the form of purification.

What was more merciful than a father who warned a child away from a hot stove with a little nudge or slap when necessary?

And if that didn't work, a stronger hint, and then stronger still.

Where there had been three major earthquakes in the 1940s and five in the 1950s, suddenly there were seven in the 1960s and three *times* that many—21—during the Seventies. In Iran, a Richter 7.7 that killed 25,000 struck on September 16, 1978, just before the Shah was overthrown and the brutal Ayatollah Khomeini assumed power.

In California, the worst earthquake in forty years shook the San Fernando Valley.

So too could one see portents in the vicious storms. About 300,000 were killed when a cyclone hit Bangladesh, and that was but one of the 19 major hurricanes, typhoons, and blizzards during the 1970s. So great were these tempests that the Blizzard of 1977, a monstrous storm that buried Buffalo and many surrounding areas, didn't even make the list (despite snowdrifts as high as the top of a telephone pole in Lockport, New York, and hurricane-force winds that, coupled with subzero temperatures, brought the wind-chill to mind-boggling levels). The blizzard, which I experienced first-hand as a newspaper reporter covering it, was a chastisement for the way industry had degraded nature in that area, and the melting snows brought landfilled chemicals to the surface at the dump known as Love Canal, sparking authorities to clean up toxic chemicals both there and at hundreds of other dumps across America.

It was purification in the finest sense of the word.

That same year Johnstown, Pennsylvania, was deluged. It was but one of 17 major floods and tidal waves during the 1970s, as compared to 16 during the Sixties, six during the 1950s, and but two during the first decade of the century.

If 68 were killed in the Johnstown flood, that was nothing next to the 5,000 to 15,000 who succumbed in Morvi, India, which was steeped in the pagan practices of Hinduism.

CHAPTER 17

Beneath the Blowing Sand

It was not so much that God was raving mad—blind rage is *not* in His exquisitely majestic nature—but rather that His protection and grace flow or ebb depending on our behavior. When mankind rejects God, it is also rejecting the force that binds the universe and keeps everything from chaos. Whether sociological or meteorological—whether war or the weather—it's God's power that maintains us in careful balance. The more we sin, the more His bonding force is withdrawn. And the more His force is withdrawn, the less stable becomes each aspect of the cosmos.

Man and not God causes imbalances. Our Lord allows the ebb of grace as a matter of divine justice. When that protection leaves—when the angels are repelled by our sin—then Satan is free to strike. He has a field day. He was a murderer from the beginning and remains the Great Destroyer. He loves war, disorder, and the misery of illness. This is seen not only in storms and quakes, not only in the external world, but also in our own biology. Many little chastisements, especially sickness, are our own doing. As technologies have increased, spewing toxics in the rush for profit, so too have nervous disorders, birth defects, and cancer increased in direct proportion. There has been a tradeoff: health for materialism. That's idolatry of money. It's also selfishness. Drug use and sexual sin have borne similar consequences. This was the decade during which AIDS entered the blood system. Unknown to doctors, there was a virus germinating during the 1970s that would one day be infamous as "HIV," spread mainly through intravenous drug use and male sodomy. It is a classic plague, like the boils, flies, and lice in *Exodus*. Its rise has tracked the rise in gay bars, transvestites, sado-masochistic sex, and transsexuals.

For thousands of years man saw events in terms of heavenly approval or warnings. Throughout the history of humankind, right back to *Genesis* and cavemen, harsh storms were seen as the Lord's admonition, while clement weather and a good yield of crops or game were seen as signs of divine approval. God's admonishments, when not spoken through intuition, or directly to prophets, came through wars, plagues, famines, poverty, anarchy, volcanoes, storms of hail, and even comets. Interaction with the supernatural, especially through geophysical events, played the crucial role not just in Noah's time, which may have been 4,300 years ago, but also in the Christian era. It is only since the French Revolution (and the arrogant scientism which followed) that such signs have been discounted simply as natural or coincidental happenings.

God has always been known, through natural events, to express His holy anger. When Israelis were guilty of murder, adultery, swearing, lying, and idolatry, the Lord warned that He was wilting their harvest, or as He put it (*Hosea* 8:7), *"the stalk has no bud."* Because Israel had made gold idols, His anger was *"aroused against them"* and He promised that *"the land will mourn."* Throughout the Old Testament natural events were attributed to God's judgment. We need only turn to Elisha and the way he explained that *"the Lord has called for a famine, and furthermore, it will come upon the land for seven years"* (*2 Kings* 8:1). So too was His withdrawal of grace obvious in *Jeremiah:* *"You have defiled the land by your wicked harlotry. Therefore the showers were withheld, the spring rain failed."* The Lord's hand in meteorology, His attempts to nudge us, through the weather, back to His embrace, is nowhere clearer than His complaint in *Amos* 4:7-8: *"I also withheld rain from you, when there were still three months to the harvest. I made it rain on one city, I withheld rain from another city. One part was rained upon, and where it did not rain the part withered. So two or three cities wandered to another city to drink water. But they were not satisfied; yet you have not returned to Me."* In addition to the weather, God withdrew His protection in times of warfare. This is seen in *Hosea* when He promises that Israel's enemies will pursue her as a chastisement. The same is true of internal enemies. He lets us succumb to our own devices, especially crime. *"Your own wickedness chastises you,"* He said through Jeremiah. *"Your own infidelities punish you."*

God uses angels to evaluate society and execute His judgments. When Israel necessitated purification, God sent a pestilence that killed 70,000. On the other hand, when they deserved *protection,* as against Assyrian warriors (*2 Kings* 19), a single angel was sent to strike an Assyrian encampment. (About 185,000 enemy soldiers were counted dead by the following morning.)

All we need do is listen to the prophets. We'll be hearing from some current-day ones in the next chapter. But let's stay with the Old Testament for another moment, as testimony that, indeed, God can exercise sacred indignation.

Said the prophet Zephaniah (2:1-3), *"Gather yourselves together, yes, gather together, O undesirable nation, before the decree is issued, before the day passes like chaff, before the Lord's fierce anger comes upon you, before the day of the Lord's anger comes upon you!"*

There are those who complain that the God of the Old Testament was too fearsome a God. They fail to see discipline as an aspect of His love. They also misunderstand the need for purification. It's true that God is love, but He is also a God Who, reasonably enough, is not about to see Satan reign over His universe. Therefore what we witness in the Old Testament is not so much the wrath of God as His call to *obedience.* Those were evil times! Blood flowed like water! It was His love that sought to stop the loss of souls and the horrendous carnage!

God loves in all circumstances, and His mercy is beyond what we can understand. Just as He suspended promises of protection given to the Israelis when they went on a wayward course, so too, conversely, on the other end of His justice, does God suspend punishment when mankind shows signs or at least intentions of improvement. His warnings of disaster are nearly always qualified and provisional. Whether a disaster ultimately arrives is up to our response. His warnings are a part of His mercy, and only New Agers or unbelievers deny this correctional justice. He does allow disasters, and He does demonstrate anger, as any good parent is firm with an unruly child. He does it so we can encounter His Light. *"I will shake all nations, and they shall come to the Desire of All Nations, and I will fill this temple with glory,"* said the Lord of hosts (*Haggai* 2:6-7).

In few places is God's fairness and also His seriousness more apparent than in the account of Sodom and Gomorrah. These two cities were probably located on a plain of the lush Jordan Valley and some theorize that they have since been covered by a southern extension of the salty Dead Sea. We know that the Lord and two angels appeared to Abraham (*Genesis* 18) and informed him that the sins committed in Sodom were "very grievous" and the outcry against them "great." Old English preachers such as Thomas Vincent have speculated that the sins included intemperance in eating, idleness, abominable filthiness, and lack of mercy to the poor. The "abominable filthiness" was in the way of adultery, whoredom, and homosexual intercourse (or "sodomy," which is named for this very city). To this we can almost surely add some sort of sorcery, for "Ishtar" and other gods or goddesses (who with huge eyes sometimes looked like extraterrestrials) were probably worshipped at Sodom.

So merciful was God that upon Abraham's plea He conceded if but *ten* righteous people could be found in Sodom and Gomorrah, He would reinstate His protective force and spare the two cities.

As Abraham returned home the two angels proceeded to Sodom, where they found his nephew Lot. Unaware they were angelic beings, Lot invited them home for the night, to wash their feet and have a meal.

It was then that the great sin of sodomy was revealed. Men of the city, old and young alike, from all quarters, converged on Lot's house and demanded to see the two "men," who of course were really angels.

"Bring them out to us," shouted the Sodomites, "so that we may know them *carnally*" (*Genesis* 19:15).

That seemed to seal Sodom's fate. Next morning the angels told Lot to gather his family and leave. Punishment was imminent. The area was to be destroyed under a hail of brimstone and fire. While there are many who claim that Sodom and Gomorrah were washed away by the Dead Sea, others have speculated that destruction may have come through an earthquake that set loose petroleum gases. Sparked by a hearth, these gases may have created a firestorm which ignited the area's copious deposits of sulfur. Hot sulfur is known, after all, as "brimstone." At any rate, smoke rose "like the smoke of a furnace."

As at Sodom, God's warnings are almost always conditional. They describe what will happen if present circumstances persist. They are not usually etched in stone. Such was also the case with Nineveh around the eighth century B.C. *"Arise,"* the Lord told Jonah, *"go to Nineveh, that great city, and cry out against it; for their wickedness has come up before Me."*

Nineveh was located in Assyria and had a population of about 120,000, making it one of the great congregations of humanity. Both before Jonah and then years later, it was, as large cities are wont to be, a cesspool of violence and depravity. The great sins here were murder and sorcery. The Ninevehites were known as a horrible warring people, conquering rival city-states in one fell swoop and burning the eyes of those they attacked or skinning them alive. They also amputated the arms and legs of noble citizens who were then displayed in cages. Treasures from looted cities were brought back and served as part of Nineveh's very foundation. The carnage was well-recorded, and so was the demonology: in the general vicinity were many works of art depicting, for example, a winged figure with a horned cap, which is a fairly standard representation of a demon. There was a large tower to the god Ashur and many sculptures or "idols" depicting supernatural beings that were half man and half beast.

Jonah traveled to Nineveh and expressed God's warning. "Yet forty days," he cried out, "and Nineveh shall be overthrown!"

That destruction was postponed when all of Nineveh responded to the warning. They fasted. They donned sackcloth. The king himself set aside his robe and sat in ashes. *"Then God saw their works, that they turned from their evil way; and God relented from the disaster that He had said He would bring upon them,"* says *Jonah* 3:10.

But not long after Jonah, Nineveh returned to the evil described above. Again they were warned, this time in more explicit tones by the prophet Nahum, whose prophecies were astounding. Nahum foresaw destruction through warfare. He saw brandished spears and smoke coming from Nineveh's extravagant chariots. "Fire shall devour the bars of your gates," he predicted. "Though Nineveh of old was like a pool of water, now they flee away. 'Halt! Halt!' they cry, but no one turns back. Take spoil of silver! Take spoil of gold! There is no end of treasure, or wealth of every desirable prize. She is empty, desolate and waste!"

Nahum foresaw countless corpses, a place laid to waste. He warned that the city, so cruel to its captives, would see the tables turned in dramatic fashion. Man the fort, warned Nahum, strengthen the flanks, for a great attack was coming. *"Woe to the bloody city, all lies, full of plunder, whose looting never stops! The crack of the whip, the rumbling sound of wheels; horses a-gallop, chariots bounding, cavalry charging, the flame of the sword, the flash of the spear, the many slain, the heaping corpses, the endless bodies to stumble upon!"* he quoted the Lord as saying (*Nahum* 3:1-5). *"For the many debaucheries of the harlot, fair and charming, a mistress of witchcraft, who enslaved nations with her harlotries, and people by her witchcraft: I am come against you, and I will strip your skirt from you; I will show your nakedness to the nations, to the kingdoms your shame!"*

This prophecy was fulfilled with startling precision when the Babylonians and Medes, two peoples often under its subjection, rose against Nineveh and beleaguered it horribly for two years. There was also a flooding of the Tigris that undermined Nineveh's thick walls. Disaster upon disaster followed in quick succession. In 612 B.C. (some say 623 B.C.) the city was overthrown and its king set himself, his women, and his treasures on fire, leaving Nineveh to disappear like Sodom beneath the blowing sand.

CHAPTER 18

Harm's Way

While the sorcery in Nineveh was more flagrant, it may not have been any more pervasive than in our own era. There was no tower dedicated to the gods Ishtar or Ashur, not yet, but our society was doing a fairly good imitation of old idols, with horoscopes—which had been invented at Babylon—in virtually every daily newspaper. Pure danger. Few deeds offend God as much as sorcery. That's why He was sending His Spirit: in an effort, as with Jonah, to pull us out of harm's way.

"In ancient Israel," notes theologian Clifford Hill, "God always raised up prophets in times of crisis."

So it is today. Around the same time Josyp Terelya had his first extraordinary experience with a light during his Soviet imprisonment, and two years before the stunning second apparition that saved him in the freeze cell, some 8,330 miles to the west, in Chicago, a Methodist missionary named Gwen Shaw had her own kind of mystical experience. I mention it because in tone and scope, it would serve as an example of what was on the way in all parts of the U.S.: a new wave of prophecy. "It was 1970 and I was praying and fasting in Chicago for the leading of the Lord, asking God for guidance," says Sister Gwen, who now directs a well-known ministry in Arkansas. "I had returned after 23 years in the mission field, and as I was seeking the Lord in a 21-day water fast, the Lord sent a young prophet to me who said God had sent him to tell me I had been raised up to the Lord to call out the 'end-time handmaidens,' that we were coming near the End Times and that the opportunity to serve the Lord was not to be much longer. When I finished my fast I felt that God had spoken to me through this means. Once the Lord visited me when my children were still quite young. That was in Hong Kong. One afternoon I was lying around with kind of the flu and I had a vision of the Lord standing over me and He said, *'Get the children ready. I'm coming soon.'"*

Largely because of that inspiration, Sister Gwen founded the End-Time Handmaidens in Jasper, Arkansas, on land they named Engeltal, which is German for "Angel Valley." Their logo became an angel holding a large hourglass. She also has received a beautiful porcelain angel with a trumpet at its mouth, which she takes to be a confirmation. Sister Gwen reported a slew of supernatural experiences. Just before her vision, at the end of the fast, suffering badly from uterine bleeding, three black "Holy Ghost sisters" came to see her and interceded with prayer, holding Gwen's hands and one of her feet. Suddenly she felt a fourth person clutching her arm in a powerful grip. Since she could see no one she took it to be the Lord. "In that moment the fire of God came down upon me and filled my body," she recounted. "I jumped out of bed and started praising God and dancing all over my apartment! The fountain of blood which had been causing the extreme weakness dried up instantly and I was healed and strengthened!"

Sister Gwen also reported an incident which had occurred in the Celebes Islands. She said that one day at noon the natives were terrified to see the sky turn suddenly dark. They ran in the houses and caves, fearing a great calamity. "Then they saw it was becoming light, so they went outside again," she wrote. "Lo and behold, they saw another light, shining in the sky, and above it were two nail-scarred hands with blood dripping from them." This was taken as a sign that Christ was coming soon—a message to that effect was claimed to have been written in Indonesian over the hands—and they thought the Second Coming would occur within the next few hours. She said tens of thousands had witnessed the sign over a large area.

She also reported a vision given in the Maritime Provinces of Canada to an eight-year-old girl who was the daughter of a pastor. "I was lying in my bed when I heard a trumpet blowing very loudly," the girl told Sister Gwen. "I jumped up and ran outside. I saw the heavens open up like two big curtains rolling apart. Jesus started coming down with a lot of angels and we began to rise up."

In Pakistan Sister Gwen, as she is known, said she heard everywhere she went of a similar sign that had appeared for several nights, a strange dagger in the sky, "as though held by an invisible hand." It was the time when Zulfikar Ali Bhutto had suddenly come to power and Pakistan was at great odds with India. There had been many skirmishes and the people were living under a suspicious truce. The air remained filled with tension. That same year a horrendous tidal flood had swept hundreds of people and their livestock to sea.

Three years after Sister Gwen's experience in Chicago, a preacher named David Wilkerson had a similar but much more elaborate vision. It was a notable event, not only for its content, which contained a number of prophecies, but also because Wilkerson was well-known in the New York City area both for his preaching and as the author of a Protestant bestseller called *The Cross and The Switchblade.*

It seemed to be a vision of five calamities soon to visit the earth. "I saw no blinding lights, I heard no audible voices, nor did I hear from an angel," he wrote in a second book, *The Vision.* "While I was in prayer late one night, these visions of world calamities came over me with such impact that I could do nothing but kneel, transfixed, and take it all in." At first he resisted the revelation, not *wanting* to take it in. The message was "too frightening, too apocalyptic, too discomforting to my materialistic mind." But it came back to him night after night, he said. "I couldn't shake it off."

What Wilkerson saw was the coming not just of more loose morals, not just remnants of the sixties, but a "moral landslide." A demonic spirit of lust, he said, was sweeping over the nations. In 1973 he predicted that nudity would be shown on network television. He foresaw pornography on cable programming. He saw the coming of magazines that would be much more explicit than *Playboy,* and this materialized a few short years later, as x-rated video magazines, along with raunchy publications such as *Hustler* and *Penthouse,* took over the newsstands. He saw the "floodgates" of homosexuality opening. He saw sex education getting out of control and students exposed to the idea that homosexual love is a viable lifestyle. "The sin of Sodom," as he put it, "will again be repeated in our generation." And like Lot, we would be vexed by the violent filth and sensuality. It would resemble what Nahum railed against in his prophecies about Nineveh. Wilkerson also saw sexual immorality entering the ministry. In other cases, as Satan played both extremes, innocent ministers would be falsely and viciously slandered. He saw nudity and occultism entering the Church itself, a prophecy which would one day materialize at America's largest cathedral, St. John the Divine in Manhattan, an Episcopalian sanctuary where New Agers have been allowed to hold winter solstice rituals (an old pagan practice popular too with witches) and where the nude sculpting of a woman on a cross has been displayed during Holy Week. He saw persecution through taxation of churches. He saw Hollywood stepping up its attack against true religion and persecution even by those in television comedy.

The response of God, felt Wilkerson, would be grace. He compared it to Noah's time, how before the Flood people were living high without much in the way of moral cares, scoffing at Noah, but when the flood came, horribly surprised. More than anything Pastor Wilkerson saw economic confusion and disarray. He saw a huge recession starting in Europe and then encompassing America, permanently lowering the standard of living. Many would seek to buy land in rural areas, away from the cities, where they could raise their own food and establish some semblance of security. For not even gold would be secure, he fretted. The only secure investment would be land. If Wilkerson's prophecies were at times a bit premature (predicting, for example, "lean years" and an economic crash "just ahead," when in fact America was soon to embark on a great expansion), perhaps that was because it is difficult to discern the order of events and determine which were due in the short term and which were in the more distant future—a time-honored problem with prophecy. He saw up and down periods in the economy—lean and fat years—and a period of false prosperity just before major events. But in general he saw a decidedly downward trend that would change the way we all live. The economic confusion, he said, would continue until the arrival of the Anti-Christ. He prophesied a new world monetary system and a "walking credit card" system. The day would come when "invisible numbers will be implanted on the forehead and forearm, and only photoscope scanners will be able to detect the numbers." He saw a revived Roman Empire which eventually would become the power base for a super world leader who would rise to restore economic order. "It is not a time to go into debt," he advised. "It is a time to prepare, a time to get clear and out from under heavy financial burdens."

As for natural tribulation, Wilkerson saw nature going "wild" with more floods, tornadoes, and hurricanes. "Sudden storms will appear without warning," wrote Wilkerson. "Southernmost regions will be gripped by record cold waves and northern areas will experience record heat waves." Severe winters and record snowfalls would become the rule. So would vicious hail storms, as in the eleventh chapter of *Revelation*. He also saw a tremendously tragic earthquake in the "not-too-distant" future and he didn't think it would be in California, but rather "where it is least expected." It might be preceded by another earthquake in a nation such as Japan. The earth was going to shake in a way that seismologists would not be able to explain. He believed that the earthquakes which had occurred in the early Seventies (there were six before the summer of 1973, including a nasty one in Nicaragua) were mere warnings. He saw a major tremor in the Aleutian Islands. There would be so many quakes that disaster funds would be depleted, a development that has already materialized among insurers in California. As with the economy, he saw a calm period after the turbulence, but a calm period that would not last. He saw strange phenomena in nature: signs in the heavens such as cosmic storms or a moon haze and large chunks of ice during those hail storms. "The world is about to witness the beginnings of great sorrows brought about by history's most drastic weather changes, earthquakes, floods, terrible calamities— far surpassing anything ever yet witnessed," he concluded. "These are exciting days for true Christians. God, in His love and mercy, is allowing disasters to strike the earth to warn all who hear that Jesus is coming back, and that it's time to get ready."

The very same year as Wilkerson's "vision," an Italian priest, Stefano Gobbi, from the lake region north of Milan, came up with a very similar evaluation. While praying at Fatima, the place where those three peasant children had encountered the angel, Gobbi began to hear an inner voice that he identified as the Virgin Mary. *"Night has now fallen upon the world, my son. This is the time of darkness, Satan's hour; this is the time of his greatest triumph,"* the sweet womanly voice told him. *"Troubles, anguish, and tribulation are bound to increase from day to day, because humanity, redeemed by my Son, is withdrawing ever more and more from God, and transgressing the laws. The Demon of Lust has contaminated everything. My poor children, how sick and stricken you are! The Spirit of Rebellion against God has seduced humanity; atheism has entered into so many souls and has completely extinguished the light of faith and love."*

The voice said that "decisive moments" were approaching mankind. Quoting his locutions, Gobbi reported that atheism, especially in the form of secular humanism and Communism, constituted the Red Dragon spoken of in the Bible. *"Read it, my sons,"* said the voice, *"because the present times are those of its realization! How many of my children are already victims of this error of Satan! Nothing can now hold back the hand of God's justice, which will soon be roused against Satan and his followers, as a result of the love, the prayer, and the suffering of the elect. Times of great indescribable tribulation are in preparation. If men only knew, perhaps they would repent!"*

Others weighed in with startling biblical interpretations. Prime among these was the highly popular author Hal Lindsay, who wrote *The Late Great Planet Earth*. Educated at Dallas Theological Seminary, which had its roots in dispensationalism (and thus the apocalyptical preaching of men like Moody and Darby), Lindsay saw great portents in the Middle East and, like Wilkerson, the coming of the Anti-Christ.

A key sign, Lindsay argued, was the rebirth of Israel, which was established as a nation in 1948.

That rebirth, said Lindsay, was forecast as a sign of the Second Coming in *Ezekiel* 38:8 and by Jesus Himself, who Lindsay claimed was referring to Israel when He mentioned the parable of the sprouting fig tree—how when its leaves are put forth, (*Matthew* 24:32-33), *"you will know that He is near."*

CHAPTER 19

The End of an Age

Such apocalyptic scenarios had to be handled with great caution, for they seemed but a repetition of numerous prophecies—premature prophecies—from past centuries. Those errors had indicated that the prophetic impulse, however legitimate at first, is often exaggerated or misinterpreted. We've already seen how Montanists predicted Christ's return 1,800 years ago, and a pope foresaw the End Times in the sixth century.

In 999 Christians flocked to St. Peter's Basilica fretting that the end of the millennium would mean the end of the world, too.

There were all kinds of similar impulses during the tortuous Middle Ages.

In the gloom of the fourteenth century, notes prophecy scholar Gary DeMar, tracts appeared with titles such as "The Last Age of the Church."

Then too, in 1300, was seen a coming Awakening. "Conditions for Jesus's return always appear to be favorable generation after generation," wrote DeMar. "As one failed set of predictions is discarded, a new but no wiser prophet surfaces to take up the banner of prophetic certainty in the belief that past generations did not have the right prophetic key. As we get nearer to the end, the signs, so we are told, become clearer and clearer. But the signs were also clear to those who believed that Jesus's return was near in their day.''

Luther himself expected the Second Coming and preached apocalyptical prophecy back in the 1500s.

So it is true. It is true that prophecies are often a case of metaphor or hyperbole. It is true that they often miss the mark, misinterpreting coming tensions and change—whether in society or the Church—as being the Final Judgment.

It's what I mean by a legitimate impulse that is embellished and made less credible.

But it is likewise true that something unusual and perhaps without immediate precedent has been going on, especially in the last half of our own century. This is not your typical era. This is a unique century. This is an era with 5.5 billion people and nuclear weapons, an era of abortion, a time when 37 million babies are terminated every year—comparable to perhaps one-third the entire world's population at the time of Christ—and the occult is broadcast over our very *airwaves,* proving that Satan is indeed "prince of the power of the air" (*Ephesians* 2:2). This is the era of snuff films (showing actual killings) and X-rated sex, a time of lust that would have satisfied the most lecherous Babylonian, an era in which supernatural events have been witnessed by a *million* people in Egypt alone, and millions elsewhere.

It is one whopper of a change coming! For sure, a day of reckoning nears and from every indication it's going to pack more of a wallop than most other such intervals. It portends to be the greatest turnover since the French Revolution and perhaps since the decline of Rome or back even further, since the fall of Jerusalem in A.D. 70, an event presaged not only by the appearance of Halley's Comet but also food shortages, a great fire in Rome, uprisings against the Roman Empire, which led to Jerusalem's destruction, and what DeMar himself says was a flurry of quakes in Crete, Smyrna, Miletus, Chios, Samos, Laodicea, Hierapolis, Colosse, and Campania, as well as Rome and Judea—yet no more and possibly far less than what we have been lately encountering ourselves.

Important too is the rumbling of prophecy, which, however imperfect, has always indicated a change of era.

This period of prophecy has been continuous now for nearly two hundred years and not only shows no signs of abating but is only expanding, unlike any other post-Christian period of which I am aware—from the great upsurge at the end of the 1700s to the special year 1830 and on to the current move of the Spirit and angels, who continued their descent throughout the 1970s. They did so to announce a beginning of sorrows, the birth pangs which often precede a change of era, as Christ Himself stated in *Matthew*, when he foretold that we would *"hear of wars and rumors of wars."*

"See that you are not troubled; for all these things must come to pass, but the end is not yet. For nation will arise against nation, and kingdom against kingdom. And there will be famines, pestilences, and earthquakes in various places. All these are the beginning of sorrows."

The angels were here to announce the beginning of the end of the Modern Age, which like any end and new beginning would involve the pains of death and birth.

Significant is the fact that Christ's words are in *Matthew* 24, which is known in the Catholics' New American Bible as the "Beginning of Calamities" and in King James as "The Signs of the Times and the End of the Age."

Something major in the chronology of Heaven was about to bust loose.

Relevant too is the Book of Joel: *"And it shall come to pass afterward that I will pour out My Spirit on all flesh; your sons and your daughters shall prophesy, your old men dream dreams, your young men shall see visions; and also on My menservants and on My maidservants I will pour out My Spirit in those days" (2:28-29).*

The Spirit manifested His gifts in a great charismatic movement that crossed denominational lines, bringing life to evangelicals, Episcopalians, and Baptists alike. There was also a huge charismatic movement among Catholics and a tremendous growth of Pentecostal churches. If, as scholars such as Clifford Hill have maintained, there was no major movement of openness to the Holy Spirit, to prophetic revelation, or to the exercise of spiritual gifts such as tongues from the fourth to the 19th centuries, the 20th century and particularly the 1970s changed all that.

"I'd say that when I came into the renewal, back in '71, the Catholic charismatic renewal, what I saw was tremendous enthusiasm and excitement, excitement because God had become far more personal through the Holy Spirit," says another expert, Ann Shields, who served on a national charismatic advisory board. "People began to realize that they really could find the comfort of a personal God. It was very, very exciting, and very new. We went step by step, relying on God for how to proceed. In 1975 we went to the first International Catholic Charismatic Conference in Rome. There were about 10,000 pilgrims from different parts of the world. And the experience was that of seeing the work of the Holy Spirit through the charismatic renewal being wed to the heart of the Church. Pope Paul VI spoke at that time to the renewal and gave his blessing, his encouragement, and we were able to praise God in St. Peter's. In fact, at one point we drowned out the Sistine Choir and they just joined us. Everyone was singing in his own language, 'Jesus Is Lord.'

"It just could not be contained. It was totally awesome. You know, that's a kid's term today, 'awesome,' but it was awesome. I was on my knees, and it's very hard to get on your knees when you're squashed together like that. At the same time, after Communion, there was a new gift being used in St. Peter's—at least new in form—and that was a prophetic gift. There were four or five prophecies, one right after the other, after Communion from the high altar at St. Peter's.

"And all of those prophecies dealt with a time of darkness coming, a time when supports that you depend on would no longer be there, things that you've depended on, resources, buildings, people, and finances, all that kind of thing, will be taken from you. *But know that when you only have Me, you will have everything.*' And then a time of evangelism will follow such as the world has never seen. That's the heart of those prophecies. Those were the two common threads."

By 1975, about 600,000 Catholics had been touched by the movement—soon to be in the millions worldwide—and similar if not higher figures were recorded in Protestant denominations. The Spirit was moving in a magnificent and telling way.

"The question that was being asked a lot was, 'Why is God doing this? Why is God pouring out His Holy Spirit?' " says Shields. "It had been done at the beginning of the Church to get the Church out of pagan times. And now, as most of us looked around at our society, we had to say that the signs were not good. The signs were that we were moving into the Post-Christian era in our societal values, education, and legal system. And so many saw the need for the intervention of the Holy Spirit.

"I see us entering the dark period. That's my opinion. We look at statistics in society and we look at the increase in natural disasters. I think God is speaking through all of this and calling us to repentance, otherwise there's a tremendous time of judgment coming for this nation. I call it 'severe mercy,' to borrow a phrase. John Paul keeps saying we're entering a new age of evangelization. He says this evangelism has yet to see its apostles and prophets. There will be new apostles and prophets. I'm not quite sure of the definition of 'End Times.' I think we're coming to the end of an age. I don't know that we're coming to the end of time. I don't know if the Second Coming of Christ is imminent. All I know is we're supposed to act like that and prepare, so when it comes, we're not surprised. I just have a sense that what we've gone through in this country since the mid-1940s is over and we're going to have to pay some dues. I don't know what God is going to do, but it seems to me that all around us God is giving us signs of the collapse of things we've depended upon: social structures, family, and all those kinds of things. We've taken so many things for granted for so long. And we've not acknowledged the blessings of God."

One of the prophecies to come out of the 1975 Rome conference, which was held on Pentecost weekend, was from a charismatic named Ralph Martin, who said the Lord was telling us that *"days of darkness are coming on the world, days of tribulation, days of trial. Things that have been supports to My people will no longer be there. Buildings that are now standing will not be standing. Supports that are there for My people now will not be there. I want you to be prepared, My people, to know only Me and to cleave to Me and to have Me in a way deeper than ever before. I will lead you into the desert, My people. You will be My people and I will be your God in a new and fuller way. I will strip you of everything you are depending on now so you depend just on Me.*

"A time of darkness is coming on the world. But a time of glory is coming for My Church. A time of glory is coming for My people. I will pour out on you all the gifts of My Spirit. I will prepare you for spiritual combat. I will prepare you for a time of evangelism that the world has never seen."

Another participant in the Rome conference said the Lord was calling for Christians to come together in His Holy Spirit from every corner of the globe, which was all but identical to what Pastor Wilkerson was getting. He saw the rise of a "supernatural Church" that will include Catholics and Protestants of all denominations. This is not false ecumenism, nor is it a call for anyone to compromise or relinquish his or her traditions and beliefs, but rather a call to true Christian fellowship and reconciliation. It would be a true Church that will outweigh a new false church or "super world church" which Wilkerson says will rise and seek political power. The false church, forming one world religion, will be composed of liberals from all denominations and it will seek moral credibility through displays of social action and charitable organizations. At the same time, however, such a worldly church will integrate occult practices into its "worship." The true Church, on the other hand, will be the work not of men nor politicians but of the Holy Spirit, who, prophesied Wilkerson, "will bring together, in one, people from all faiths and walks of life."

A glorious day is coming, said Wilkerson, even for those behind the Iron Curtain. Those who had lived under Communist persecution were going to enjoy "a limited period of freedom," predicted Wilkerson in 1973. "God's Holy Spirit will split the Iron and Bamboo curtains and will seek out and find hungry hearts in Russia, China, and Eastern Europe."

At this very time, in Romania, was a Pentecostal

preacher named Dumitru Duduman who had received the same heavenly encouragement. Dumitru and his wife Maria pastored a small country church near the Russian border and, over the period of almost two decades, delivered thousands of bibles to the Soviet Union. Duduman had once been granted the vision of a young, tall, and handsome angel dressed in white and identified as the Archangel Gabriel.

"Behold, man!" said the spirit. *"I've come to tell you that you are being prepared for a special ministry... Do not stop seeking the face of the Lord. You cannot understand everything now, but you will understand later on. Very, very soon the work will begin."*

Duduman had prayed after the vision and when the angel returned, he told the baffled Romanian, *"I am the chief commander of the heavenly army and I have come to tell you more good news. Come fasting and praying before God, and through you the prayers of many Christians will be fulfilled. Don't fear that you will not be able to do what you're asked because of its difficulty. The Lord will teach you all you need to know."*

And the Lord, said the angel, would help us conquer everything, against any and all odds.

Chapter 20

Sea of Sorrow

But before the victory there was to be more turmoil, much more turmoil. The same year the charismatics were in Rome, so too was Bishop John Shojiro Ito at the Vatican, trying to learn how to proceed with a series of revelations occurring at an obscure convent on the hill of Yuzawadai at the outskirts of Akita, Japan. The events involved a holy nun named Sister Agnes Sasagawa who was encountering angels and also strong and even startling words of warning.

Sister Sasagawa's experiences commenced on June 12, 1973, when she was in a small chapel praying before the tabernacle. As Sister Sasagawa later put it in an account to Bishop Ito, "an overwhelming unknown light suddenly shone forth. Seized with emotion I prostrated myself immediately with my face to the floor. Evidently I no longer felt the audacity to open the tabernacle. I remained perhaps an hour in this position. Subjugated by a power which overwhelmed me, I remained immobile, incapable of raising my head, even after the light had disappeared. When I came back to myself and I was finally able to reflect on what had happened, I asked myself if Jesus, present in the Host, had manifested Himself to enlighten my soul in the state of sin or if I had been simply a victim of hallucination."

The Akita event was important to all denominations. While Protestants and Catholics are often wary of each other, especially in regard to each other's mysticism, there was already the joining—a supernatural union—that Wilkerson saw. For in different ways, all active Christians, especially those with a sense of the Pentecost, were entering into a period of extraordinary illumination. Two days after her first experience, on June 14, Sister Sasagawa again saw a light—this time rather much a flash—and it was surrounded by a red flame that seemed to encompass the rays coming from the tabernacle. More than a week later she again saw an illumination she described as a "blinding light" and something like smoke or fog began to gather around the rays of light at the altar. It was reminiscent of the "incense" at Zeitun, Egypt. Suddenly Sister Sasagawa saw a multitude of beings that looked like angels, surrounding the altar. "These were not human beings, but one could see very clearly that they were an adoring crowd of spiritual beings," she later explained. "Absorbed by this surprising spectacle, I knelt down to adore. Then I was seized with the thought that there could be a fire outside. Turning around to look through the bay window in the back, I saw that there was no fire outside. It was indeed the altar which was enveloped in this mysterious light. The brightness from the Host was so brilliant that I could not look at it directly. Closing my eyes, instinctively I prostrated myself. When the hour of adoration was over I remained in the same position without noticing that the others had left."

Soon Sister Sasagawa was visited by an angel who took the form of a woman and identified "herself" as the nun's guardian. She felt the angelic influence at the chapel, where in addition to the angels, she claimed to hear a motherly voice: *"Many men in this world afflict the Lord. I desire souls to console Him to soften the anger of the Heavenly Father. I wish, with my Son, for souls who will repair by their suffering and their poverty for the sinners and ingrates. In order that the world might know His anger, the Heavenly Father is preparing to inflict a great chastisement on all mankind."*

Thus was the first startling warning. That was August 3. *"A great chastisement."* Two months later, on October 13, Sister Sasagawa again saw the brilliance as she was praying and could detect a heavenly fragrance. The date was highly significant, coming as it did on the anniversary date of the supernatural experiences to those three peasant children on October 13, 1917, at Fatima, Portugal. The voice continued where it had left off: *"As I told you, if men do not repent and better themselves, the Father will inflict a terrible punishment on all humanity. It will be a punishment greater than the deluge, such as one will never have seen before. Fire will fall from the sky and will wipe out a greater part of humanity, the good as well as the evil, sparing neither priests nor faithful. The survivors will find themselves so desolate that they will envy the dead."*

Prayer, penance and "courageous sacrifices," said the voice, can soften the Father's anger. Prayer is necessary even in secular institutes, said the Virgin Mary. Fervent prayer is necessary to console God. The work of the devil would infiltrate even into the Church, Sister Sasagawa was told, "in such a way that one will see cardinals opposing cardinals, bishops against others bishops." The Church would become full of those who accept "compromises"—an obvious allusion to modernists who in the wake of Vatican II sought to bring secularism and radical rationalism into the Church—and the demon would be "especially implacable" against souls consecrated to God.

If sin continued to increase, the nun was warned, the period of mercy and pardon would come to an abrupt end.

Although the apocalyptic tone caused wariness, it seemed more than coincidence that Sister Sasagawa, Father Gobbi, and David Wilkerson all experienced such visions the same year, 1973, even though they were in different denominations. Wilkerson, who was soon to have a huge ministry in midtown Manhattan, also made references to the Flood. "People in Noah's day didn't believe a flood of judgment was coming to the earth, and they spent their time in revelry, laughing at the crazy prophet who was preaching a vision," he wrote, citing biblical prophecy which he interpreted as predicting that countries would become ungovernable and cities would become unmanageable, as the world reeled "out of control." Normal times would disappear, he predicted, "and there would appear the addict, the prostitute, the homosexual, the thief, and the street-gang killer." He saw "total terrorism and violence." He saw coming a plague of "malignant sores or skin cancers," which bears similarity to Kaposi's sarcoma, the skin cancer now known to those suffering from AIDS. He also prophesied an episode of international blackouts, bloodbaths in Israel, major pollution in the ocean, and food shortages. He foresaw a "United States of the World" and a phony dictator who would deceive us. In addition to meteorological disturbances would be "a final world war."

While there was nothing said at Akita about Armageddon or the Antichrist, the tone of Sister Sasagawa's message certainly addressed a *spirit* of anti-christ, and sensing the urgency of the Akita phenomena, Bishop Ito took the issue to Rome, where he was informed that authority for determining the validity of Sister Sasagawa's message would rest with his own office. On April 22, 1984, a full 11 years after the onset of phenomena, and after the formation of two separate investigative commissions (the first of which reported back negatively), Ito concluded that Sister Sasagawa's experiences were not due to the paranormal faculties of a human being—were not "psychic"—and did not involve deceptive machinations of the devil. They were both holy and inexplicable. "After the inquiries conducted up to the present day, one cannot deny the supernatural character of a series of inexplicable events," said the bishop formally.

Far from cooperating with demons, Sister Sasagawa was attacked by them. As she was going to the chapel on August 4, she had felt something violently pull her back by the shoulder and when she turned to see who had grabbed her, the nun caught sight of a tall dark shadow that dominated her entire height. She tried to free her shoulder from the satanic grip but wasn't able until she prayed and invoked her guardian. "Save me!" she cried out. An angel appeared and the dark force immediately left. It was one of many struggles.

Most galvanizing to the bishop was how the stark message of Akita seemed to be an extension of the 1917 prophecies given by the Virgin to the peasant children in Portugal. In addition to predictions about the rise of Communism and the coming of a second world war—prophecies that were fulfilled—those young seers had also been given the third message or "secret" which has never been publicly revealed. Were the messages similar? Did they carry the same prophecies? Could anyone tell him? There were only three living humans known to be familiar with the "third secret" and they weren't talking. These were the original visionary, Lucia dos Santos, who in 1973 was in a Portuguese convent, Pope John Paul II, who studied the third secret with special earnest after the 1981 attempt on his life (which also occurred on an anniversary of the Fatima apparitions), and Joseph Cardinal Ratzinger, prefect of the Sacred Congregation for the Doctrine of the Faith, the high Vatican office which among many duties oversees reports of supernatural occurrences. When in 1988 Bishop Ito traveled to Rome for another meeting about Akita, where remarkable conversions and medical cures were occurring, he reported that Cardinal Ratzinger—a man of unquestioned sagacity, respected by Catholics and non-Catholics alike, and arguably the second most powerful figure in the Catholic Church—showed no disapproval of his pastoral letter and according to some accounts indicated private support, even enthusiasm, for promulgation of the message. Surely he favored that part of the communication calling for repentance. What, if any, portion of the Akita warning corresponded to the Third Secret of Fatima remained, however, a great mystery and became a matter of intense speculation among a small group of Catholics who were conversant with both incidents. That the second warning at Akita occurred on October 13 found significance in that it was the anniversary date of the great Fatima "miracle" reported not only by the three Portuguese children but also an estimated 50,000 to 70,000 onlookers who, during the children's apparition, had claimed to have seen the sky, particularly the sun, act in an inexplicable manner. It had been as if the sun was pulsing, spinning, throwing off colors, and moving in zig-zag fashion from its normal position, so as to seem at one point as if it was going to crash to the earth. For a terrifying moment the witnesses in 1917 had thought it was the end of the world. When the phenomena ceased, their clothes, damp from hours of rain, were suddenly dry. Even seasoned journalists had found it difficult to explain away the 1917 happenings that now seemed to link, in at least some small way, to Akita in 1973. Said a Portugal newspaper called *O Seculo:* "Before the astonished eyes of the people, whose attitude carries us back to biblical times and who, full of terror, heads uncovered, gaze into the blue of the sky, the sun has trembled, and the sun had made brusque movements, unprecedented and outside of all cosmic laws." The visionaries claimed that it was at this particular juncture, during the solar miracle, that they had seen an apparition of the Infant Jesus with Mary and Joseph, and also a vision (this seen only by Lucia) of an adult Jesus grieving as when He met His mother on the way to Calvary. The girl could only see the upper part of His Body but said Christ had looked upon the crowd and blessed the faithful.

If the coincidence of the October 13 date was not enough to connect Akita to Fatima, and also to Father Gobbi, whose locutions had *begun* while praying at Fatima, there was also the experience Sister Sasagawa reported during hospitalization for a fever that had swept her into a coma years before. Upon administration of the sacrament of the sick during four days of unconsciousness, Sister Sasagawa, it seems, had amazed the priest by reciting the Lord's Prayer (*Matthew* 6:9-13) and other supplications *in Latin,* a language she did not know. Her mother recounted that as she prayed, her face seemed to glow. Sister Sasagawa recalled having a vision at that time of "a beautiful person in a place which seemed like a pleasant field." The vision beckoned her, inviting her to approach. She also noticed a mysterious and "gracious" person next to her bed. This gracious visitor taught her a beautiful prayer, one she had never heard: *"Oh my Jesus, forgive us our sins, save us from the fires of Hell, lead all souls to Heaven and especially those who are most in need of Your Mercy."* Therein was another key link to Fatima: the prayer is nearly *identical* to a prayer the Portuguese children had been taught to recite in 1917 by *their* celestial visitor.

Those who speculated about similarities between Akita and Fatima noted that in addition to the prayers, parts of Sister Sasagawa's warning were strikingly similar to a controversial version of the third secret that was supposedly leaked to a European periodical. The Vatican, which kept the real secret under tight lid (often in the pope's very apartment), declined to confirm the speculation and indeed tried to calm fears and false rumors that it had to do with some form of massive calamity. When asked by an Italian journalist named Vittorio Messori why the secret was not released, Cardinal Ratzinger responded elliptically: "If this decision has not yet been made, it is not because the popes want to hide something terrible."

Then was there "something terrible" in the secret?

"If that were so, that after all would only confirm the part of the message of Fatima already known," replied Ratzinger. "A stern warning has been launched from that place that is directed against the prevailing frivolity, a summons to the seriousness of life, of history, to the perils that threaten humanity. It is that which Jesus Himself recalls very frequently: Unless you repent you will all perish" (*Luke* 13:3).

Ratzinger added that the pope deemed that the secret would add nothing to what a Christian must know from *Revelation.*

To publish the secret, said Ratzinger, "would mean exposing the Church to the danger of sensationalism, exploitation of the content."

But indications are that the secret, like the Akita warning ("cardinals against cardinals, bishops against bishops"), has to do with problems in Christianity, which during the 1970s saw its priests and ministers begin to compromise with the strong forces of modernism. Faced with an almost overwhelming scientism that scoffed at the supernatural, these ministers began losing their faith, replacing spirituality with psychology—a trend that was already causing an emptying of the pews. They also began listening to radical feminists and the rising homosexual movement. Old Christian strictures became cumbersome, while liberal theology seemed suddenly and curiously benevolent. Belief even in Christ's miracles fell into scientific doubt. Simply put, the shepherds were losing the Spirit and along with that, they were losing their flocks.

Poor ministers! Poor priests! They were islands in a raging storm.

Struggling to regain their audiences, such preachers became all the more psychological and "progressive," preaching Dr. Feelgood prosperity sermons that they hoped would make churchgoing more palatable.

It was the era of gurus!

It was the era of "positive thinking!"

It was the era of prosperity!

Who needed an old strict myth called God?

Secular humanism, an old heresy, began creeping into Christianity, and there was something yet more unnerving entering the picture: occultism. Along with the psychology came hypnotism and then a dangerous Christian openness to gnostic phenomena. Church leaders began tip-toeing toward ancient mystery religions, and soon a renegade priest named Matthew Fox would open a place called the Institute of Culture and Creation Spirituality on the grounds of Holy Name College in Oakland. Fox spoke at New Age gatherings (including in a hall which had a retractable ceiling in order to accommodate UFOs) and had on his faculty a practicing witch named Starhawk.

The gods of Babylon, the worshippers of Baal, and the witch of Endor were now poised, 2,500 years later, to make a major reentry.

"This is the hour when the abomination of desolation is truly entering into the holy temple of God." said Gobbi's locutions. *"They are no longer the salt of the earth, but a salt without savor, corrupted and nauseating, good only to be strewn on the ground and trampled underfoot by everyone. They are no longer the light on the candlestick, but darkness which makes the night even more obscure. They are all poor ailing priest-sons of mine, because they have fallen under the dominion of Satan. My beloved son, how can my heart not be submerged in an infinite sea of sorrow?"*

CHAPTER 21

Valley of Decision

"In this night," added Gobbi's message, *"darkness covers everything, and silence has now dimmed every sound, when suddenly a new light pours forth from Heaven and the festive voices of angels resound along the deserted roadways of the world."*

The heavenlies were lending their touch, singing their sweetness, placing a dome of protection over us. If they hadn't, mankind would have succumbed long ago. The angels arrived like celestial bodyguards and do so today. This is especially true when we feel alone and vulnerable or when we face danger on what Gobbi called life's deserted roads. To repeat what it says in *Psalms* (91:10-11), *"No evil shall befall you, nor shall any plague come near your dwelling; for He shall give His angels charge over you."*

Angels are there when we are deserving and particularly when we call for them. Sin puts them at a distance and gives Satan room in which to operate. Sin causes us to be envious and to misunderstand others. Sin also blinds us to the spiritual. That is why so many people, despite their intelligence and education, cannot see or comprehend the supernatural reality all around them. They are wearing spiritual blinders. They cannot see the wrongfulness of abortion or promiscuous sex because they are not in touch with the Light.

129

Yet angels are everywhere, strong and full of love—
touching us with the sweetest of sensations because it is
the touch of God. They surround us when we ask them to
surround us, and they bequeath to us special gifts and talents.
That is why anyone with pride and arrogance—anyone who
is "puffed up" with ego—shows a misunderstanding of
Christ. These gifts are *not* from us—are not our own doing—
but are from God. No matter what it is we do right, it is
because through free will we have allowed God's inspiration to work through us. Only God creates. Only He heals.
Only He inspires. Those who possess the gift of healing
or serve as prophets do so *not* through faculties of their
own but through intervention of the Spirit and His special
angels, who are assigned special tasks. Everyone has special angels. And they have the potential for performing miracles. We are the ones who limit them. We are the ones who
create division (criticizing the beliefs of others who differ
from us in often small ways). We are the ones who, in so
doing, put angels at a distance and invite demons instead.

Everyone on earth is loved by God and everyone forsak-
ing sin has special access to His Spirit or Paraclete. "To
the great gift of forgiveness God adds also the great gift of
the Holy Spirit," says Billy Graham. "He is the source of
power who meets our need to escape from the miserable
weakness that grips us. He gives us the power to be truly
good. If we are to live a life of sanity in our modern world,
if we wish to be men and women who can live victoriously,
we need this two-sided gift God has offered us: first, the
work of the Son of God *for* us; second, the work of the
Spirit of God *in* us."
That power is set free when we have true faith and when
we praise and thank the Lord.
Praise You, almighty God, praise Your very Name. We
praise You and thank You, dear Lord. We beseech Your
divine protection. Praise You, dear Lord. We praise You,
Lord Jesus Christ!
Angels come when we praise God because that's their
favorite past-time. When they come, they do so not to titil-
late us, not to play games with us, not to feed us constant
predictions, locutions, or visions, but to shield us as we
walk through this glorious and difficult test called life.

Angels come when they are invited and when we experience humility and love.

If you see a demon-creature in the dark of night, see also a brilliant and pure angel, chasing it away with the Light of the Holy Spirit.

We need always invoke the Holy Spirit, Who we already see as so active in countering the evil deceptions.

We need always invoke the Blood of Jesus!

Praise You Jesus! We praise Your Name! You are King of kings and Lord of lords, above all power and principality, above all deception. We invoke Your strongest help, dear Lord and Savior! Send Your legions! Show us the way to Your courage and away from our own cowering and doubt.

Such power was invoked at the foundation of America. To deny the spiritual is to erode the very concrete of our republic. During the Second Continental Congress, Benjamin Franklin urged that its sessions begin with prayer, and James Madison was equally cognizant of the Lord's power, writing that the establishment of our great and blessed nation revealed a "finger of the Almighty Hand." As newspaper columnist Don Feder, a Jew, has pointed out, "America was founded by religious people—'fundamentalists,' 'evangelicals,' yea, even the colonial equivalent of the dreaded 'religious right.' New England was settled by Puritans and Pilgrims." In God did we profess our trust. Our institutions presuppose a Supreme Being and no less than Daniel Webster once warned: "If we and our posterity neglect religious instruction and authority, violate the rules of eternal justice, trifle with the injunctions of morality...no man can tell how sudden a catastrophe may overwhelm us that shall bury all our glory in profound obscurity."

Yet as the Seventies turned into the Eighties, as hippies gave way to yuppies, as materialism graduated to a new and vulgar level, America and much of the world, neglecting the Spirit, risked precisely that forewarned obscurity. In the darkness of secularism and the occult, with mainstream religions dabbling with yoga, with nuns and young mothers turning to psychology instead of the Spirit, with the media marching ever stronger to an agnostic and then an anti-Christian drum, any new "light" was desperately necessary, any light to give a sliver of guidance along the shadowy passage. Not only the Church but society in general—indeed, *especially* society in general—was wandering in a strange forest of new dangers. This nation called America, founded by Christians, was being taken over by an anti-Christian minority which cleverly seized America's infrastructures of education, legalism, and communications. They propagated loose morals and made sure Christ—that same Christ so important to our Founding Fathers—was booted out of our mainstream establishments. There was something of an interlude in the 1980s—only 13 major quakes as opposed to the 21 in the Seventies—and God *was* acknowledged by the White House, which reached out to the nation's many evangelicals. But this period of mercy was not going to last. It was an interlude during which decisions were to be made and the good were asked to begin a public witness, to divorce themselves from the rampant and rising wickedness. *"Put in the sickle, for the harvest is ripe,"* says the Lord in *Joel* 3:13-14. *"Come, go down; for the winepress is full, the vats overflow—for their wickedness is great. Multitudes, multitudes in the valley of decision! For the day of the Lord is near in the valley of decision."*

It was a time for decision. It was a time to choose sides. It was a time when matters were coming to a head. Such was also spoken by modern-day prophets like Josyp Terelya. On July 17, 1983, the imprisoned Ukrainian, still held for his Christian activism, sent a letter to his wife Olena describing a vision he had of the Archangel Michael. The vision occurred at a moment when he was crouched in the corner of a solitary cell, down in spirits, the cell small, raw, and cold. It was a different Soviet prison, one he had been sent to after a string of incarcerations that had followed the attempt to freeze him at Vladimir. And though this time he wasn't being frozen, he was lonely and oppressed and needed the heavenly contact. In the vision, Terelya saw himself in the center of a meadow at a famous shrine called Zarvanystya in the western region of Ukraine. All of a sudden an intense light illuminated the meadow. Terelya smelled what seemed like the pleasant aroma of apple blossoms. In the distance was an old man dressed in white.

It was this man who identified himself as the angel Michael. He didn't have wings, nor was he young. There was no silver breastplate, nor any sword. He came as a man of ancient bearing and he explained the nature of the times. He also addressed the decisions facing mankind. *"The Lord is now gathering the good men against the evil,"* he told Terelya. *"The world would long ago have been destroyed but the soul of the world would not allow this. As the soul preserves the life of the body, so do Christians preserve the life of the world. There are many false teachings and false churches. And the false churches are preparing for the degeneration of the peoples. There are many pious people who are confused and are falling into the darkness of false beliefs or faiths because people have lost the true faith. There are many faithful and even members of the hierarchy who will fall into neo-paganism. God needs fervent and constant sons. Prayer will help you to find a solution to difficult situations. Great miracles will take place and the testimony of hundreds of thousands of Christians of the true faith will verify your words. In the end God will punish the apostates, because only through this punishment will God be able to bring man back to sound reason. Times of persecution will begin. The world will be divided into the messengers of God and messengers of anti-christ."*

God and anti-God. Christianity versus secularism. It was indeed coming to a head. And the prediction of "miracles"—of coming great events—already was materializing to the south in the Bosnia-Hercegovina region of Yugoslavia, which like Ukraine was under the oppression of Communism and where, two years before, in 1981, at Medjugorje (which means "valley" or "between the hills"), six peasant children began encountering daily apparitions of a celestial visitor who, as at Fatima, was described as the Virgin Mary. Within ten years not thousands but millions would journey there on pilgrimage, including a great Pentecostal leader named David DuPlessis.

The vision was radiant, accompanied nearly always by angels and occasionally by the Christ Child. Miraculous healings and signs abounded. The messages were urgent and sent directly to Pope John Paul II. The apparition called herself the "Queen of Peace" and warned that despite outward appearances, despite hopeful signs among political forces, the peace of the world was in a state of crisis.

No one understood, she said, how hideous things could get.

The miracles from God were both a gift and a warning.

A coming war in Yugoslavia?

It seemed unlikely in 1981.

At the time, tranquility reigned in Bosnia-Hercegovina, where Croats, Serbs, and Muslims had learned to share communities. And Yugoslavia, of which Bosnia was a part, seemed poised, among Communist nations, to make the easiest transition to democracy and capitalism. Indeed, there was no real sign of coming conflict. Yet the celestial visitor warned that without true conversion in Christ mankind faced a series of disasters.

Such events were prophesied to the peasant visionaries in a number of messages that to this day remain as secrets.

"A great struggle is about to unfold," said the apparition. *"Light and darkness are fighting each other. Many live in darkness. Show them the light. Excuse me for saying this, but you must realize that Satan exists. One day he appeared before the throne of God and asked permission to submit the Church to a period of trial. God gave him permission to try the Church for one century. This century is under the power of the devil, but when the secrets confided to you come to pass, his power will be destroyed. Even now he is beginning to lose his power and has become aggressive. He is destroying marriages, creating division among priests, and is responsible for obsessions and murder. You must protect yourselves against these things through fasting and prayer, especially community prayer. The hour has come when the demon is authorized to act with all his force and power."*

Each visionary at Medjugorje was to receive ten secrets. The first to do so was a 17-year-old girl named Mirjana Dragicevic. She received her tenth secret on Christmas Day in 1982 and indicated that the first three secrets involved events that would come as warnings to mankind, along with a great sign or miracle to convert unbelievers. The first warning is especially severe, she says, and will be known around the world. But it does not sound like a global disaster. She indicates it is something that will happen on a *regional* scale. She once compared it to a dam collapsing: not a global disaster but something awful enough that you wouldn't want to rush to see it. "There will be events on the earth as warnings to the world, before the visible sign is given to humanity," is the way Mirjana put it. Between the first and second secret is a time for conversion, she says, but the time between secrets may in some cases be very brief. Scientists and the media will try to rationalize the first secret as a natural event, but the trend will soon become apparent to those watching for signs of the times, especially after the second secret. While the middle secrets seemed to be of a personal nature, or to concern the Catholic Church, the last several pertain to the world at large and the final two seem especially severe. Already the seventh secret had been eliminated or lessened through prayer and fasting. The eighth had a similar opportunity. But less so the final ones, which seemed much harder to lift, for one could not expect all of mankind to suddenly repent.

Indeed, the world if anything was moving in a more sinful and thus a more precipitous direction.

While the event in the first "secret" would be severe, as would certain of the subsequent ones, their unfolding would mark the breaking of Satan's special powers this century and as such would mark the end of the era, these visionaries were told.

Whatever these events are, they're to occur within the lifetimes of the Medjugorje visionaries, meaning sometime between now and around the year 2040.

"Before the visible sign is given to humanity, there will be three warnings to the world," wrote a priest named Tomislav Vlasic, quoting Mirjana in a December 16, 1983, letter to Pope John Paul II. "The warnings will be in the form of events on earth. Mirjana will be a witness to them. Ten days before one of the admonitions, Mirjana will notify a priest of her choice. The witness of Mirjana will be a confirmation of the apparitions and a stimulus for the conversion of the world. After the admonitions, the visible sign will appear on the site of the apparitions in Medjugorje for all the world to see. The sign will be given as a testimony to the apparitions and in order to call people back to faith. The ninth and tenth secrets are serious. They concern chastisement for the sins of the world.''

They declined any comment when asked if these secrets had anything to do with End Times or the Second Coming, leaving followers to their own speculations.

The seers were given certain dates, although certainly no date pertained to the Second Coming, about which, we are told by Christ, no one—not even the angels—knows the hour (*Matthew* 24:36).

Were the secrets related to Akita, Garabandal, or the third secret of Fatima?

No one could say.

Was it the end of the world? Was there anything relative to a ''rapture?''

There was no indication of that either—but they did seem to involve large catastrophes and perhaps not just one but a number of unusual miracles.

Should we be frightened?

''Not at all,'' said Mirjana. ''I've seen Heaven! Nothing of the earth is worth one moment of worry. We are God's children! If people only realized how much He loves us, and what He has prepared for us, they would be filled with such peace!''

CHAPTER 22

Along the Deserted Roads

It was serious stuff, but it had a happy ending: a new and joyful time would follow the current period of tribulation. God will be glorified as seldom if ever before. It will be a great spiritual awakening. The bonds of evil will be broken. We will worship as in ancient times.

Many non-Catholics had great problems with the Virgin Mary, and in fact a number of such apparitions seemed fabricated or diabolical. But when David DuPlessis, the Pentecostal leader, visited Medjugorje, he felt "the whole place charged with the love of God. You can feel it, and you can see it. I told myself that if there had been anything wrong with what was happening here, there would not be the manifestations of the Holy Spirit that I could observe." He concluded that Medjugorje was "of God."

There were incredible signs there, signs that were seen by the millions who visited and also signs that paralleled those in biblical times. In 1981 a mysterious fire was seen on a hill known as Podbrdo. It could be seen from surrounding hamlets and appeared to consume the large hillside, where the apparitions first occurred. Yet when the peasant villagers went to see what happened, nothing seemed burned. There was no sign of incineration in the hillside scrub. It was as in *Exodus* 3:2 when Moses witnessed an angel in the burning bush, *"and behold, the bush was not*

consumed." There were also strange signs in the sky. Stars
split and turned colors. The sun pulsed and spun as at
Fatima. Images of Christ and the cross were discerned in
the clouds. At Podbrdo, one man with whom I spoke, an
old villager whose daughter is one of the visionaries, himself saw an apparition of Christ from the waist up.

As was reported by the Methodist missionary Gwen Shaw
in the Celebes Islands, there was writing here too—actual
writing—in the sky. On August 24, 1981, the peasants saw
an inscription above another rise called Mount Krizevac.
The luminous letters spelled *"MIR,"* which is Croatian for
"PEACE." Strange columns of smoke were seen to rise from
Krizevac and this too reminded me of *Joel* (2:30): *"And I
will show wonders in the heavens and in the earth: Blood
and fire and pillars of smoke."* I myself saw that and a
number of phenomena during four visits there, including
a moon that seemed to split in two and a strange light shaped
something like a dove.

The warning that peace—*mir*—was in danger rang across
the small hamlet in Bosnia-Hercegovina throughout the
decade. Mankind had not reconciled with each other nor
with God. As a result, we faced danger. *"You cannot
imagine what is going to happen nor what the Eternal Father
will send to earth,"* the Virgin said. *"That is why you must
be converted! Renounce everything. Do penance. You must
warn the bishop very soon, and the pope, with respect to
the urgency and the great importance of the message for
all mankind. I have already said many times that the peace
of the world is in a state of crisis. Become brothers among
yourselves; increase prayer and fasting in order to be saved."*
Now was the time for conversion. We must pray for
unbelievers. We must repent before it is too late. Prayer,
fasting, penance, conversion. That was the main message.
"Every family must pray family prayers and read the Bible,"
said the celestial visitor. *"Pray, dear children, so that God's
plan may be accomplished, and all the works of Satan be
changed in favor of the glory of God."*
In addition to the possibility of deception, Protestants also
worried that the Virgin was given too much attention, almost
to the point of usurping Christ. Still, a good number of non-
Catholics were nonetheless fascinated by how closely these

words of knowledge fit with what had been coming out of the non-denominational and other charismatic movements. It seemed that the Holy Spirit spoke in accordance with religion and culture—to different people in different ways.

Most fascinating was the idea of imminent events, implicitly world disasters. Since the Virgin came wearing 12 stars as a crown—12 lights above her head—was this, wondered Catholics, a fulfillment of *Revelation* 12?

It was, if nothing else, a message of prayer. It was a message to "address yourselves directly to Jesus" (9/4/82). It was a plea to fast, for through self-denial and prayer, said the vision, "One can stop wars, one can suspend the laws of nature." It was a message to bring peace into the heart— the tranquility of love and God. It was a message, like Terelya's, that the time had come to choose for Christ. It was a warning that Christians had to stop carping at each other. *"There is only one mediator between God and man,"* said the Virgin Mary, *"and it is Jesus Christ."* But she said it was up to God and only God to judge various religions. Every person is equal before Him. She emphasized prayer not from the brain, not through rote repetition, not in false praise, but from the *heart.* When she appeared, her pose was in the charismatic pose of palms facing up. *"The devil tries to impose his power on you, but you must remain strong and persevere in your faith. You have to pray and fast. Begin by calling on the Holy Spirit each day. The most important thing is to pray to the Holy Spirit. When the Holy Spirit descends on earth, then everything becomes clear and everything is transformed."*

Many were those who claimed miraculous cures at Medjugorje, but more important was the peace in their hearts. Many too encountered angels. The visionaries saw them with Mary, and others noticed two or three lights like tiny meteorites that arrived just before the apparitions. This too I saw with my own eyes. Ivanka Ivankovic described the angels as appearing there "small, like babies." She said it is up to us to accept or refuse their help. "These angels," said the visionary, "are especially caring to babies and the elderly, the sick and the weak, and those in trouble." Their job is to "keep prodding us to get back on the path to

Heaven.'' They come when we ask and were assigned to us before time. "Where God is," she said, "all is eternal now. There is no time. The angels are with God.''

Pilgrims encountered them in the form of mysterious peasant women. These accounts I heard from priests and laity alike. "I was there in September, 1989," says Debbie Womack of Louisville. "We were walking to the church and our group was kind of scattered. I was lagging behind with a friend. I noticed this woman. She was so tall it was like she was huge. And yet she was so natural. When I noticed her, she was walking with her head down. And then she turned to her right, which would be to our left, and I just stopped dead in my tracks. Something just told me in my heart that it was an angel. As soon as I had that thought, she turned around and she looked right at us. Both of us stopped. Her eyes were blue—so blue you couldn't imagine, so clear—and she looked like an old woman, yet her eyes were very young, and she had the most beautiful smile. She looked at me and I could *feel* it. She looked like a peasant woman, but with a smile and eyes like I had never seen. It was so beautiful. There was so much joy. All I could think was how wonderful God is! As I turned to look at my friend, my friend said, 'An angel!' We turned back and looked and she disappeared. There was nothing but a dirt wall."

That same year, a woman named Bonnie Lewis of the Cincinnati area also had an encounter at Medjugorje, this time on Mount Krizevac itself. She was heading to the top, a challenging climb up a path of sharp stones, when she encountered a plump little old lady who needed help. "She appeared to be around seventy years old," said Bonnie. "Anyway, as we began the long climb to the top I grabbed this woman's arm and helped her up the mountain. Another girl also helped her, for she really needed two people, one on each side of her."

Once at the top, they parted ways and, falling into prayer and praise, melted into the crowd.

"As we began the climb down the mountain," says Bonnie, "I looked around to see if I could spot the old woman and was relieved when I didn't see her. I was so tired by that time that I didn't feel I had enough strength to help her down the mountain. I even remember saying to God in my heart that I hoped that I wouldn't see her because I was just too tired to help her. No sooner did I say those words than she appeared right in front of me. For some reason, I just couldn't keep from going to her assistance. I grabbed her arm and slowly but surely, down we went. As we said goodbyes she grabbed me and held me in her arms. She then looked me straight in the eyes and it was as if she were saying to me, 'I've known you all your life.' I felt those words so strongly, accompanied by a tremendous love.''

So too did those returning from Medjugorje find themselves in closer contact with the spiritual world. During a special service in Jersey City commemorating an anniversary of Medjugorje, a little girl of six or seven kept raising her hand as if in a classroom, according to Jon Zielenski, who wrote me about it. "Her mom," says Jon, "swiftly pulled her hand down. From then till the end of the homily that little hand kept popping up and at times took on a waving motion. After the talk, all returned to normal. After Mass we all gathered outside the church for a little small talk. Nearby was the frustrated mom and her little girl. She questioned her daughter about her behavior in church. 'But mommy, I just wanted to talk to the man.' ''

Her mother explained that the man couldn't speak to her. He was giving his sermon.

"No, mommy! Not the priest—the man standing beside him—the one with wings!''

In another part of the same state, Keith and Kathleen Werner, two others with close ties to Medjugorje, were on the way to give a presentation about the apparitions to a group in the town of Hopewell. They had just prayed for angelic protection when one of their tires blew out. "To get a front flat tire on the driver's side of a front-wheel drive vehicle at near-highway speed is usually a catastrophe," said Kathleen. "We were just entering the slow-down lane off I-95, heading for exit 31. Keith calmly told me to brace myself as he felt he had blown the left front tire and he had to hold the wheel tightly. I hardly felt anything wrong and we seemed to ease our way over, and it was a side street across from a real estate service.

I looked at my watch—we'd be late for sure. Yet I felt in my heart that this was going to be a very special presentation. Little did I know!

"I got out of the car to assess the damage, when I noticed a man drive up in an old battered pickup truck. He was in his sixties, I guess, and very frail-looking. Yet he had a strength about him I could not describe. 'I've come to help you change that tire,' he said. 'I have a hand lift right here in the truck.'

"In my mind I was a bit skeptical as I was sure he would never be able to even lift the tire out of the trunk," continued Kathleen. "Just then another car drove up. A younger man, I'd say in his early thirties, came up. He was in his jogging shorts and looked as though he had just come from the local health spa. Looking at the older man, he asked if he could help. They agreed and opened my trunk to get out the spare.

"When Keith and I do our presentations, we have boxes and boxes of material with us, as well as our TV and VCR for showing a short video. As they began to remove the articles, I felt a bit of embarrassment, because to take everything out was a lot of work. I saw Keith coming our way and begged them to wait as he could do the work of removing things. The younger man then looked at me. I had never seen such piercing blue eyes. In the most sincere voice he said, 'No, you and your husband have a presentation to do, and he must not get dirty in his suit. We'll take care of this flat and you will be on your way.'

"I never saw a flat changed so easily and all was neatly packed back into the truck. We tried to pay them but they flatly turned it down. We couldn't thank them enough. We were only twenty minutes from our destination but were thirty minutes from the time we were to begin our presentation. So we wasted no time getting back on the road.

"It wasn't until we were pulling away that it hit me. 'Keith, do you know what that man said to me? He told me we were going to do a presentation and that you had to keep clean for it.'

"There was no way this man could have known this.

We had not said nor done anything to indicate where we were going or what we were doing with boxes of papers, books, a TV and VCR. I said, 'I have the strangest feeling we just met our guardian angels.' ''

So too did Joan Zugelder of Pueblo, Colorado, have an angelic experience after visiting Medjugorje. "I was driving home from work in my van. It was on a Friday evening and it was dark and very cold. My route takes me on the outskirts of town, and my car just died at the bottom of a hill at an intersection. Everything was totally dead—battery, lights, everything.

"I sat there and many things flew through my mind in a few minutes: I was in this intersection in this dark place at least a couple miles from a phone. I was not dressed for this weather. It was bitterly cold. I could feel the cold seeping in already. Cars were going by me on both sides. I was afraid to get out of the car. I was afraid to stay there. I was afraid of getting hit from behind by this Friday night traffic. I wanted someone to stop, but was afraid of who it might be. I really did not want a man to stop.

"Suddenly I spontaneously prayed aloud, 'Lord, please send me an angel!' Not a minute later, a car pulled around me, stopped on the side of the road, and a lady walked into the intersection, to the driver's side of my van, and asked if anyone was helping me. I said, 'no,' and I asked her if she would please make a phone call for me. She said, 'Oh, no. I will push your car out of the road and give you a ride to a phone.'

"This pretty, petite woman with long blonde hair (she even looked like an angel!) walked around to the back of my van, in spite of the fast-moving traffic coming down the hill behind us in the dark. She started physically pushing my van to the side of the road. A man stopped just then momentarily and gave her a hand. Then he left. I'm sure she could have done it herself. She then told me to get in her car and she drove me to the nearest phone. I was so astonished, I could not think of what to say. I finally said how grateful I was that she stopped. She smiled and said, 'Oh, I do this for people all the time.' I never saw the lady or her big, gold car again, even though I have looked for her on the road many times since. She was definitely the answer to my desperate prayer!''

While I am getting ahead of myself in that some of these accounts happened in the 1990s, they all tie into the miraculous events that started in the 1980s. From Wentyville, Missouri, came the touching account of a mother, Ann Wilson, at the side of her daughter Monica during a blessed and miraculous death. Monica was only 22 and a cancer patient who traveled to Medjugorje.

"She came back very weak, but with a greater faith and inner peace," recalls Ann. "She said that Medjugorje was like a little Heaven on earth. When one of her sisters asked how she could stand being sick, she replied, 'I'm happy. Jesus is with me.' She never complained, even though she vomited constantly and was never able to be comfortable. She was not able to hold anything down, not even water. She kept losing weight and the hospice nurse said she was living on faith and a strong will to live."

The night of her death, Ann tried to comfort her as best a mother could.

"She was sitting in the chair in the living room with my daughter Mildred on her left. I was on her right and my husband Grover was at her feet. All of a sudden, she said, 'The Light. The Light.' She was moving her head and I was so upset that I took her in my arms and her head rested on my breast. I was crying and I cried out. She raised her head and looked at me, her starry eyes full of suffering, then laid her head back on my breast. I felt I was holding a bundle of peace. She seemed to be asleep so I laid her back on the chair.

"Suddenly, a great hush or stillness descended on the room and I felt that time stood still. I could not move. I felt I was frozen in time. Have you ever been in a room by yourself and someone came in, and although you did not hear or see them, you felt their presence? I felt the presence of royalty and I felt that Jesus, the King of Peace, and Mary, the Queen of Peace, and their attendants had come. I felt a great awe.

"Suddenly I saw a flash of a bluish gray and then a clear form came from Monica's head and went up and disappeared. I saw the movement as it went up. It was surrounded by a golden light with a thousand tiny twinkling lights. I don't know if the lights were around the golden light or on it or in it. It lasted only two or three seconds and then disappeared. I looked down at Monica and saw that she had died."

CHAPTER 23

"It's An Angel!"

If there is any one center of angelic activity, it may well be Mount Gargano near the east coast of Italy. It is a place where the Archangel Michael has manifested since A.D. 404. A cave there serves as a basilica, and the sensations of heavenly power are extraordinary. Heading for this site a few years ago, on the way from Assisi, the famous nun Mother Angelica, who founded Eternal Word Television Network (EWTN), experienced one of the most dramatic angelic experiences on record. She was in the company of three other nuns and a deacon named Bill Steltemeier.

It wasn't just one angel they happened across. It was a carload.

They were about 20 miles from the cave when the five travelers found themselves at a crossroads and couldn't decide which way to turn. There was a road to the left and a road to the right. But there were no signs, and it was something of a dead end. All that was around were the stony hills and occasional livestock.

"I slowed down as I came to the intersection," says Deacon Bill, who is president of EWTN. "All of a sudden we saw a car coming very fast from the left. It was speeding. I rolled down my window. I wanted to ask him directions. He slowed down to probably thirty miles an hour. There were a whole bunch of handsome men in that car, three in the front and three in back—in this small car. I'm trying to wave at them. They were all looking at us, smiling. All of a sudden a young man just jumps out of the back seat on the other side of the car while it's going 30 miles an hour and heads straight for us. The car never stopped! It just kept going. All of a sudden he comes out the back. I was just flabbergasted! As he walks to me, I see he is just so handsome and as I'm wondering about how he got out of the car, Mother Angelica is saying, 'It's an angel! It's an angel!'

"I'm just totally surprised. I knew Mother Angelica was saying it was an angel, but I had never seen one. I'm ready to ask him the way to the top of the Gargano when he points to the mountain to the right and says, 'That way to Gargano,' in perfect English. But he was as Italian as anyone I ever saw! He was extremely handsome, maybe 22 and very dynamic, yet extraordinarily young. I knew there was something about him that was different—just so handsome in a way I had never seen.

"I asked if he wanted a ride. He said he would go back to the intersection—where there were no houses and no humans for 25 miles. It was desolate—just livestock on the hillside."

Bill recalled that the sisters were all excited. Mother Angelica kept repeating, "It's an angel!" They started up the hill, Bill driving, the nuns looking back at the strange young man, this man who looked 22 and yet *didn't* look 22. As they watched, the stranger walked in a pattern that formed a cross—15 feet one way, then up and down. A cross! He did that six or seven times.

All of a sudden the nuns cried out in unison, "He's gone!"

The helpful man had vanished before their eyes.

One can only guess at the many other occurrences that have been witnessed near the Gargano in the past 1,600 years. The history of the Archangel Michael's appearances there and at nearby Siponto is said to go back to 404. It was then that a wealthy man who had a herd of cattle grazing encountered the supernatural. According to a popular account published by the Daughters of St. Paul, "One day a steer went astray from the herd and did not return with the rest of the cattle at the usual time. The owner and his hired men went in search of the steer, and finally found him on the summit of the mountain, lying at the entrance of a cave. The animal refused to leave the spot. At length the owner, exasperated by its stubborness, took up his bow and sent an arrow toward it. However, the arrow whirled about in the air, and, coming directly toward the archer, wounded him.

"All were frightened at this strange incident, and no one ventured to approach the place. They went directly to the bishop of Siponto and related the incident to him. The holy prelate, after serious reflection, decided that there must be some mystery connected with it. He therefore prayed fervently that God's Holy Will might be revealed. Thereupon St. Michael appeared to him in great splendor and said, *'I am Michael, the archangel, who ever stands before the Lord. I am keeping this place under my special protection. By this strange occurrence, I wish to remind men to celebrate the divine service in my honor and that of all the angels.'"*

The night preceding an attack on the area by Neapolitans, Michael again appeared to the bishop and prophesied victory. This apparition occurred after a three-day fast.

"As soon as the attack began, all Monte Gargano was violently shaken," said the Daughters of St. Paul pamphlet on the archangel. "The entire summit was enveloped in dark clouds, from which flashes of lightning, like fiery arrows, flew toward the enemy, who, in consequence, took to flight. In joy and gratitude, and amid devout prayer, the conquerors entered the sacred spot. They found the cavern to be perfectly formed for a church."

There have been many such interventions of Michael since, from Constantine the Great (whom he helped in the battle with the pagan Maxentius) to Joan of Arc. Many theologians are of the opinion that Michael surpasses just about any other angel in glory and power, possessing the highest and most perfect degree of love and zeal. These are the characteristics of what some consider to be the highest order of angels, known as "seraphim." Others believe that "archangel" is a high-enough ranking.

"Michael is now the angel above all angels, recognized

in rank to be the first prince of Heaven," remarked Billy Graham in his book, *Angels.* "He is, as it were, the Prime Minister in God's administration of the universe, and is the 'angel administrator' of God for judgment. He must stand alone, because the Bible never speaks of archangels, only *the* archangel. His name means 'who is like unto God.'"

Michael is thus really much higher in rank than what is commonly thought of as an "archangel." He is involved as Prince of the Angels and is the counterpart, the great nemesis and defeater, of Lucifer *(Revelation* 12:7-8). Some say he's also the author of *Psalm* 85. In Jewish lore it's even believed that the fire Moses saw in the burning bush may have had Michael's appearance. In the Dead Sea Scrolls he is referred to as "Prince of Light." In the apocryphal Book of Enoch, Michael looks down upon earthly sorceries and calls for a purification. (That was just before the Flood). Both in the Old and the New Testaments, the holy angel Michael, this vast power from Heaven, whose presence is not to be taken lightly, is called guardian of the people and guardian of Paradise. As Graham points out, he is also herald of the "general judgment." God revealed to Michael the designs of His justice and mercy. He is often associated with two other "archangels," Raphael and Gabriel. To this day, Jews invoke Michael as the principal defender of the Synagogue. He is the protector of individual Christians and entire Christian nations. Michael is also important in Islamic writing. According to the prophet Daniel, the holy angel will *"stand up" (Daniel* 12:1) at the *"time of trouble."*

Thus do we see that the presence of Michael in particular and angels in general is itself a sign of the times and often a prelude to God's judgment. It was angels who warned about Sodom and who, at the other end of the Bible, gave John the Book of Revelation.

While they have always been around, their appearances in the 1980s, and also the beginning of the next decade, were without a doubt on the way to some sort of crescendo.

The accounts, many from average people of good spiritual and community standing, continue to amaze me. One of my favorite stories involving Michael occurred to Patricia "Pam" Larson of Ann Arbor, Michigan. Pam and her husband had been waiting 11 years to adopt a baby and finally had found one in Costa Rica. They were going through an excruciatingly long adoption process and so there she was, alone in Costa Rica for nearly four months when the process was supposed to have taken but six weeks.

"The policy there is that the adoption must be finalized before you leave the country," says Pam. "We were running into all kinds of complications. I had two other children and a husband at home, and I don't speak Spanish, so to say it was a test is putting it mildly. The process was that the adoption would be finalized and you would present the Costa Rican papers to the U.S. Embassy and it would have to clear.

"The day finally came when I had the adoption papers in hand. I called the embassy to make an appointment. But they didn't have the approval documents. This was before the fax. It was 1985. The woman said she couldn't take a copy, she needed our packet of paperwork. So I called my husband who called the Detroit immigration who called Washington who called here and said that somewhere between Washington D.C. and Costa Rica, probably in a diplomatic pouch, was all the paperwork. Until it was found we couldn't proceed. I was like hysterical. They had lost it!"

Pam wandered into the garage at the home where she had been staying. The garage had a high ceiling, perhaps 15 feet.

"I used to laugh that this was my prison, because I used to walk around in there when I didn't feel good. After I talked to my husband, I went into the garage and all I could do was pace. I couldn't pray. I just needed to move. I knew I couldn't handle being there another three months. So I'm pacing and pacing and saying, 'God have mercy, God have mercy,' and thinking this must be what it's like to have a nervous breakdown.

"Totally helpless, I was saying 'God have mercy' and when I made one of my turns, there were two sets of feet standing there. We're talking big feet. Logically they didn't fit in the space because we're talking 12-to-15-foot ceilings and I could only see the feet *up to the ankles*. I could see the bottom of the robe, and the toenails. I knew they were angels and I had no fear. It was in color. They were huge. The one close to me, his big toe was split, the feet were dirty. I could see hair on the ankles and the toes. They were not like I thought angels were. These were tough warrior angels. The robe was white and had a belt with a knot and I could see the tip of a sword. The hem of the robe had little holes woven, and the feet were in sandals. The hair was blondish, nearly brown—as if blond from the sun. I could see a left ankle bone and the blood vessel. I didn't hear a voice so much as inside: 'My name is Michael and we're here to do battle for you.' I remember kind of stooping down trying to see more of them, and of course I couldn't. And I had no sense of time. The other one didn't identify himself. I remember thinking, 'Warriors. These are not like the little cherubs you see in church. These are manly warriors.'"

It was as if Pam had been momentarily pulled into a parallel reality.

Huge angels, such that their ankles seemed more than ten feet high.

As far-out as it seems, Pam sounded like a highly credible and prayerful woman and we must remember that the unlikeliest of images accompany the supernatural. Angels can appear however they want to appear.

Right after, Pam felt compelled to call the consulate, where a woman named Gabrielle came on the line.

"I said, 'This is Pam Larson,' and she said, 'Are you a Christian?' I was like looking at the phone. I said, 'Yes.' She said, 'Do you pray?' And I started to cry because I knew. She said, 'Does God always answer your prayers so fast?' By that time I was really crying. She said, 'The strangest thing happened. When we spoke half an hour ago and hung up the phone I turned around and the messenger was at my desk with the diplomatic bag. It was the funniest thing: in the bottom of the pouch was all the paperwork. We were frantic trying to reach you.'"

The baby was named Michael.

Another account of warriors, or at least sentry angels, came from a Canadian businessman named Tony Van Hess. "In February 1975 at the age of 36, I decided to open up a personnel recruiting and consulting business in Dundas,

Ontario, which catered predominantly to the manufacturing industries throughout southwestern Ontario," Van Hess told me. "On November 24, 1979, I experienced an outpouring of the Holy Spirit in my life which dramatically changed my focus and business ethics to this date. Along with dealing with many of the executive and high-tech professional requirements in the industry, I quickly realized that the business was to be used as an evangelization tool, where extensive inner healing took place and where people once again were built up mentally to face challenges and tasks ahead.

"In 1983, while I was in my office, an angel suddenly appeared standing beside the entrance door of my office. This large, human-like figure, approximately seven-feet high, wearing a grayish white full-length robe, stood silently and perfectly still and looked directly at me. I did not see his lips move, although suddenly a very audible message was given to me: *'Know that every person who comes into this office has already been pre-screened and sent.'*

"At the same moment I witnessed in the eyes of my spirit standing outside of the entrance of our offices two angelic figures standing as sentries watching over those who are coming and going. These two figures were a little shorter in height and appeared to be steadfast in carrying out their responsibilities.

"Since 1983 I have walked with a new self-confidence and an assurance of the vocation that I have been given and the awareness that those who enter my office are already on God's bonus plan."

There were also instances, as in World War One, when angels appeared on actual battlefields. One such case involved a Marine who was wounded in Vietnam and found himself encompassed by a "beautiful shining light" that took away all his pain. To this day he experiences a glimmer of light at difficult moments which brings him a "joyous peace." There were also cases in which angels were reported during "NDEs," or near-death experiences. I read about a Yugoslavian man who "died" during an operation and was even taken to the morgue. There he awoke with a cry, summoning the astonished medical per-

sonnel. During his unconscious state he'd heard heavenly
music. "Many angels came," said the man, "and sang a
beautiful chorus, and Jesus was with them. He kissed me
three times and said to me three times, *'You must return
and preach and tell the people I am coming soon.'"*

In churches the angels were "seen" in great adoration,
suspended in devout postures, especially near the
Eucharist, and when a ten-year-old Chinese girl named Sen
Ching had an NDE, according to Gwen Shaw, a "presence"
talked to Sen Ching about lies she had told during her life,
mentioned her impatience, and also brought up disobedience to her parents. But she professed faith in Christ and
was set upon a bright road.

"I was very happy," said the girl. "The place was as
bright as the middle of the day. The first things I saw, after
coming inside, were the beautiful, very high houses made
of jewels and gold. I saw God's light. Heaven is brighter
than the noonday sun. Many hundreds of times brighter.
Jesus then came and changed my clothes to white. "

Sen Ching also saw angels with wings and halos. Each
held a gold trumpet, "and when they played them, the
music was so lovely nothing can compare to it. The Lord
Jesus's clothes were whiter than anyone else's. Whiter than
the angels' and whiter than (those) who had come to
Heaven with me. A brownish-golden light shone all around
Him. It seemed to shine from the jeweled crown which He
was wearing. His halo was bigger than the angels' halos
were. His whole body shone, even His fingernails."

CHAPTER 24

Ancient Wisdom

They came as handsome young men. They came as beautiful women. They came as plump older ladies or as peasants. They came as cops or disheveled beggars and street people. Never was there more reason to refer to *Hebrews* 13:1-2: *"Love your fellow Christians always. Do not neglect to show hospitality, for by that means some have entertained angels without knowing it."*

One time, during a trip to New York, William Howley, a sales representative for religious goods, was staying at Southgate Towers right across from Madison Square Garden. Every morning he'd scoot over to seven o'clock Mass at a Franciscan friary.

"Out on the side street, the Franciscans feed all the street people—probably 2,500 to 4,000 a day," says Bill. "They give them coffee and a sandwich. I'd go across the street and see all these street people getting lunch and breakfast—a sandwich for the afternoon—and they have a collection. I had five bucks in my pocket and I was going to put it into the pot. But for some reason the Franciscans didn't come down the aisle I was on. I went bouncing out the door and there was this guy with a beard who looked a little rough. He said, 'You know, it's an awful cold morning.' I said, 'Yeah, it is.' He said, 'A warm cup of coffee is really in order. You know, it's tough out here on the

154

street in February.' I said, 'Look, if I give you some money
will you promise not to use it for alcohol or drugs?' He
said he wouldn't. He said, 'By the way, I'm a doctor by
profession, but due to certain circumstances, I ended up
here on the street.' I said, 'I'm really sorry. Look, here's
five bucks. Tomorrow I'll be going to Mass. If you're
around I'll take you for a nice breakfast with me.' He said,
'Okay. The Lord will always be with you.' I said, 'Huh?
Can I ask your name?' 'Well,' he said, 'the street people
call me Angel.' He turned around and I never saw him
again.''

A friend of mine who works in Manhattan's financial district was a bit down and out, having lost his job in the wake
of the 1987 market crash. He was out of the financial circuit
for a couple years. While circulating through midtown
Manhattan trying to land another job, he ran into a beggar
but all he had was a twenty—and the beggar had no
change. My friend really couldn't afford the whole twenty
but finally said, "Keep it."
Right afterward he found an excellent job—and soon
after that he ran smack into the same mysterious beggar
again but far away from midtown, this time near his new
job, as if punctuating the fruit of his kindness.

A woman named Kristi Schmit from Canby, Oregon, told
a similar story: How once, in downtown Portland, she
noticed a very disheveled and dirty man rooting through
a large trash can. "I watched in horror as he pulled out
a discarded soft-drink cup and began to sip someone's left-
over soda pop," says Kristi. "People dressed nicely in their
pearls and suits and ties were completely oblivious to this
poor, obviously hungry fellow human being! Everyone was
walking past him, paying him no notice whatsoever, as if
he weren't even there. Moved with compassion I
approached him and said, 'Sir, are you hungry?' He looked
at me in the eye with a sad but humble expression and
replied, 'Yes, ma'am, I am.' I reached in my purse and
grabbed two or three dollars and handed it to him. He
thanked me, we both turned away, and as I stepped to the
curb to cross the street, I turned to see where he was
headed. He was gone! There were no crowds on the side-

walks at all. I could not see him anywhere!''

That was an angel placed there by the Lord as a test but other times they came, as we've seen over and over, to help or offer advice at moments of need. Maria Snyder of Winston-Salem, North Carolina, told me how an old woman named Roberta Walch, the grandmother of a friend, was sick in a hospital when two men dressed in white visited her. One stood watching, never saying a word, while the second informed the elderly woman that she would have six months to a year to live and that her job during that time would be to lead her family to God.

An angel spoke to Kevin Valaika of Lincoln, Nebraska, and may have saved his life. The account is reported by his wife Mary. One Wednesday before Easter, Kevin got out of bed to take medication for sciatic pain in his thigh and hip. ''He drives for a living, and has an occasional flare up of sciatica due to his job,'' explains Mary. ''He went back to bed and woke up an hour later, feeling 'funny'—he was having an allergic reaction but did not recognize the symptoms. He got a drink of water and went back to bed. He awoke again an hour later, in serious trouble, still not knowing what was happening to him.

''His lips, tongue, and throat were swelling, hands and feet were itching and tingling, his lungs were swelling, his blood pressure was dropping, and his thinking was seriously affected by oxygen deprivation due to the dropping blood pressure, in a reaction known as 'anaphylactic shock.'

''Untreated, anaphylactic shock results in complete collapse of the circulatory system, cardiac arrest, and death.

''Kevin staggered down the hall to the kitchen and fainted, hitting his head on the kitchen counter and sustaining a one-inch laceration on the back of his head. He does not remember hitting his head. He came to, got up off the floor, dizzy, thinking foggy, short of breath, and decided what he needed was more air, so he thought he would just go outside and get some fresh air, and then he would be fine.

''He did indeed need air, but that was the wrong solution. If Kevin had gone outside the house, we would have found him dead on the front lawn the next morning.

"Kevin had his hand on the front door, on his way outside, when something spoke to him and said, 'No, go get Mary.' He argued with the angel (don't we all!), thinking, no, I won't bother Mary. I'll just go outside and get some fresh air and I'll be fine. Something spoke to him again, much more insistently, in a command. 'No! Go get Mary!' So he came down the hallway, opened the bedroom door, and turned on the light, calling for help, and promptly passed out again.

"I ran over to him, saw how swollen his lips and tongue were, and called for my children. We called 911. We had the firemen and the ambulence crew, and EKGs and IVs and all sorts of excitement in the next 15 minutes. My husband's blood pressure dropped to 55/35. I am a medical secretary, working for a busy family practice. All three doctors I work for came up to me the next week and said Kevin was no more than five minutes from death."

I received another account of a Trappist monk who was saved by his angel long before, during construction of a new monastery. The monk, Father Thomas Francis of Conyers, Georgia, had been told by the foreman to get a crow bar and take apart the cement hoist used for that section of the building up on the roof.

"As I inserted the bar into the lead of the long nail, I noticed that I was leaning over quite a bit, but still thought I could manage it," said Father Francis. "The nail did not budge when I applied pressure, so, without my realizing it, I leaned farther out and suddenly realized I had passed the center of gravity over the building and should have fallen at least thirty feet below on the concrete. It surely would have killed me. But an amazing thing happened: just as I became aware that I was about to fall, a force, a wind, a sudden push, from *an invisible agent,* pushed me back onto the building."

Many such rescues involve cars. Somehow roadways are prime parcels for materialization. "I was driving with my two small children in the back seat during a winter snowstorm in February, 1986," says Diane O'Malley of Omaha, Nebraska. "I was on the interstate when I decided it didn't seem too slick out, so I was picking up a little speed. All

of a sudden I swerved out of control. I tried to turn the
wheel so we didn't slide into a ravine. I completely turned
my car facing the on-coming traffic and slid completely
across three lanes of traffic into the median into the deeper
snow.

"I just knew we were going to be hit by all the oncoming
traffic and felt like I was moving in slow motion waiting
for the crash. What I saw was that the traffic was way
behind me. When I was on the median and trying to get
back out into the lane of traffic again, there was no way
for me to gain enough speed with the ice and snow to cut
in front of all the cars that seemed to be flying by. Out of
nowhere a police officer appeared and stopped traffic so
I could gain admittance."

I heard other stories of angels materializing not only in
unusual human forms and not only near automobiles but
also in tow trucks and snow plows. An angel can take
whatever form necessary, and can actually suspend the
reality around us. Some of the images may be like holo-
graphs but others are real objects materialized out of
nowhere. Indeed, so human do angels usually appear that
it is almost anomalous to hear accounts in which they are
luminous or winged.

Many of the celestial visions are reported in near-death
experiences. While I don't trust all NDEs (many sound New
Age and too few of them mention judgment and negative
afterlife experiences such as Hell, while others may be little
more than the effects of anesthesia or erratic temporal lobe
activity), there are a number of near-death episodes that are
exceptionally interesting. And the NDEs often involve
what seem like angels. These are cases of men and women
who were revived after clinical death and claim to have
caught a glimpse of eternity. When they "come back" they
describe the process of ascending above their corpses
(where they were able to float freely and sometimes actually watch nurses and doctors trying to revive them), then
being whisked through a sort of "tunnel" to an indescribable light that symbolized Christ or an angelic presence.

The angels or spirit "beings" often show NDEers a
"review" of their lives like a moving picture that includes
every little action and decision they've made and shows

how those actions affected other people. The most stirring and controversial case is that related by a Seattle area woman named Betty J. Eadie who had two brushes with death, one as a youngster and one at the age of 31, while hospitalized for a partial hysterectomy. During her first experience, Betty said she encountered a man with a beautiful and fascinating white beard—hair that seemed to sparkle with luminosity. "He gently rocked me, cradling me in his arms, and although I didn't know who he was, I never wanted to leave him," said Betty, who believed he was her angel and felt "perfectly calm and happy with him."

But Betty recovered and grew to adulthood and motherhood. Then came the hysterectomy and an unexpected complication that caused her to "die" a second time, with no doctors or nurses around.

This time she saw *three* men at her side, wearing gold-braided belts and gorgeous light-brown robes. They looked like monks. One even had a hood at the back of the head, and each of them glowed. (See page 309.)

"I was not afraid," says Betty. "The men appeared to be about seventy or eighty years old, but I knew somehow that they were on a time scale different than earth's. The impression came to me that they were much older than seventy or eighty years old—that they were ancient. I sensed in them great spirituality, knowledge, and wisdom."

Betty saw different types of angels. She saw them answering prayer. She saw the prayers of humans rising like beams of light, and the spirit beings rushing to answer them. She saw the great joy with which they worked. She saw how prayers said with intensity and faith were answered first. She saw how elimination of doubt freed prayers to bear fruit. She heard pure voices and glorious music.

In Heaven, light was not reflected; it supposedly came from *within* the objects. Betty saw beautiful and loving people weaving on ancient-looking looms. They seemed to be making cloth that shimmered and sparkled, "like a mixture of spun glass and spun sugar." There were also "living" waters and plants that seemed to sway to a subtle but unforgettable music, praising God. "When the heavens scrolled back," said Eadie, "I saw earth with its billions of people on it. I saw them scrambling for existence, making mistakes, experiencing kindness, finding love, grieving for death, and I saw angels hovering above them."

She also saw magnificent spirits "dressed like warriors, in head dress and armor, and I saw that they moved more swiftly than other angels."

Nothing evil could daunt them, she felt, and they seemed to rush away on missions.

I don't endorse any particular NDE. I mention them as a point of discussion. When Betty returned to earth she was hounded by beings that were half animal and half human, like old Babylonian devils. But a huge light came around her like a glass dome of protection. The creatures fled when her angels, appearing again as monks, returned to her hospital room.

"Satan desires to have us, and sometimes when he marshals his forces against one of us, that person will need special protection," said Betty. "We can protect ourselves by controlling our thoughts, by allowing the light of Christ to enter our lives. As we do this, the light of Christ will shine through us and will actually appear in our countenances."

CHAPTER 25

Jesus Everywhere

There are those who criticize phenomena that are outside of their own churches. There are those who look askance at near-death experiences and even wonder if occultism has seeped into accounts like the one you have just read, or if such cases are a deception like UFO abductions. There are Catholics who are nervous about Protestants and Protestants who are nervous about Catholics, especially alleged apparitions of the Virgin Mary.

But I have a simple policy. Anyone who believes in Christ is my brother. Anyone who loves God is my cousin. Anyone who fights the devil is a friend. I have worshiped with different Christians and have seen tremendous similarities across Christian and even some Jewish denominations.

In the 1980s there was a remarkable proliferation of spiritual experiences that weren't confined to any one site, any one set of circumstances, nor any one system of belief. And a sense of growing urgency—tempered during the first part of the 1980s, but growing with each passing year—was one element that active Christians, especially evangelicals, charismatics, and old-school Catholics, had in common.

Mankind was on a crash course and Heaven, ever patient, continued to foresee it.

The angels were often accompanied by a feeling of great peace and the aroma of something similar to roses or lilies.

There were also luminous signs that again raised passages such as those in *Luke* 21:11, which spoke of *"great signs from Heaven."* In Medjugorje, the sun continued to pulse and spin on a daily basis, and there were also reports of the moon splitting into two "moons," one with an image that was tentatively connected to a bearded portrayal of the prophet Elijah. Stars were seen to wiggle about in the sky and split into three separate stars, each a different color and each then wiggling about the night sky themselves, until rejoining and once more forming a normal white star. In Texas, strange rays of sun seemed to detach and descend to the ground, looking like tongues of fire. There were also strange clouds and flashes of light as in *Exodus* 13. On January 12, 1986, Florence Gray of New Providence, New Jersey, saw "flames of clear, bright, white light" break out around a nun. She related it to not just *Exodus* (3:2) but also *Matthew* 17:2, which describes a heavenly transfiguration. Many were those who saw such signs as unusual harbingers. In Russell, Kansas, a housewife claimed in 1984 that an angel was warning there was little time to choose for Christ. The End Times, she insisted, are at hand. She said the angel warned that the "abomination of desolation" as spoken by the prophet Daniel in the Old Testament and Christ in *Matthew* 24 will soon take place, followed by the Great Tribulation. "The true Anti-Christ is preparing his advent into the world scene, awaiting the right moment to deceive many and destroy many peacefully."

While discerning such messages remained the most challenging of tasks, and while a number of such prophecies seemed like a demonic attempt at confusion, there was no shirking the Christian duty to search for gold amid the dross, nor was there any ignoring the supernatural explosion that occurred throughout the 1980s. A number of observers believe it was the greatest outpouring since Pentecost. Highly striking was a series of reports from deep Africa starting on November 28, 1981, and continuing for the next several years—reports from a group of young people in Kibeho, Rwanda, who reported visions and apparitions that contained messages about future calamities. As at Fatima and Medjugorje, the villagers in Rwanda noticed an oddly spinning sun and interpreted this as yet another warning that historical and possibly horrible events were just beyond the horizon. Already terrible carnage had occurred in neighboring Uganda under the rule of the tyrant Idi Amin, who had seen that UFO at Lake Victoria in 1973 and soon after had turned to sheer savagery. These negative phenomena—angels from the dark side, often in the form of UFOs—were in active contention with apparently holy visions occurring in places such as Kibeho, where a pagan man, Emmanuel Segatashya, was converted to Christianity after encountering an apparition of Jesus on July 2, 1982. Emmanuel had his experience in a field on the way home from picking beans. Once more, the prophetic impulse was of an apocalyptical nature. "He taught me the Lord's Prayer," claimed Emmanuel of his alleged rendezvous with Jesus. "And how to pray from the heart. He filled my heart with such joy. When I saw Jesus, He was surrounded by a bright light. He told me we don't reach Heaven by special gifts or compromises, but only through prayers coming from the heart. There's not much time to prepare for the Last Judgment."

Jesus in Rwanda! Jesus in deepest Africa! Whatever the final discernment, we could conclude this much: Where UFOs often left witnesses feeling confused and frightened (particularly when accompanied by the so-called "men in black" or by creatures with demonic bug eyes), the holy apparitions seemed to have the opposite effect: of peace and clarity. There were at least seven visionaries in Rwanda and the other six were Catholic and Muslim females who were told by their heavenly visitor that if the people of Rwanda, and by implication all the world, did not forsake godlessness and promiscuity, terrible events would soon occur (a warning that came just before the AIDS epidemic began wiping out entire African villages, such that by 1994, 2.5 million cases—more than *half* the world's AIDS casualties—would be in Sub-Sahara Africa).

"*The world is on the verge of catastrophe,*" said a vision of the Virgin Mary on March 27, 1982, to a girl named Marie Claire.

"*I have come to prepare the way to my Son for your good and you do not want to understand,*" she said during other apparitions. "*The time remaining is short and you are absent-minded. You are distracted by the goods of the world which are passing. When I show myself to someone and talk to them, I want to turn to the whole world. If I am now turning to the parish in Kibeho it does not mean I am concerned only for Kibeho or for the diocese of Butare, or for Rwanda, or for the whole of Africa. I am concerned with and turning to the whole world. Do not forget that God is more powerful than all the evil of the world. Tell the youth not to spoil their future by the wrong way of living, which can weigh heavily on their future. Don't lose Heaven for the world. The intellectuals have received learning to help others arrive at the truth, which is God. To profess atheism is to insult and mock God. To those with incurable illnesses, remember that nothing is more beautiful than a heart which offers its sufferings to God. Pray, pray, pray. Follow the Gospel of my Son."*

Most of the messages were given to a seer named Alphonsine Mumureke. As in Bosnia-Hercegovina at Medjugorje, the Rwandan seers received indications of coming mayhem. In one vision that lasted eight hours they saw terrifying images of people killing each other, and bodies thrown into rivers. They saw abandoned corpses with no one to bury them. They saw bodies without their heads—decapitated. They were weeping and crying and the witnesses who crowded around the seers were left with an unforgettable impression of fear and sadness.

If Rwanda did not come back to God, said the vision, there would be a "river of blood."

That seemed to be a prophecy of riots or war—societal chaos in Rwanda. More difficult to discern was Segatashya's extreme claim that mankind faced a "final judgment." That wording had not come from the Virgin Mary but rather during his alleged experience with Jesus. If the translation was correct, and if Segatashya was accurately conveying what he was told or saw (as opposed to lending his own interpretation to the vision), there was a potentially troublesome similarity between his prediction and the equally extravagant ones during other moments in history, especially during the 13th and 14th centuries. "The 13th century was a very interesting time, and especially around 1260, a time chosen by Italian followers of a mystic named Joachim of Fiore," said one skeptic with whom I spoke, Dr. Michael Grosso, a philosophy professor at Jersey City State College and an expert on millennial emotions and imaginal psychology. "Joachim predicted that the end of history would somehow come to pass in the year 1260 and that caused a tremendous furor. But actually, there are dates upon dates upon dates. In the United States of America, 1844 was the big year of the so-called Millerite movement. This farmer, William Miller, read the Bible and figured out by analyzing all kinds of rather obscure numbers that 1843 or 1844 was the year in which the end would occur and the Lord would descend and a rapture would take place and so forth. When it didn't happen, curiously enough, the followers of Miller evolved into the Seventh Day Adventists and some of them evolved into the Branch Davidians."

As with any mysticism, one had always to remember the stark warning that Christ gave in *Matthew* 24 about false prophets showing great wonders and signs so as to deceive, if possible, even the elect. These experiences needed to be tested and retested through prayer and fasting. In the 1980s there were already questionable copycat apparition sites in Italy, Ireland, Chile, and the United States—as well as the city of Split in Yugoslavia, where a young man claiming dubious visions was trying to collect large sums of money.

But Rwanda was more credible than Split, and its eschatology was not dissimilar to prophecies pouring out of evangelical missions. Decoding the Bible, Protestants too looked with a certain trepidation upon the end of the millennium, which they envisioned as much more momentous than other such periods. The signs in the sky seemed startlingly mindful of *Luke* 21:25, which clearly named *"signs in the sun, in the moon, and in the stars"* as indicating the coming of the Son of Man. All three of these signs were reported at places like Medjugorje. The *Luke* passage was basically a summary of the incredible prophecies in *Matthew* 24, where, after quakes, famines, plagues, wars and rumor of wars—and after the *"abomination of desolation"* stands in the holy place—Christ said would come the Great Tribulation and advised those in Judea, which is a part of Israel, to *"flee to the mountains."*

Parts of the *Matthew* prophecy had been realized repeatedly through history. Especially was it realized in A.D. 70, when Jerusalem was surrounded by the Romans and devastated. And many were the other historical epochs such as the sixth century that, through war or pestilence, could claim partial fulfillment of Christ's prophecy. While none had yet seen the Great Tribulation, as time progressed the cycle of prophecies in *Matthew* not only repeated itself around the world but gained in intensity. The more it repeated, the closer it came to fulfilling the complete passage of Chapter 24. And once that occurred—whether years or centuries from now—we could indeed expect an apocalypse.

But still it fell short, especially in that the sun and moon had not yet darkened, as prophesied in Verse 29, and the Gospel was not yet known in every remote corner of the globe, which is known as the "Great Commission" and which is a requirement of Verse 14, which reads: *"And this gospel of the kingdom will be preached in all the world as a witness to all the nations, and then the end will come."*

Likewise, there was the famous parable of the fig tree. Not until it sprouted would Christ be ready to return. *"Now learn this parable from the fig tree: When its branch has already become tender and puts forth leaves, you know that summer is near,"* Our Savior said in Verse 32. *"So you also, when you see all these things, know that it is near, at the very doors. Assuredly, I say to you, this generation will by no means pass away till all these things are fulfilled."*

Many were those in evangelical circles, especially among dispensational Protestants, who believed that the "fig tree"—in the form of the reborn state of Israel—had finally sprouted its leaves during our century. As a result they, like the one seer in Rwanda, believed that a great tribulation was near, to be followed by the Second Coming. While there were many disputes about exact details, such adherents often saw the coming sequence of events as involving a rapture of the Church during which the faithful would be *physically* removed from earth (an idea that seemed to gain special currency during the 1800s, after the woman heard the rapture prophecy while speaking in tongues), along with rise of the Anti-Christ from a revived Roman Empire in Europe. He would sign a covenant or peace agreement with Israel but then would breach it three and a half years later. The Anti-Christ would declare himself world leader and install himself in the rebuilt temple of Jerusalem as the abomination of desolation. This would spark the Great Tribulation—war and other forms of judgment such as natural disasters—which would end with the Second Coming of Jesus and the defeat of the Anti-Christ during the great foreseen battle of Armageddon.

Most important to many fundamentalists is the new status of Israel. It is their belief that it is symbolized by the fig tree. Israel was reborn in 1948 and Christ had said that once the fig tree sprouted, *"this generation will by no means pass away till all these things are fulfilled."* Since a biblical "generation" is held to be forty years, many expected that the Rapture and Second Coming—the End Times—would occur within forty years of Israel's rebirth, which meant by 1988.

While that date came and went with no cosmic event—as did most prophecies set for specific years, months, or even days—many were those who still maintained that the Messiah would return around the end of the current century. "After almost 2,000 years of dispersion and according to many prophecies, the nation of Israel has been reestablished only in this century," argued one prophecy buff, Ret. Air Force Lt. Col. James D. Bramlett, who works as a special assistant to the president of the Campus Crusade for Christ. "Never in history has a nation been destroyed and the survivors scattered around the world, then have their nation later restored, especially after nearly 2,000 years. In itself, the nation of Israel is a modern-day miracle. And the Bible itself seems clear—at Christ's return, Israel will be intact as a nation, something impossible until the last half of this century! In my opinion, as Satan used Herod to kill all the Jewish babies to try to thwart Christ's first mission, Satan used Hitler to try to kill all the Jews to prevent Israel's rebirth, a prerequisite to Christ's return.

"Israel is God's 'time clock,'" continued Bramlett. "Jesus Himself expressed such a view. He spoke prophetically of Israel and the future, saying that Jerusalem would be destroyed and the Jews scattered, which actually happened forty years later in A.D. 70. He said Jerusalem would be trampled down by the Gentiles *'until the times of the Gentiles are fulfilled'* (*Luke* 21:29-31), and that *'this generation will certainly not pass away until all these things have happened'* (verse 32).

"If the fig tree is, indeed, the nation of Israel, it began to sprout in 1948 when Israel was re-established. And in the miraculous Six-Day War in 1967, Israel recaptured Jerusalem from 'the Gentiles,' some believe fulfilling Jesus's prophecy about *'the times of the Gentiles'* now being complete.

"While world data is not available, it is a known fact that the United States has been in a precipitous cultural and spiritual decline precisely since—yes, the 1960s."

Bramlett went on: "It is astonishing to find that even the scholarly writings of the Jews express the view that the Messiah would come at the end of our present century. After the Bible, the Talmud is the most authoritative source of Judaism. The view frequently expressed in the Talmud, according to researchers, is that the world as we know it would last only 6,000 years. Rabbi Ketina said in *Gemara,* a commentary on the Talmud, 'The world endures 6,000 years and 1,000 it shall be laid waste (that is, the enemies of God shall be destroyed), whereof it is said, 'The Lord alone shall be exalted in that day.'"

The thousand-year reign of Christ that comes after the Great Tribulation is known as the "Millennium." While paleoanthropologists analyzing fossils in China and Africa believe that modern man rose not 6,000 years ago but more like 200,000, and while many others, including a good number of devout Christians, viewed words like "millennium" as more symbolic than literal, there were those who stayed with literal interpretations and as for paleoanthropology maintained that its dating methods are in error and that human history is much briefer, going back only to 4004 B.C. (a figure calculated in 1650 by Archbishop Ussher), with every 2,000-year period carrying a special meaning.

As Barnabas once wrote, there were 2,000 years from Adam to Abraham and 2,000 years from Abraham to Christ, "so there will be 2,000 years for the Christian era and then would come the Millennium."

The seventh millennium, like the seventh day of the week, would be a time of remission.

As it says in *Psalms* 90:4 and *2 Peter* 3:8, noted Bramlett, a thousand years to the Lord is as a day.

If others, knowing how many times such specific prophecies had failed to materialize in the past, stayed away from prophesying for the specific year 2000, there were those like Bramlett who argued that the End Times were close at hand because fulfillment of the Great Commission, the one remaining requirement for the Apocalypse, concerning the global teaching of Christianity, was about to be realized. As apocalyptic writer Grant R. Jeffrey pointed out, the Bible has now been translated into more than 1,700 languages! According to one expert I interviewed, Dr. David Barrett, editor of *World Christian Encyclopedia* and an expert on missions for the Southern Baptist Foreign Mission Board in Richmond, Virginia, of the world's 5.7 billion people, only 1.5 billion—3,000 of the world's 12,000 linguistic groups or "peoples"—have *not* been evangelized. If only the populations in northern Africa, the Mideast, and Central Asia could be reached, along of course with China, there is a chance that the name of Christ will one day be known to the 22 percent of the world which has not yet heard of Him.

Would doing that take years or decades?

At a Christian think-tank called the Sentinel Group near Seattle, there was hope that the Great Commission could be accomplished by 2005. According to George Otis Jr., president of the group, approximately 364,000 people around the world hear the Gospel for the first time each day. While at the end of the first century the ratio of non-believers to Christians was 360 to 1, today it is seven to one. And every year, Christianity realizes 44,000 new churches. "Many are praying, planning, and working toward a fulfillment of the Great Commission by the year A.D. 2000," writes Otis.

He and an assistant named Michael McCausland cite a

plethora of supernatural occurrences as signaling a possible denouement during the next decade. The phenomena are both heavenly and diabolical, symbolizing the great spiritual warfare. Says McCausland: "A lot of the missionary groups are mainline denominational and they're seeing phenomena that they just can't explain. The list goes on and on. Here's an example of a supernatural occurrence that took place. We interviewed a Tibetan who runs a Christian radio station in northern India. He'd heard there was a Tibetan Buddhist monk doing a demonstration in a town nearby, so he went with his wife and they entered discreetly.

"There were about 300 people in the room and they saw the Buddhist monk up front with a person sitting on the floor in front of a bed of coals. This person was a spirit medium. As they started, the medium went into a trance and all of a sudden levitated up off the ground! He also swallowed hot coals, which sizzled! The Christian and his wife started praying, rebuking the spirit, and the spirit left the medium and he came out of his trance.

"The monk asked what happened and the medium sat there a minute and went back into a trance, pointing to the Christians. The Buddhist monk went up to them and politely asked them to leave."

Few places were more difficult to penetrate than the Himalayas, and as a result, few places stood as such an impediment to the Great Commission. It is the Himalayan region, along with Iran and Iraq (harkening back to ancient Babylon), where they have seen some of the greatest demonic strongholds and thus the greatest spiritual warfare. Tibetan translators of the Bible have died mysteriously. In Nepal, a manuscript disappeared on the way to a point of transfer. "In the Old Testament it talks continuously of high places and the devil likes high places," says McCausland. "If you go to these Tibetan Buddhist places all along the Himalayas, every high ridge has Buddhist prayer flags and altars on it—the prayer flags are everywhere waving in the breeze, on top of every mountain peak. The Himalayas, being the rooftop of the world, are a very intense place. Some of the oldest covenants between man and the spirit of darkness exist in the Himalayan region. The Tibetan Buddhists are extremely, extremely devout in the serving of their demonic protective deities."

But at the same time, there has also been an avalanche of what seems like holy phenomena. Among them is the seemingly outlandish claim of the dead raised to life as with Lazarus. Such accounts appear totally fantastic until one equates them with the many thousands of claims to what we've called NDEs or the near-death experiences. Protestant missionaries also observed miraculous healings similar to what Catholics were seeing at sites of Marian apparition. McCausland claimed that one revived man had been dead for two hours, another for six hours—which is also about how long Betty Eadie claimed she had been in an unconscious state during her NDE in 1973.

"There are tremendous numbers of healings taking place, and supernatural visitations," says McCausland. "One night in a village in Algeria every man in the town received the same vision, Jesus standing before them telling them they were following the wrong person and they came out the next morning and started talking and figured out they'd all had the same dream. That became reported and many didn't believe it, but when they checked into it, it wasn't just the village but the whole surrounding area. There's a lot of supernatural phenomena taking place on both sides. Most of the reports we get here we try to validate first-hand, from the people who have actually been there."

While there can be little doubt of a supernatural upsurge, it is difficult to discern its degree compared to past eras simply because we have few records from past generations. Too, the phone, fax, and laptop computer have brought reports from the missionary field with far greater ease and frequency. Nonetheless, McCausland and Otis sensed something in the wind. In a book called *The Last of the Giants,* Otis reports that 35 percent of recent Turkish converts "describe having had spiritual dreams and visions in which Jesus has appeared to them as the Son of God. In Soviet Central Asia, several Turkish Uzbeks and Kirghiz have also reported physical healings, while workers among Bulgaria's Turkish minority have shared extraordinary tales of the dead being raised to life."

Many Muslim converts in Algeria reported supernatural intervention, and the story was told of a former Pakistani Muslim named Gulshan Esther who was approached by Jesus in a vision and healed of crippled limbs.

The reports came or were soon to come from Tunisia and Soviet Central Asia and the Comoro Islands.

"First evidenced in the early 1980s, many observers report detecting a significant surge in both the frequency and scope of these occurrences around 1987," wrote Otis. "Accounts from Muslim converts and missionaries in the field tend to fall into three basic categories: dreams and visitations, miraculous healings, and special deliverances (both physical and spiritual)."

It was in 1983, reports Otis, that the supernatural episode in which God manifested to nearly everyone in the vicinity occurred in a village 125 miles east of the city of Algiers.

"Moving from house to house, and communicating through a combination of dreams, visions, and angelic visitations, He did not rest until every member of this Muslim community was properly introduced to His only begotten Son, Jesus."

Once word got around, the experience led to a reported 400 conversions.

It was in that very area, coincidentally, that a Spanish missionary was once stoned to death in 1315 by Muslims who didn't like his preaching.

McCausland also saw signs of the times in mundane developments and told me, "Mankind now stands in a position where we have knowledge unbridled by wisdom. Knowledge on the face of the earth is currently doubling every two and a half years. Only two times in history has that happened before, and that's in the Garden of Eden when man named every animal that existed on the face of the earth—there are literally millions of species, so he had to have had the ability to do that—and the second time was at the tower of Babel. Ours is the first generation to bridge the language gap worldwide."

CHAPTER 26

War of the Witch Doctors

The importance of the Great Commission cannot be overstated, but in looking for those signs forecast by Jesus and the prophet Joel, I was most keen on the reported phenomena—visions and dreams—from the missionary field.

McCausland had said that "when you start talking to the mission people who are working on the front lines, nobody's going to deny that there's supernatural stuff going on. They weren't taught that back in seminary, but when they get out there and face it head on, it's pretty hard to ignore."

Ever wary of possible deception, and not knowing the final answers of discernment—not able, in fact, to *absolutely* prove anything to be both authentic and of God—I nonetheless tallied other accounts of the supernatural. To me both the outpouring of the Holy Spirit and agitation from the dark side continued to be the most salient indicators of special times. Bramlett's own organization, Campus Crusade, which had done as much as anyone in striving for the Great Commission (reaching 500 million in 276 translations with an evangelical film about the life of Jesus), itself reported many extraordinary occurrences. They confirmed an upsurge of the Spirit in the waning days of a larger era that started with Christ's Resurrection and could be called the Feast of the Pentecost. It was as if God were punctuating the Pentecost before we begin a new "feast" or era. There was a very strong current of mysticism.

A number of the most intriguing cases reported by Campus Crusade involved the spiritual tension between local occultists (in Africa occult religions of voodoo and animism are rampant) and the newly converted or missionary Christians. The film project's director, Paul Eshleman, described how, while evangelizing the primitive Massai in Kenya and Tanzania, he'd heard the anecdote of a converted Massai warrior named Mattayo. This man belonged to a people who still roam the savannas naked, with spears to fend off lion or wild dogs, and live in small mud-and-dung huts. Their most authoritative leader, and certainly the most feared, is the local witch doctor. Yet Mattayo himself had no such trepidation. He had first come to Jesus at a mission station where he sought help for a friend who had been mauled by a lion. The man had died but Mattayo left the station a convert. Now he traveled from manyatta to manyatta seeking to turn other pagans into Christians. In one such village, the witch doctor had ordered him to leave. Mattayo refused. Instead he ministered to the witch doctor. He told him that Jesus is more powerful than black magic. And as he went on about Christ, according to Eshleman, the witch doctor fell to the ground, trembling, as if in an altered state of consciousness—as if he had suddenly heard or seen something. When Mattayo returned the next day the witch doctor told a group in his hut that when Mattayo had spoken about Jesus it was like "a big cross came out of the sky, went down through my body, and cleaned all the bad out of me. I must tell you I am now a follower of Jesus."

During the showing of their film in the village of Djurukturu, Indonesia, members of the project ran into another witch doctor, this time one who conjured a curse against the film and those from the village who dared to accept it. The hex was invoked in a hut with covered windows. He would show these "Christian" followers.

But much to the conjuror's befuddlement, the curse boomeranged. The ones who became ill—who were struck by the curse—were not the new converts nor members of the film project but a number of those from the village who had *refused* to turn to Jesus.

They were healed, says Eshleman, only when the Christians who were showing the film prayed over them, as they writhed on the ground in intense pain.

In Whitefield, India, missionaries had constant trouble with film equipment after a follower of the occult guru, Sai Baba, levied a similar curse. When crew members stopped and prayed, however, the witch doctor, Sathya Sai Baba, jumped to his feet and fled from the building.

The projector was turned to the screen and showed the film without further incident.

In Thailand, hostile inhabitants made it so the film team had no place to sleep but a Buddhist temple said to be haunted by a particularly malicious demon. Others who tried to sleep there had run out before morning and there were rumors that some had even died in there. In fact, there was an evil spirit. "Shortly after drifting off to sleep, they were awakened all at once by the immaterial presence of a hideous beast," wrote Eshleman. "There in the corner of the room appeared the most frightful image they had ever seen. Fear struck them all like an icy fist."

But instead of fleeing they practiced what they preached, casting the demon away in the name of Jesus.

"Early the next morning the villagers came to the temple to look for the team's equipment," says Eshleman. "They were certain that, like the others, these too had been driven away in the night, or killed. When they found them all sleeping undisturbed, they were confronted with the undeniable fact that God is more powerful than any other force."

So too did a staff member in Burma shoo away a cobra that had slithered from the underbrush and onto his feet. As the audience gasped, this missionary sent up fervent prayers, until the serpent slithered away, leaving the man unharmed and the people amazed. *Away in the Name of Jesus!*

There were also angels, angels who protected film members in a bus accident, or who, as in the New Hebrides Islands, stood guard against hostile natives. "Near a village in Thailand where *Jesus* was being shown, a gang of thugs decided to rob the team of their equipment, hock it, and make some quick money," said Eshleman. "Creeping into the village during the night, they scouted the hut where the team's equipment was stored. Security was simple. It would be an easy job. But as they approached the entrance, they were startled by two brilliant white beings filling the doorway. Both were over eight feet tall and brandished flaming swords. Frightened, the robbers ran into the darkness."

These experiences of supernatural rescue were joined by cases of supernatural conversion, many of which were precipitated by precisely what I was looking for: visions and dreams. According to Bruce Bradshaw, a missions researcher for World Vision International, Africa is particularly prone to such reports because the culture is conducive to what he calls "transrational" experiences. Such is particularly true, he says, of the apocalyptical Christians in the Yoruba groups or organizations such as the Church of the Twelve Apostles in Ghana. "I've met several people, especially in folk Islamic cultures, who have become Christian, and you ask them why and they say, 'Oh, because I had this dream!'"

When I asked another Christian, Chris Alberts, a pastor from South Africa, if there has been an upsurge in spiritual activity on the Dark Continent, he responded, "Emphatically, yes. There are phenomenal signs and wonders. We've seen this first-hand. We see demonic situations where people are manifesting the evil. We pray over them and deliver them and you would actually see the manifestations, especially where there is witchcraft, the tearing of flesh, frothing at the mouth, wild eyes. We plead the Blood of Christ and they scream out and froth at the mouth and then are set free. I believe there's going to be a massive outpouring of the Holy Spirit and very soon. We're seeing it already. The Glory of God is going to be just awesome. God is pouring out His Spirit. Children are experiencing incredible things, both in Africa and America."

I also heard about Mahesh Chavda, a Kenyan born Indian who accepted Christ, got Bible training in the U.S., and is into healing, based now in North Carolina. He had what must stand as the most remarkable confrontation with sorcerers. "In my work in Africa, I have found that many regions are under the domination of sorcery and witchcraft," he said. "Masses of Africans live in mortal fear of the local witch doctors. This is not without reason: these witch doctors wield terrifying spiritual power to bring sickness, calamity, and death upon the people. I often teach special seminars to the pastors about the power and authority we have, in Jesus's name, over the works of darkness."

Like the film teams for Campus Crusade, Chavda found himself in what seemed like an unending series of spiritual challenges. Once, in the Kananga region of Zaire, which is known as an especially intense center of witchcraft, Chavda was ministering a healing service in the city of Mbujimai, unaware that among the throngs was the chief sorcerer of that city. He had been sent to levy a curse on Chavda by the other witch doctors in the Kananga region. As Chavda moved through the crowd praying over the people in the name of Jesus, he kept getting closer and closer to the sorcerer, without knowing it. "Finally, I reached the place where he was standing, and I reached out to place my hands on him," recalled Chavda. "As I did, I suddenly heard this strange noise coming from him. It sounded like several animals all crying out at once."

When Chavda blessed the sorcerer, this witch doctor was flung to the ground, squirming and twisting but unable to regain his feet. "He couldn't get up," said Chavda. "It was as though an invisible angel were sitting on him."

At the end of his Kananga crusade, Chavda conducted a prayer renouncing witchcraft and pulling down the demonic strongholds in that area. The next morning he was told a remarkable event had occurred. It seems that as he was leading the people in prayer against evil, a group of witch doctors were gathered at a spot about seven miles away, calling down curses on Chavda's meeting and on those who followed Christ. The place where they met was marked by an enormous tree that was notorious throughout the vicinity as the "Sorcerer's Tree." It was about thirty feet tall.

"Suddenly, as they were talking and we were praying,

they saw fire streak across the heavens," said Chavda. "It seemed to be coming from the general direction of our meeting. It shot across the night sky and fell upon the Sorcerer's Tree. The leaves and branches were consumed, leaving nothing behind except the charred trunk." Chavda added that it looked "like the remains of a huge match stick, burned from the top down. The trunk is not split, as it would have been had it been struck by lightning. The first several feet of the trunk are untouched, which would not be the case if someone standing on the ground had set the fire."

Bizarre as many such accounts sound, they often are consistent with other widely circulated accounts among the missionaries. Some of the more lucid and spectacular ones come from Israel and involve Reverend Gerald Derstine, an internationally known evangelist who has ministered to thousands of Israeli Arabs despite death threats and other hazards. For example, Derstine recounts the story of a fanatical Muslim who had been offered a $4,000 reward to kill him. This started in 1987 and the Arab carried Derstine's photograph everywhere he went. He asked all around Galilee for the minister, hoping to make the lucky find and collect the bounty. Find Derstine!

Then, on April 30, 1989, while resting on his bed at about one in the afternoon, an absolutely mind-boggling irony occurred. It seemed a case of bilocation. As the Arab watched in sudden, paralyzed astonishment, Reverend Derstine—his very quarry!—walked into his room and sat next to him.

The would-be hitman was stunned. Here was Derstine in his bedroom trying to preach to him! He recognized him from the photograph and listened as "Derstine," reaching into the Muslim's suddenly guilt-ridden and nervous heart, began explaining Jesus and His kingdom. He spoke in a clear Cana Arabic dialect. The Moslem terrorist was assured that his sins would be forgiven if he sincerely asked God for mercy. When he was told this he felt a warm sensation flush his body of all evil, enlightening him, making him feel clean.

Right then the Arab was born again, and he was sure it was Derstine who had come to see him until, running into

Derstine months later, he learned that the minister *had not been in Israel* at the time.

Reverend Derstine had been in Melfort, Saskatchewan, which is half a world away in Canada. At that very moment a group of the preacher's intercessors had been in morning prayer.

It was an angelic visitation, Derstine concluded, "a sign and wonder of the End Time."

There were blinding lights. There were healings of paralytics. There was the revival of an accident victim. There were demons cast out of occultists. There were mysterious voices—angelic voices—that led to conversion in the dark of night. Derstine's take on this was again apocalyptical. "God spoke to us prophetically, saying, 'There will be revival coming upon the face of the earth as no man has ever witnessed—even greater than what took place on the day of Pentecost.'"

Most difficult by far to believe was Derstine's account of a Samaritan woman whose baby was born uttering praises to God. "Suddenly, all those present were startled to hear a voice," wrote Derstine. "At first the people thought the sound was coming from outside the house, but they soon realized it was the voice of the baby coming from inside the mother! The cry became louder, and distinct words could be heard—words of praise to God in their ancient Samaritan language. They were bewildered, startled, and amazed when suddenly the child birthed, coming forth literally shouting the praises of God, its tiny arms waving and its eyes wide open. The infant, a boy, was alert and lively, appearing as large as a two or three-month old child, according to the priest. The women in the room fell on their faces in awe. They told the priest that when they looked at him, the priest, his body was glowing with light—so much so that the whole room seemed to be brilliantly lit." Derstine believed the alleged miracle bore historical significance, reflecting back again on the parable of the fig tree. "Israel celebrated its fortieth year of statehood on May 14, 1988," he said. "The entire world has experienced dramatic changes since 1988—and the miracle in Samaria, which began in 1988, was the first of many to follow."

In Indiana, Robert Colver, a pharmacist and associate at Pike Christian Fellowship, also claimed to have inclinations about Israel. These inspirations, he feels, have been confirmed by a number of meaningful coincidences. Colver, a Methodist who now considers himself a Messianic Jew, feels a close affinity to Israel because the very day he turned of voting age, November 19, 1947, was also when Palestine was partitioned by the United Nations. He says the Lord once explained to him that his father was born in Bethlehem, his mother in the land of Goshen, and that he was born in "The Door." He had taken the "door" to mean Jesus. He was also told his wife would come out of Lebanon. This was all interesting because, indeed, Colver's father had been born in Bethlehem, Pennsylvania, his mother was born in Goshen, Indiana, and Colver himself was born in Laporte—which means The Door. Moreover, he and his wife were married in a town called Lebanon.

In 1988, Colver had a vision. "I was working at the pharmacy on Lafayette Road here in Indianapolis and about 9:30 a.m. I was in a cubicle, filling prescriptions and praising the Lord, thanking Him, and all of a sudden, bang, this thing hit for just a few seconds," he says. "When it was over I said, 'Lord, I know that was You, but what does it mean?' It took me a while to delineate just exactly what was going on. I had seen myself high upon a tower and the only city I could express it to be was Jerusalem. I believe what I saw was a broken-down wall. As I looked down upon this broken-down wall, everything was lit up. I saw these two gates and it was like a burst of revelation or light. Are you familiar with *Nehemiah*, where Nehemiah comes and helps Israel restore the Jewish people to their original roots? That period took 12 years and when Nehemiah comes to the city what he sees in these night visions is a city that has been destroyed. Nobody has the gumption to rebuild the walls and gates. It was a prophetic vision. It was 1988, which happened to be 12 years before 2000. In the meantime the Lord has shown me that there is a 12-year period between 1988 and 2000 where He's going to restore His Church."

Referring again to the Book of Nehemiah, Colver emphasized three biblical feasts as symbols of major eras. There was "Passover," which started with Abraham and Isaac and ended with Christ's Crucifixion. That was our atonement and salvation. It was followed by the era which is now beginning to end, "the Feast of Pentecost," which saw the outpouring of the Holy Spirit and thus revelation of the full Trinity. That outpouring is now approaching what (with all the miracles) seems to Colver like a grand finale. It will be followed, says Colver, by the "Feast of the Tabernacles," which he feels will come by 2000.

In the Old Testament the Feast of the Tabernacles was a time for holy convocation. It seemed to indicate the end of one time and the beginning of another (in *Exodus* 34:22 it's directed that this feast take place "at the year's end"). There are those who feel it's a feast picturing the coming millennium—establishment of the fullness of the Kingdom of God on earth, as one pamphlet explained, and "the reaping of the great harvest of souls for 1,000 years." Just as Pentecost pictured the early harvest, now did this approaching feast picture the full harvest. It seemed to imply the return of Christ and living waters flowing, as Colver envisioned, from a rebuilt Jerusalem.

Was it yet another warning sign?

Using a logic that was somewhat arcane, involving as it did both private revelation and calculations based on prophetic (360-day) years as opposed to regular years, Colver computed from a day in 1896, the year he said the new Israel was envisioned by a Budapest lawyer named Theodor Herzl, and counting off 99 prophetic years and nine months, he felt something was going to begin to happen on June 9, 1994, which we'll discuss in a few chapters.

Would it be relevant to *Nehemiah*, where there is a scene with the Wall of Jerusalem, as in Colver's vision? That description (*Nehemiah* 2:13) is followed by a passage known as "The Feast of the Tabernacles" which immediately precedes a third passage in which the children of Israel fast in sackcloth and confess their sins like the Ninevehites after Jonah's warning.

Was the same not true of all the nations, including the United States? That we needed to plead repentance?

In addition to *Nehemiah*, was not our era relevant to *Jonah* and *Revelation?*

Colver's response was to the point. "I don't see *Revelation* like I used to, as a progressive thing. I don't see it in a seven-year realm. I see it as an eternal thing. This is the End Times, but the end of an age, not the end of all time. There will be prophetic and apocalyptic things happening. I see the red horse of the Apocalypse possibly coming from Yugoslavia. When it's done, it will come to America. We'll experience what they're experiencing. We're long overdue—probably thirty years overdue. A judgment is coming."

CHAPTER 27

Visions of Armageddon

I heard the same from many in America, where the mysticism was becoming as pervasive and apocalyptic—boy was it getting apocalyptic—as in Africa. In the U.S., too, a "trans-rational" way of perceiving reality was beginning to replace the shallow way of scientism. Long asleep to the spiritual, lulled by science since the 1800s, the public was suddenly waking to the spiritual dimensions.

Unfortunately, most of the initial phenomena, most of what first entered public consciousness, was from the dark side. Spiritual deceptions. They included UFOs, psychics, or unsolved mysteries like reincarnation. Adapting to social currents, the occult kept refining itself during the 1980s. Reincarnation became known as "past-life regression," and spirit mediums had turned into crystal-gawkers or channelers. Now, instead of sitting around a dark seance room, they took journeys into mind control or, deep in meditation, chanted to nature "gods." In 1987, thousands of New Agers gathered at various "power" spots around the world to call forth spirits in what was called a "harmonic convergence." They met at Machu Picchu, Central Park, Mount Tamalais in California, the Gizeh pyramids, and Stonehenge to usher in a "new world order."

That was what television focused upon, the New Age. Really they were invoking demons. Again, there were reports of abductions by UFOs—from the first few sketchy ones to now *thousands*. I spoke with one woman whose daughter had such experiences in her own bedroom. She saw a number of creatures around her bed, chanting like witches. Many were those who were approached at night by strange-looking and ghostlike "aliens." The "UFOs" seemed to hover over deserts or woodland used as ritual sites by satanists and warlocks, which in itself hinted at where they really came from. They were also blamed for mysterious crop circles near Stonehenge and reports arrived from places like Botucatu, Brazil, where a man named Joáo Valerio da Silva claimed he was taken up by a beam of light and upon return found that his home had become a center of poltergeists and his skin was plagued by strange lesions.

Another abductee, Whitley Strieber of New York, was haunted in 1985 by an extraterrestrial who had bulging eyes and looked like an insect.

No wonder the big films of the decade included one called *Gremlins*.

It was in the midst of such spiritual confusion, with angels from both sides buzzing around, that prophecy turned so apocalyptic. In the new wave of visionaries was the Pentecostal seer Dumitru Duduman from Romania. Duduman pastored that small church across the border from Russia, and like Terelya, smuggled Bibles to the underground despite the constant threat of arrest and the already realized consequence of beatings. Duduman, who was exiled to Fullerton, California, in 1984, claims that the precise date of his departure was given to him in a dream by "a man in white clothes" who "had a trumpet in his hand." He perceived the "man" as an angel. Finding his way to Fullerton, he began to record increasingly spectacu-lar visions of the future, visions every bit as alarming as Terelya's. In one dream he saw himself back in Romania. It was the afternoon, yet there was darkness and he was terrified to see a volcano erupting. As the lava poured around him, Duduman and his wife were rescued by an American helicopter. The pilot was "the man dressed in white; the angel of the Lord." Duduman remembers the angel saying nothing at first. When finally he spoke he said simply, "Look down." When he did, Duduman saw Romania covered with tanks, aircraft, and machine guns. They were poised for battle. This was very similar to the visions Terelya had had in the Soviet Union, prophecies which implied a war that would involve surrounding nations.

Next Duduman was shown several cities he had never · visited, including Los Angeles and San Francisco. "I had no idea there were such places in California, or even in the world," wrote Duduman. "But I still remember the exact names. At last we were over Fullerton where we now live. 'You can go home,' said the angel, 'but I want you to tell what will happen. You have seen a number of cities. The day will come when I will punish the citizens of those cities because of their sins. Their sin has reached into Heaven. God will punish them just as He punished Sodom and Gomorrah.' "

Duduman believed that the destruction would come in part by way of a surprise Russian attack. One day, he prophesied, that country would lead an all-out assault against the U.S. from the ocean and from remote bases in places such as Cuba. "The Russian government will have all the information regarding the whereabouts of American missiles," the angel allegedly said.

When he awoke, Duduman began a 21-day fast, praying that if the dream possessed any validity—if it was something more than his own restless subconscious—he would experience the dream again. Soon after his fast, Duduman was in a state of despair. He and his family hadn't been able to find a furnished apartment, and his children were sleeping on the luggage. Wandering outside to cry and implore God, Duduman sat on a rock when suddenly he saw a "bright light" approach, which at first he believed to be an oncoming automobile. He bolted up from the rock but saw that it was no car. Instead the light, wherever it came from, surrounded him in a way that reminds us again of the light surrounding Saul.

A voice asked Dumitru why he was in such despair. The voice told him to climb up. He didn't know where he was going but obeyed. There were of course elements of this that brought to mind UFOs. Duduman insisted, in his book, *Through the Fire Without Burning* (published in its first edition by Christ Is Creator Ministries in Titusville, Florida), that this was neither a dream nor a vision. Nor was any flying saucer mentioned. "I was as awake," he said, "as I am now." Again he was shown California and told, "This is Sodom and Gomorrah! All of this, in one day it will burn! Its sin has reached the Holy One."

Next Duduman was taken on a spiritual expedition to Las Vegas and told that city too would burn.

He was shown the state of New York and told the same.

Ditto for all of Florida.

It was not a pleasant "journey."

Duduman was told that America was in special disfavor because Americans worshipped themselves instead of honoring Christ.

The churches were in moral decay.

There was abortion among Christians, as well as widespread divorce and adultery.

Again, the prospect of nuclear war was brought into the scenario. Duduman asked the angel how the good would be saved.

"Tell them this," said the voice. "How I saved the three young ones from the furnace of fire, and how I saved Daniel in the lions' den, is the same way I will save them."

In the Book of Daniel is the account of how three of Daniel's compatriots were condemned to a fiery furnace for refusing to worship a golden statue. Thrown into an unusually hot fire, the three men were able to walk around unharmed thanks to the protection of an angel. When Daniel himself refused an order to desist from righteous prayer, he was thrown in the lions' den. *"My God sent His angel and shut the lions' mouths, and they have not hurt me,"* he explained when he was found unharmed the next morning.

Duduman said the angel also referred him to *Jeremiah* 51:8-15, which seemed relevant to the vision of New York and Los Angeles. It contains a description of Babylon's utter destruction. *"Set up the watchmen, prepare the ambushes,"* it says. *"For the Lord has both devised and done what He spoke against the inhabitants of Babylon. O you who dwell by many waters, abundant in treasures, your end has come."*

Duduman was also told to study Chapter 18 of *Revelation,* where, in a chapter headed "The Fall of Babylon the Great," we find another description of a city that could be New York, San Francisco, or Los Angeles.

It is a city that has become *"a habitation of demons, a prison for every foul spirit, and a cage for every unclean and hated bird!"*

In the chapter, a mighty angel takes a stone like a great millstone and throws it into the sea, saying, *"Thus with violence the great city Babylon shall be thrown down, and shall not be found anymore."* The chapter describes how residents glorify themselves and *"live luxuriously"* as *"merchants of the earth,"* peddling *"gold and silver, precious stones and pearls, fine linen and purple, silk and scarlet, every kind of citron wood, every object of ivory, every kind of object of most precious wood, bronze, iron and marble"* (Verse 12).

The merchants are the great men of the earth, said *Revelation,* and by their sorcery all the nations have been deceived. *"For all the nations have drunk of the wine of the wrath of her fornication, the kings of the earth have committed fornication with her, and the merchants of the earth have become rich through the abundance of her luxury. And I heard another voice from Heaven saying, 'Come out of her, my peoples, lest you share in her sins, and lest you receive of her plagues' "* (Verses 3-4).

Duduman said he was told that America had failed to halt the spread of pagan gods, many of which had been brought in, he said, by superstitious immigrants. A once Christian nation, he was told, was now following strange gods and using freedom as a vehicle for wickedness.

In later visions, Duduman saw a man on a red horse explaining that there would be wars in various places. The "man" said he had been sent down by Gabriel. He wore a helmet and carried a sword. It was his to take peace from the earth.

Still later, in June of 1989, while praying in tongues, Duduman saw a mountain. Half of it flourished with green trees. The other half was barren and desolate. He heard a voice say that California was burning.

In December of the same year, he saw a large star while

he prayed. For a few seconds it would remain high, then at great speed would fall to the ground. This vision recurred more than a dozen times.

"Do you see this star?" asked a voice. "It represents America. This is how fast the fall of America will be!"

Duduman claimed that during his previous experiences a voice told him that after America "burns," the Lord will raise China, Japan, and other nations against the Russians. This is what was so similar to Terelya's visions: China versus Russia. In 1972, many years before Duduman, Terelya had a vision of the Amur River, which separates Russia and China. On the north or Soviet side of the river he saw Chinese tanks. The obvious conclusion was that China was attacking Russia's eastern flank.

While Duduman's visions came by way of angels, Terelya's had been through the Virgin Mary, who allegedly showed him the future after saving him in the freeze cell on February 12, 1972. "I saw a map," recalled Terelya. "I saw a map and parts of it were burning. Russia! There were fires erupting all over Russia. Surrounding countries were also involved. There were flames in various parts of the world. It was what could happen if mankind does not come back to her Son. I saw entire landscapes. I saw a river I recognized, the Amur. I don't know how I knew it was that river. I saw many islands there. I saw tanks on the Soviet side—but not the Soviet type—and a city in flames. Siberia was on fire to the Ural Mountains. I saw Moscow, and the people there had faces that were twisted and deformed. Moscow was sinking, and throughout the city were strange creatures running down the streets."

Although it was not entirely clear where it would fit into the sequence, both Terelya and Duduman also believed Russia, joining forces with a confederation of other nations, would attack Israel. That was a classic scenario for Armageddon. Duduman said he was referred to *Zechariah* 14 and told that when Israel realized she could no longer count on America's strength—because America was no longer strong—it would turn to the Messiah for deliverance. Then, felt Duduman, would come what sounded like the Rapture as the world prepared for some kind of Armageddon.

CHAPTER 28

Flags of Warning

More reserved though not necessarily less strong were the warnings coming from Pastor David Wilkerson at Times Square Church in New York City—Babylon itself. On May 2, 1988, the non-denominational pastor in Manhattan issued a newsletter full of prophecy and entitled "Sudden Destruction as Travail Upon a Woman With Child." He was a prominent preacher. He was also a pessimistic one. I'm uncomfortable with too much pessimism—there are some *good* things in the world—and I'm especially uneasy with those who are so sure that a cosmic event such as the Second Coming will occur around the year 2000, along with Armageddon. I don't buy all the sensationalism. Any extreme one way or another indicates spiritual imbalance. Wilkerson too saw a massive war coming, one that would be far greater than any previous world war, but he wasn't overly dramatic and what I appreciated was that he seemed to argue that purification would arrive a bit more gradually. He likened it to birth pangs. A woman is pregnant for nine months and has plenty of notice before labor. When birth pains first come they can be an hour apart, he noted, then thirty minutes, then just ten minutes apart, until the woman is rushed to the hospital.

The pain is great but so is the exhilaration of a new child. Likewise, pangs and sorrows—the beginning of sor-

189

rows—will take hold before mankind experiences purification. Before the Church is reborn, before the glorious era,
will come the agony of delivery. Use of the term "pangs"
seemed to be an allusion to the Book of Isaiah wherein the
prophet saw the tumultuous noise among nations
"gathered together" and issued God's proclamation
against Babylon.

There is a gradual build-up. Events occur with greater
and greater intensity. There are smaller warnings followed
by larger ones until, one day, a climax or a series of
climaxes, perhaps even mega-climaxes, occur.

Thus did prophets grope for symbolism to express the
essence of what might lie in our future. The passages in
Isaiah describe the sun darkening and the earth moved out
of its place. The darkening sun can be a symbol for the
Lord withdrawing His Light. The earth moving out of its
place can mean major societal upheaval or natural events
like earthquakes, which to ancient man seemed like the
earth leaving its orbit. A volcano can cause the sun to lose
its shine. Wilkerson identified the woman as "a lost,
wicked, godless society," and he made no bones about the
fact that the wicked society was America. He saw the U.S.
as a "crumbling" empire. Taking an especially pessimistic
approach in another newsletter written in 1989, he saw the
nation in the throes of an "incurable" ailment and cited
two newspaper cartoons, one showing the Statue of Liberty
weeping in shame, her head in her hands, the other a hand
inscribing prophetic writing—the word "Anarchy"—on
the wall.

Wilkerson also quoted *Zephaniah,* who spoke of *"a day
of the trumpet and alarm against the fortified cities, and
against the high towers."* That seemed like an allusion to
large cities and skyscrapers. God would uproot all traces
of Baal. He would also cut down the merchants and those
who handle money. When a nation turns against God, said
Zephaniah, replacing Him with occult and materialistic
idols, *"the whole land shall be devoured by the fire of His
jealousy."*

For his part, Wilkerson looked forward to it. Only sinners needed to worry. "According to Scripture, God's people are to earnestly desire this fiery day of sudden

instruction," said the pastor. "As the labor pains increase it means something glorious to Christ's bride! It is one crisis closer to home! It is *their* countdown to destruction; it is *our* countdown to glory!"

Yet, before anything, the Lord issues repeated warnings. He sounds a trumpet of alarm through His angels to their watchmen or prophets. The people in Noah's era paid their warnings little heed. Society in that time was also full of materialism and violence. The Lord saw that *"the wickedness of man was great in the earth, and that every intent of the thoughts of his heart was only evil continually (Genesis* 6:5). Thus came the chastisement. For 120 years before the Flood, God had given that corrupt society ample time to reform. The same is true now. If a similar time-frame is at work today, 120 years put us back to the 1800s, when indeed pleadings and signs had commenced at places like LaSalette in France and Knock in Ireland (where the apparition of John had what seemed like the Book of Revelation in his hand).

Pointing elsewhere in the New Testament, Wilkerson noted that within Paul's warning to the Thessalonians, the word "peace" can be translated as the Greek "eirene," which implies "prosperity." The word "safety" can likewise be interpreted as "security." He saw those two words as a warning to the prosperous nation. *"For when they shall say, 'Peace and safety!' then sudden destruction cometh upon them, as labor pains upon a pregnant woman"* (*1 Thessalonians* 5:3).

The feeling of "safety" and "prosperity" had also corrupted the Church, creating a preoccupation with materialism, charged Wilkerson. He wrote at a time of scandal, when televangelist Jim Bakker was found to be bilking followers out of millions and Jimmy Swaggart was accused of patronizing a prostitute in a seedy New Orleans motel. We had grown worldly. We had become at ease in Zion. "The Church once stood before the world as a testimony against greed and materialism, against the love of things, against self-love, against hoarding and covetousness," complained Wilkerson. "But now the world sees the church as its biggest competitor for the good life! The world laughs and mocks at Christians and rejects the sufferings of Christ and Paul to indulge in the riches of this age. Sudden destruction can mean more than a hydrogen holocaust. By one sudden event, one single catastrophe, the American dream can become a horrible nightmare. The judgment that has so suddenly fallen upon God's house will fall on the nation.''

Although spoken in starker terms, such concerns were not far away from those of Pope John Paul II, who was driven by his foreboding that the world is headed for a moral apocalypse. That foreboding was buttressed with statistics provided by the Heritage Foundation. The divorce figures, less than ten per 1,000 married women in 1960, had more than doubled by 1980 and the teen suicide rate, at 3.6 per 100,000 in 1960, had climbed to 8.5 in two short decades and to ten by 1985—again, more than doubling. So too did teen pregnancy rates rise. By the late 1980s, nearly one unmarried teenage girl in ten became pregnant, and now they had the treacherous option of abortion. Where only twenty per thousand chose that route in 1972, the floodgates had since opened such that more than twice the number—45.9—opted for abortion in 1985. By that time, a total of 1,588,550 abortions were being performed in the United States each year, equivalent to the combined populations of Dallas and Buffalo. Who needed nuclear warheads? Who needed the Big One? Each year the equivalent of a large metropolitan area was already being destroyed. At an international level, every two years brought more deaths via abortion—about 70 million—than there were deaths in all of World War Two.

The level of frenzied teenage sexuality, sparked in large part by what was put before our youth by Hollywood, was also reflected in the fact that 60 percent of all black births were to unmarried women by 1985. SAT scores reached a low at the beginning of the decade while television viewing, up from five hours a day in 1960 to seven hours a day in 1985, continued its foreboding rise. That brought violence with it. And this is a statistic that affected everyone: where there had been about 290,000 violent crimes in 1960 and 740,000 in 1970 (when we last looked in Chapter 11), the total was now nearly 1.3 million.

No, there was little need for a tidal wave; we were already chastising ourselves. If, as Wilkerson said, we were experiencing birth pangs, and the "woman" was our society, judgment was coming out of our very own womb. "Thousands will attempt to flee from cities," he had noted in his 1973 vision, "hoping that a return to the land and nature will provide security." But Wilkerson, who was accused of "doom and gloom," saw no refuge. He listed some of the curses named by Moses in Chapter 28 of *Deuteronomy*. He saw a curse on the cities. He cited the statistic of a crime in New York City every twenty seconds and a murder every five hours (actually soon to be every 3.7 hours). Soon there would be a public notice posted on the boardwalk of Coney Island warning of rapists. There was a preppie who killed his girlfriend during "rough sex" in Central Park. Gangs of youth terrorized storeowners after school, literally taking control of their shops. Sidewalk slashers knifed pedestrians who looked at them the wrong way. Unwanted babies were left in trash bins or burned as in one case in a Bronx oven. Cars had to put signs in their windows ("No Radio") so no one would bother breaking in. Apartments were turned into dead-bolt fortresses. Tourists were slain in the subways. There was a precinct in Brooklyn that was probably as dangerous as Beirut.

Yet, instead of harnessing the criminals, instead of dealing firmly with evil, New York's twisted system of jurisprudence tilted in favor of shoplifters, drug traffickers, and thieves, giving criminals probation instead of jail terms and in one case *awarding* a criminal $4.3 million in damages because he was shot by a cop while fleeing a violent robbery. (He had just assaulted a 72-year old man who ended up in the hospital.)

Wilkerson also saw a curse coming upon America's economy and foreign relations. He saw America shrinking before previously insignificant enemies (*Deuteronomy* 28:25-26). He saw the curse of divorce (28:30). He saw the loss of an entire generation (28:41). He saw the nation becoming a debtor nation *("He shall lend to thee, and thou shalt not lend to him; he shall be the head, and thou shalt be the tail"*—28:44). He saw bankruptcies. He saw the curse of incurable illness. *("The Lord shall make the pesti-*

*lence cleave unto thee. . . with a consumption, and with a
fever, and with an inflammation—28:21-22. The Lord will
smite thee with the blotch of Egypt. . . and with the scab. . .
whereof thou canst not be healed.")* He related this to
AIDS, saying that "the mark of AIDS is the purple blotch—
the incurable boil!"

He could also have cited *Revelation* 16:2, which mentions "loathsome," "malignant sores." There were plenty
of those infirmities in New York, which along with San
Francisco was bearing the brunt of the AIDS epidemic. In
the mid-1980s, a third of all the American cases were in
New York. There was a frightening jump in a drug-resistant
strain of tuberculosis that is common among those found
to be HIV-positive. This was frightening because TB can
spread through the air, through sneezing and coughing.
The obituary page of *The New York Times* was just full of
young designers, singers, artists, playwrights, novelists,
photographers, decorators, dancers, and actors who were
succumbing to the plague.

*"Come out of her, my peoples, lest you share in her sins,
and lest you receive of her plagues."*

More than anything Wilkerson saw economic confusion
coming. He saw it striking Europe first, then affecting
Japan and the United States, until a "meltdown" occurred.
He said that tall glitzy buildings such as Trump Tower
represented pride, competition, and greed. They were
morally vulgar. The day was coming, he warned in a 1989
newsletter, when many such buildings would be full of
homeless people or would stand empty, like "giant, decay-
·ing tombstones." He saw America as a modern-day
Nineveh, its merchants traveling the world as the Ninevehites had, exporting glassworks, textiles, spices, carpets,
ivory carvings, gems, silver, and gold. But before long, as
at Nineveh, an invading force would swoop upon America,
spread themselves over the rich spoil, and flee with the
loot. He felt Japan, Taiwan, Korea, and Germany would
take their money out of the United States.

"The stock market has become one gigantic gambling
casino," complained Wilkerson. "Millions of Americans
play numbers, the lottery, hoping to get rich overnight.
Why such obsession to make it Big? Because everyone

knows a storm is coming! The entire world awaits with anxiety that one day when a financial meltdown hits.''

Wall Street, he prophesied, would become "Wailing Street.''

One must remember that these gloomy economic forecasts came just after the October 19, 1987, crash of the stock market, which fell more than 500 points. The market's plunge was a clear warning. There was an absolute frenzy of money in the booming Eighties, as Wall Street, shuffling paper on the foreign exchange and engineering monumental corporate mergers (by floating junk bonds), vacuumed huge dollar amounts out of the credit-crazed economy. While it is no sin to earn good money, and while for decades the American system was designed to reward those who *contributed* to the overall public well-being, the system had twisted itself to the point where thousands were making a killing on mergers that *hurt* mainstream Americans whose employers were stripped of cash by the Wall Street carnivores.

Somehow, *destructive* tendencies were now what was rewarded.

And it is a sin to benefit economically at the cost of another person.

Not everyone could take vows of poverty; not everyone is cut for the monastic life. There is nothing wrong with monetary reward. But wasteful spending and the hoarding of money—reaping millions or even billions at the expense of others—was not what Christ had in mind when He said He had come to give us life more abundantly, nor was a materialistic obsession part of the Christian walk.

There was a difference between making good money and looting society.

Manhattan was so awash in paper money that one man, the "king" of junk bonds, made as much as $600 million in a *single* year. Anyone making under $100,000 a year was considered nearly at poverty level. There were wall-to-wall millionaires on the Upper East Side of New York and throughout the sprawling suburbs.

This great excess of paper money and the greed it provoked were captured in the movie *Wall Street*. God's indication that He didn't like the trend—His admonishment that materialism had reached an unimagined and wasteful extreme—was the 1987 crash, which jarred many of the yuppies and junk-bond traders. As it says in *Romans* 1:18, *"the wrath of God is revealed from Heaven against all ungodliness and unrighteousness of men,"* specifically those who serve and worship created things rather than the Creator Himself. Man cannot serve both God and mammon. The crash was also a signal to America that her great bounty could be stripped overnight, the wealth she had been blessed with because she was a nation founded upon God. It was a minor warning. If matters didn't change—if Americans continued to view life in terms of the dollar sign—there would be more warnings to come.

It was also a signal that the Lord was not happy with societal trends such as abortion, adultery, and homosexuality. Just eight days before the 1987 crash, there was a large gay-rights march in the nation's very capital. As with so many trends, the gay movement had its origins in New York. There, in June of 1969, a police raid on reputedly illegal sexual activities at the Stonewall Inn, a bar in Greenwich Village, led to a small riot as militant homosexuals swore at police and threw bottles. This "riot" marked the radicalization of the homosexual movement. Henceforth they would use intimidation as the quickest route to societal acceptance. They also forced the American Psychiatric Society into removing homosexuality as a mental disorder from the Diagnostic and Statistical Manual of Psychiatric Disorders. They would *make* us accept their sodomy, cross-dressing, and often sado-masochistic practices. They would do this even though the Bible expressly states in *Leviticus* 18:22 that *"you shall not lie with a male as with a woman. It is an abomination."* They would do it even though in the very same passage of *Romans* that warns of God's wrath over excessive materialism—in the same passage that seemed so relevant to Wall Street—the Bible also explicitly condemns *"men with men committing what is shameful, and receiving in themselves the penalty of their error which was due"* (*Romans* 1:27).

It was heart-rending to see so many talented young men dying in droves. The Bible calls homosexuality an "abomination," and it was back in *Daniel* that the angel Gabriel mentions that *"on the wing of abominations shall be one who makes desolate"* (9:27). Surely no one reading the newspaper could argue against the fact that homosexuality is barren and that wanton sex of any kind causes desolation. Homosexuals needed love, and they needed help in healing their hearts. It was the sin—not the sinner—which was the abomination, as other sexual sins are also.

Yet still they persisted and included groups such as NAMBLA, the North American Man/Boy Love Association (which openly advocates sex with consenting minors) and Dykes on Bikes, a radical lesbian group, in their gay-rights parades. "God Is Gay," said a sign held by a man in San Francisco's Gay Freedom Day Parade, while in Manhattan gays attacked St. Patrick's Cathedral.

In 1979, Reverend Chuck McIlhenny, pastor of the First Orthodox Presbyterian Church in San Francisco, was sued under a gay-rights ordinance by an organist he fired for being a practicing homosexual. While McIlhenny eventually won that lawsuit, the media attention stirred up the radical homosexual population such that the McIlhennys and their children received "obscene phone calls, dozens of threatening letters, pornographic materials mailed to us, and death threats, some of which described the children in detail—their names, ages, what they looked like, where they attended school, and what sexually deviant acts were going to be performed on them before they killed the children." More than once the McIlhennys were forced to leave the city for safety. Occasionally, a threatening caller would identify himself as "Satan." On May 31, 1983, their home was firebombed, and as McIlhenny's wife described it, the flames "roared up the alleyway wall and burst through the window into the bedroom, breaking the quarter-inch pane of glass." The firemen told them the intent was to kill. The downstairs of the church was burned out, and everything in the home itself was covered with black soot. Their bed was completely destroyed and most heart-wrenching, some of the photos in their wedding album had been destroyed.

No one was questioned for the arson. In San Francisco, gay politics are such that the flag for the group called Queer Nation has actually flown over city hall. There and elsewhere homosexuals have also been ordained as ministers or have created their own choirs and church services. One gay newspaper advertised "Secret God's Church: Ancient Phallic Rites of Gnostic Christianity: An Orgy of Brotherly Love." During one confrontation between lesbian pro-choicers and Christian pro-lifers, the lesbians hissed and cursed the Christians, beating a drum and chanting, "We do it for the goddess. We do it for the goddess."

These were serious dangerous signals, as serious as anything in New York—or back in ancient Sodom. The term "abomination of desolation" is mentioned in *Daniel* in "The Prophecy of the End Time" (12:11) and, most forebodingly, in *Matthew* 24: *"Therefore when you see the 'abomination of desolation,' spoken of by Daniel the prophet, standing in the holy place,"* said Christ, *"then let those who are in Judea flee to the mountains."*

CHAPTER 29

"We Are Coming!"

There were meteorological signs. There were record tornadoes in the south-central states. There was a scorching summer that wilted much of the nation, raising concerns about global warming. There was the frightening disaster when a nuclear reactor caught fire at Chernobyl. The nuclear accident tainted soil for hundreds of miles and made scholars nervous for more than environmental reasons. Some of them began to read *Revelation* and especially Chapter 8: *"Then the third angel sounded: And a great star fell from Heaven, burning like a torch, and it fell on a third of the rivers and on the springs of water; and the name of the star is Wormwood; and a third of the waters became wormwood; and many men died from the water, because it was made bitter."*

What made Soviets uneasy was this curious "coincidence": wormwood is a bitter herb used as a tonic in rural areas of the Soviet Union. The Ukrainian word for wormwood is "chernobyl."

Although Richter 7 quakes dipped in the 1980s, the total number of tremors rose steadily upward. In 1982, 7,747 were recorded and 12,290 the last year of the decade. On October 7, 1988, as Mikhail Gorbachev was meeting at the United Nations, an enormous quake struck the southern

Soviet republic of Armenia. It killed more than 55,000, so terrible a disaster that Gorbachev cut short his visit and returned home. The destruction hit the cities of Spitak and Kirovakan, splitting buildings in two and creating mounds of rubble. Whole apartment complexes were reduced to piles of brick. *The New York Times* called it "one of the worst earthquakes in Soviet history."

In the United States there was a discernible link between societal trends and similar disturbances. As writer John McTernan pointed out in Sister Shaw's magazine, during the summer of 1989 there were major abortion developments as a result of the Supreme Court's Webster decision. That decision had opened the way for individual states to limit abortion. Florida was one of the important test cases. In September, during the debate's most heated moments, Hurricane Hugo lashed at the South, as if in warning. But no one saw it that way and on October 11, 1989, the state of Florida declined to limit abortions, granting pro-choice forces the momentum. The U.S. House of Representatives followed suit, voting to widen funds for abortion. Two days later, on October 13, 1989, the anniversary of the great warning at Fatima, President George Bush, who had run as a staunch opponent of abortion, began hinting at compromise and "flexibility" on the issue. The Dow fell 190 points that day and did so in a way that, even to secular observers, was eerily similar to the crash two years before. At the same time, a nearly bizarre storm hit Charlotte, North Carolina, felling so many trees that officials asked parents to keep their children home on Halloween. ("From an airplane it looks like a forest that got hit by a hurricane," said Assistant City Manager Don Steger.) Soon after, a second hurricane battered good old Galveston in Texas, and the day of *that* storm, October 15, a number of governors signed a joint "pro-choice" declaration, granting yet more steam to the forces of infanticide. There was also a rally of pro-abortion forces at San Francisco's city hall.

Within 48 hours of these developments, San Francisco was jarred by a devastating quake. The tremor measured 6.9 on the Richter—same as the Armenian quake—and shook buildings for two hundred miles. Residents were described as "too frightened to show fear." It was the greatest wake-up call since 1906, rumbling through at 5:04 p.m. and destroying a section of Interstate Highway 880 in Oakland. Dozens were killed, as if the city had been hurled, said one newspaper, into some "twilight dimension." The city's quirky charms crumbled in a moment. People made a mad dash out of the same city hall where the pro-abortion rally had been held. "If you look at the newspaper articles for the day of the quake, you will see it clearly states people came running out of city hall in terror," said McTernan. "The very spot that was used for organized rebellion against the Lord and was used to promote the killing of His children, two days later became a spot of terror and fear."

There was terror throughout "Babylon on the Bay" as residents, shop owners, hospital patients, and office workers rushed to the streets. They were in a collective stupor. When dark came there was no electrical power. Gas supplies were disrupted and homes in the Marina district collapsed onto the sidewalks. The epicenter was in a region that is famous not only for its occult and homosexuality but also for genetic-engineering. Scientists tinker with DNA, the bluprint of life, and seek evolution theories that exclude God.

At the 4,000-student University of California just above Santa Cruz, books in the library came tumbling down.

Bricks from buildings smashed through skylights and communications systems were out.

In San Francisco, fans watching the World Series had to flee Candlestick Park. One of the greatest sporting events ground to an incredible halt. It was doubly interesting because at the time homosexuals were seeking to pass a domestic partners law to provide them government benefits and the proposed law was ardently supported by Mayor Art Agnos, who was also campaigning for a new ballpark. "In what he thought was a shrewd political move," remembered Pastor McIlhenny, "he teamed the two ballot issues together in order to get both passed in November. He elicited support from the gay community for the ballpark, in exchange for support from the 'new ballpark advocates' for the domestic partners law. One issue would support the other—and vice versa."

The earthquake changed all that, slowing down the campaign for gay legislation and at the same time causing the city to second-guess the idea of a new ballpark in the vulnerable Marina District, where the quake hit hardest.

Both the ballpark initiative and the domestic partners law failed at the polls the following November.

Soon after the quake, America began to see a great rise in what Catholics call "locutions" and what Protestants refer to as "words of knowledge." In plainer English, they were claiming that the Lord was speaking to them through an interior "voice" or even through auditory locution—words of warning. There were also dozens of reported apparitions in the wake of Medjugorje. The common theme: as Colver said, a judgment was coming—or had already started.

I knew from first-hand experiences, including some negative experiences, that a good number of such locutionists were simply listening to their own subconscious. They fantasized spectacular End-Time scenarios and then related them as words from God. But their collective effect stood, like the impulse in the 1300s, as another warning. "We're realizing how close we are to the fulfillment of those prophecies that have been given during former times, to the Catholic Church as well as different people in the Protestant religion—even prophecies given to Hindus and Muslims," said Sister Gwen, the Methodist missionary who had seen her share of signs and miracles. "I was preaching on signs of the End Times in India one time at a great outdoor meeting and a man came up to me and said, 'Sister, everything you said is true.' I said, 'How do you know it's true? Are you a Christian?' And he said, 'No, I'm not a Christian, but you could have been quoting from some of our own ancient holy books. All these things have already been written by our ancient religious writers.' And I remember standing once on a balcony in Alexandria, Egypt, just looking out at the sea, and suddenly there was another Muslim man standing on another balcony looking over at me. We began to talk and when we got to the subject of what's happening, he said, 'Lady, all I can say is that we're running out of time. And these are certainly the last days. We can see the fulfillment of our Scriptures.' We are getting all kinds of reports into this office. In fact one of our recent reports in our newsletter was the report of one lady who had seen an angel with a trumpet at its mouth. At Christmastime someone sent me a beautiful porcelain angel with mighty wings and the trumpet right at its mouth. It was absolutely amazing that it went along with the prophecy."

Sister Gwen printed the account of a Bible smuggler in China. Waiting one day to get through customs in Hong Kong, a large, impatient crowd began to stampede. Said the missionary: "All these people started pushing and running, and I fell to the ground. Many of them walked or ran over me. My whole body was in serious pain, yet no one would stop. I felt I was suffocating, and all I could do was call upon the name of Jesus. The minutes seemed like hours as I lay on the ground. As I called the name of Jesus, I heard a loud voice as if it spoke through a loud speaker. I looked up and saw what looked like a Chinese man. He was just radiant, dressed in white clothes—glowing white, indescribable—and as he spoke a Chinese word, it was as if the people were pushed back to make a circle around me. He looked at me, and without saying a word he gave me his hand to lift me up. As he brought me to my feet, all the pain in my body left."

There was also the story of an Arkansas insurance salesman named David Bergman. "In the spring of 1982, I was kind to a stranger who happened to be an angel," he recalled. "As an insurance salesman I was used to driving all over the state. I had never picked up a driver before nor since in my many miles of traveling. It was a Monday morning and I had just left my home office. It being the first day of the work week, I was trying to get my enthusiasm and positive mental attitude up for door-to-door canvassing. Passing through Western Grove, I saw a hitchhiker on the side of the road. That was it. I would pick him up—be kind to someone and be off to the right start. I pulled into the next drive, turned around to pick (him up), and he was gone. A car right behind me had picked up my friend. So much for being off to a good start. I was depressed. Reluctantly, I got back on the highway to head back to my next town. What could I do, I couldn't go to work like this, down on myself? I was praying what to do next. Not one mile down the road from the last hitchhiker was another one. Wow! This could be my day after all.''

The new hitchhiker was about six feet tall, 180 pounds, with straight blond hair. He also had the fairest skin Bergman had ever seen. He appeared to be about 25 to 30.

''I slammed on the brakes, backed up the car, and my good deed jumped in. After introducing ourselves, I found out that he wanted to go to the next town. No problem. I'd just sit back and drive. Right out of the blue this guy asks, 'Well, David, where do you go to church?' I thought, what's this guy? I don't know him from Adam. He's asking me where I go to church. I answered him truthfully. 'I'm not going regularly anywhere. I'm bouncing around from Baptist to Assembly of God.' While I was telling him the sad truth, I thought, who is this guy? I'd never seen him before and he's asking me personal questions. I'll get even with him. I'll ask him where he goes to church. So I did, and he replied, 'The church of St. Paul,' and just as if he was reading my thoughts, he added: 'where Jesus Christ is the cornerstone.' ''

Others received messages about Satan and how everyone would be tested in every possible way. The saints would be specially tested. ''So take care,'' the Lord allegedly said. ''Keep your eyes on Me. Every day will become a testing day. Every day will become a day when you must stay very close to Me, because the devil is going around like a roaring lion seeking to devour the saints in these last days, and if he can't get them to lose their salvation, he certainly will do all he can to get them to lose their rewards. So stay close to Me. Stay filled with love.''

On April 23, 1988, Sister Gwen had a mystical experience as she stood to prophesy. It was punctuated by a clap of thunder. ''Even in this time, even in this day of grace, yea, the Lord would say unto His people, I will appear unto this nation as I never appeared unto it before,'' she spoke. ''For I am coming, saith the Lord, even as I came up to Jerusalem to cleanse the temple! I came at the beginning of My ministry, yea, and I came with fire and I came with zeal. I made Myself whips, and with these whips I whipped out the place. I overthrew the money changers and I freed the dove.''

Shaw urged a reading of *Isaiah* Chapter One, hinting that it was particularly relevant. The missionary saw a day when the glory of God "shall be seen over vast areas of these states." He was coming, she said, "in the judgment." She believed that there was not enough righteousness in America to make our country worthy of a good leader. "Know that there is no man," she prophesied, "to stand in this White House." She was especially concerned about a coming persecution of American Christians. She saw it arriving through a "world church organization" that sounded similar to Wilkerson's premonition of a "super world church." It was not an idle concern. At the United Nations Environmental Program, workers would soon send out literature on ecological spirituality to thousands of churches, with suggestions for their Sunday sermons. Dozens of non-Christian organizations began to form during the late 1980s and early 1990s in an effort to unite religions under the banner of environmental awareness, which soon deteriorated into earth worship.

Persecution was also prophesied by Dumitru Duduman, who in a dream saw a black bird of enormous size, its wings spread, coming swiftly to the earth. "When I looked, I saw something was written on the wings," recalled Duduman. "It said, 'Power has been given to me to be able to come against the Christians in a short time.'" And like Shaw, he saw some form of Christlike manifestation. "Not many days will pass and the One Who is to come will come and He will not tarry. The days are coming when the kings of the earth will wail loudly. Tell My people in the U.S.A. to be prepared and be careful, says the Lord, for everything I have decided will happen. Do not say in your hearts that the Lord has said many things that have not happened yet, because all things are decided by Me and everything has its appointed time. Draw closer to the Lord your God and cease doing evil things, that I may give you victory. I the Lord will work in ways that you cannot even imagine, but be holy. The sins of the great whore have spread throughout the world. The stench of her sin has reached Me and it will not be long until I will raise the whole Arab world, the Russians and the other countries against her, that they may destroy her."

Whatever their individual reliability, these many locutions were reaching the point where the 1980s stood as an
eruption of End-Time prophecy that was more than a match
for that of the 14th or any other recent era. There were also
signs in the way of human warfare. The number of armed
conflicts again reflected upon Christ's mention of *"wars
and rumors of wars"* in *Matthew* 24. According to the
researcher Nelson Pacheco, a mathematician and computer
scientist who'd worked for the Air Force (but whose
research in this realm was purely a private spiritual
endeavor), the number of major battles showed a fairly
steady rate for the first thousand years A.D. as Christianity
spread throughout Europe. But the spread of Islam coin-
cided with upward spikes and the battling began a determined upward trend after 1300, skyrocketing starting
around 1650, a century before the French Revolution. Sister Gwen quoted the director of the Stockholm International Peace Research Institute as saying that there has not
been a single day in which a battle wasn't being fought
somewhere in the world since 1745. Others said the continuous battling was since World War Two. This much was
clear: from 1800 to the present, the amount of human warfare had increased in large, unnerving jumps.

While much of that could be attributed to the simple fact
that there were now more people on earth—the population
was expanding—this did nothing to negate Christ's warning of *"famines, pestilences, and earthquakes in various
places."* Such trends had taken centuries to develop, but
developing they were. "The 14th century was particularly
hard hit by famine combined with the notorious Black
Plague," noted Pacheco. "Nevertheless, even the rate of
famine during that century pales in comparison with the
famine rate in the 19th and twentieth centuries."
So too was Billy Graham quoted as saying that while
some signs have appeared in the past, our time may be
the first in human history when all the signs are
converging.
And Sister Gwen said the Lord prophesied, *"I will yet
do two great things in this nation. I will send judgment
with much persecution, but I will also send out of the
judgment a pure, clean, holy revival."*

In Florida, Jim Bramlett noted that it was dangerous to set times and dates. There had been many miscalculations already, most notably the unfulfilled expectations of 1988. But Bramlett still maintained that the millennial change was biblically significant and that according to Hosea's prophecy we could expect full restoration of Israel in light of the presence of the Messiah on the "third day," around the year 2000. (Actually, older calendars would place the millennial change at more like 1996.) Some thought this "change" would be birth pangs. Others described it as the Great Tribulation.

An evangelist named A. A. Allen had long before warned of a vision that involved the Statue of Liberty, its torch torn from its hand and replaced with a cup that Lady Liberty was forced to drink from. As she imbibed the bitter dregs, a voice said, "Should ye be utterly punished? Ye shall not be unpunished: for I will call for a sword upon all the inhabitants of the earth, saith the Lord of hosts." The Statue of Liberty grew powerless to defend herself. She staggered and lost her balance. It reminded me of George Washington's alleged vision. "Far to the northwest, just out over Alaska, a huge, black cloud was rising," said Allen. "As it rose, it was black as night. It seemed to be in the shape of a man's head. As it continued to rise, I observed two light spots in the black cloud. It rose farther, and a gaping hole appeared. I could see that the black cloud was taking the shape of a skull, for now the huge, white, gaping mouth was plainly visible. Finally the head was complete. Then the shoulders began to appear, and on either side, long, black arms."

The "cloud" stretched one of its arms toward the east and one to the west. It stopped above the Great Lakes and turned its face toward New York. Out of its "mouth" came wisps of smoke. Then it turned its attention to the West Coast. After the horrible images—the vapors that also swept over places like Kansas City and St. Louis—and what seemed like a rocket attack with huge explosions, Allen encountered a strange silence followed by sweet music. "There was joyful shouting, and sounds of happy laughter," said Allen. "I looked, and there, high in the heavens, above the smoke and poisonous gases, above the noise of battle, I saw a huge mountain. It seemed to be of solid rock, and I knew at once that this was the Mountain of the Lord. The sounds of music and rejoicing were coming from a cleft, high up in the side of the rock mountain. It was the saints of God who were rejoicing. It was God's own people who were singing and dancing and shouting with joy, safe from all the harm which had come upon the earth..."

The vapors seemed like a symbol, and if they were, if they were true revelation and not the product of imagining, they represent the dark powers, the anti-christ spirits, that rule over cities and nations. And their activity indicates the coming of a great evil force. In Israel, a well-known mystic named Mother Barbara, abbess of the Russian Church Convent of Saint Mary Magdalen, on the Mount of Olives in Jerusalem, recounted her fears of the Anti-Christ himself. In 1978, at the age 90, she told Sister Gwen a story about her spiritual father and confessor, Father Aristocoli, a bishop of the Kremlin, known as a *staretz* or prophet. When she asked him if she would see the Anti-Christ, the prophet said, "No, no. You will live a long, long, long time. But you will not see the Anti-Christ. There will be a time between. It will be a good time and God will be merciful. He will again give help to the people. But you know human beings are not faithful to God. When it's quite good, they forget Him and they begin to live carelessly and do those things which they should not do."

"Will it be a long time?" she asked.

"I don't know," he answered. "But perhaps about fifty years, and the Anti-Christ has come."

When Christ comes, he said, there will be a light over the whole world and it will come from the East.

Aristocoli also prophesied a "terrible revolution" in Africa. Echoing the prophecies in Rwanda, he said Africa would be "a sea of blood," but no country would be without its trials. "China and Russia will fight," he said. "On the border where three frontiers meet, India, China, and Afghanistan, there will be a terrible explosion...terrible, terrible, terrible. On the borders of Russia's three frontiers, near Tien Shan. That is where it will take place."

When Mother Barbara went into her own reverie, she envisioned a cloud open.

From it came rays of light.

They were enormous.

And out of them stepped many angels.

"The devil has an enormous army, and he is leading his army to kill souls," said Mother Barbara. "But his army is not as great as Christ's army, which is under the orders of Michael the Archangel. I saw Michael, and he said, *'We are coming, coming now!'*"

CHAPTER 30

Sound of the Choir

Such themes, largely Protestant or Orthodox, were strikingly similar to what was heard in Catholicism. At a place called Betania (which means "Bethany"), witnesses testified to a plethora of otherworldly phenomena. And these wonders were all the more significant in that the local ordinary, Pio Bello Ricardo, who as Bishop had the authoritative say on its validity or lack thereof, deemed on November 21, 1987, after personally interviewing or taking signed statements from more than five hundred witnesses, and after spending three years praying for discernment, as well as consulting directly with Cardinal Ratzinger and Pope John Paul II, that "to my judgment these apparitions are authentic and of a supernatural character." He declared Betania, which is near Caracas, Venezuela, "sacred" ground.

The phenomena at Betania included the spinning sun and the sounds of an angelic choir. Near a hillside clearing in a rainforest, the mellifluous sound of angels came as from nowhere! Many were those who claimed to see manifestations of light taking the form of Jesus or Mary. Often the shapes seemed as in vapor, like the apparitions near Cairo. And like the Zeitun phenomena, hundreds saw manifestations with their own eyes. Medical doctors attested to miraculous cures, including Dr. Vinicio Arrieta,

who had been director of the School of Medicine at the
University of Zulia (and also educated at Harvard). Dr.
Arrieta was himself healed of an incurable prostate cancer
which had spread to his spinal column.

The chief visionary, Maria Esperanza Medrano de Bian-
chini, an aristocratic woman in her sixties who had
experienced supernatural phenomena since childhood,
believed that mankind is approaching a "serious
moment." She called for a reconciliation between religious
denominations as we approach "this hour of decision for
humanity." She told me that at some point in the not-too-
distant future, Christ is going to manifest in such a way
that His presence would be felt—or in some way
witnessed—"from east to west and north to south." She
saw societal upheaval. She was especially concerned for
the youth. She feared revolutions breaking out everywhere,
especially in South America and her homeland of
Venezuela. She foresaw "little quakes and certain others."
She felt the earth's core is "out of balance." She believed
the United States would be among the nations to suffer.
She predicted a sexually-transmitted disease that would
kill in days or hours. A judgment is coming. It would not
be the end of the world, she emphasized, but a difficult
moment that would purify us. She called it a "good test,"
as anything from God is good. Although it was unclear
whether she was alluding to a manifestation of Jesus, a special outpouring of the Spirit, or the Second Coming, she
said, "Perhaps I will not live to see this, but the Lord is
coming. He is coming—not the end of the world, but the
end of this century's agony." I emphasize the word
"manifestation." Perhaps in a subtle way, during coming
decades, Christ's grace would be more manifest. In a striking parallel to Duduman, she warned of Cuba and missiles
that may one day be fired in a surprise attack. She made
clear that these were only possibilities—that events could
be changed if mankind responds to God. And like both
Duduman and Terelya, she worried about the Mideast. "I
hope Israel makes peace with the Muslims, that they make
peace between them, because there is a nation within those
people that may provoke a war—a very great war," she
said. "This could be very serious. And comes Russia,

Germany, and then England, and so many nations to defend themselves, and this is going to be a catastrophe." She felt the "yellow races will stand up" and worried about a surprise from that corner of the world—including the possibility that it would involve quiet China. "Be careful," she warned the U.S., "especially when all seems to be peaceful and calm. Russia may act in a surprise way, when you least expect it." The manifestation of Christ, she felt, would in some way carry worldwide implications. Mankind is on the verge of a renewal or "awakening"— what Sister Gwen had called revival—and Maria wrote an incredibly majestic song by precisely that title: "The Awakening."

What is coming, she emphasized, is "not a bad test and most of us are going to see Him, to notice this event, and it's beautiful."

There were equally astonishing wonders in the Soviet Union. At Hrushiw, where the peasants saw phenomena in 1914, signs had returned at the chapel known as Blessed Trinity. Closed for seven decades under the oppression of Communism—which had been prophesied both there and at Fatima—the chapel showed sudden and remarkable life as thousands and perhaps *tens* of thousands claimed to witness the supernatural. It started on April 26, 1987—the first anniversary of the Chernobyl disaster. Attention was first called to the chapel by an 11-year-old peasant girl named Maria Kizyn. According to a government official I interviewed, Ivan Hel', who at the time was deputy chairman of the Lviv Regional Council of People's Deputies, much of the phenomena, including the appearance of angels, occurred during the spring and summer. Hel' said there was an inexplicable glow around the chapel that the Communist police—the militia—tried to drown out with a searchlight. Others described the glow as a lambent luminosity. It was silver and yet not quite silver, and it seemed like this gargantuan field of light enveloped the chapel's surroundings, causing even trees and people to appear slightly phosphorescent, with a reflection different than that of the moon, yet at the same time similar. "When I got there, there were about 5,000 people," said Hel.' "I believe there were up to 150,000 during the course of certain days, during the course of holidays. (The major phenomena) lasted until October.''

First in a trickle, then in droves, as surrounding villages heard about the manifestations, Ukrainian peasants began to congregate around Blessed Trinity. It was the hour of the fire of the Holy Spirit. There was the unusual if some-times nearly invisible and stereoscopic glow around Blessed Trinity, and according to at least one witness, there was also, as at Betania, the sweet song of angels.

Pilgrims representing several Christian denominations claimed they saw a large cross above the church, along with copious other divine or at least paranormal manifestations—witnessed by Orthodox, Catholics, Bap-tists, Jews, Pentecostals, and atheists alike, including a number of KGB and militiamen. The interior of the chapel, closed for many decades by the Communists, also seemed strangely illuminated. Pilgrims were cured of eczema and cancer.

Not everyone saw supernatural manifestations, but the crowds were unstoppable, desperate to feel the Hand of God, starving for spirituality. Hrushiw was only one of more than a dozen spots that suddenly reported activity behind the Iron Curtain. In chapels, churches, and monasteries throughout Ukraine (where Chernobyl is located) came reports of supernatural lights glowing around the abandoned religious structures. The events in 1987 at places such as Zarvanystya, Pidkamin, Buchach, Hoshiw, Ternopil, and Pochaiv, as well as Hrushiw, seemed to indicate that a major change was in the offing and with it an end—at least temporarily—to the hideous suffering.

This was before the fall of the Berlin Wall, yet everyone seemed to sense that change in the wind. Signs and wonders were abundant beyond my ability to enumerate. At Hrushiw, witnesses claimed to have encountered a sweet older woman who mingled with the crowd, gave them advice, especially about health—and then vanished, like the mysterious "peasants" in Medjugorje.

I was acutely aware, in such manifestations, about the danger of deception. I knew that besides interaction of the subconscious, there is often cause to wonder if deceptive spirits are involved. Of the top five reported cases of the Virgin appearing in America, there were indications of significant and perhaps grave problems with at least three of them. Bad fruits. And demonic plagiarism. In New York, a bishop formally disapproved of apparitions at a place called Bayside. In another, more recent case, a visionary told me about UFOs that had once landed in front of her house, with small entities milling around. She had also encountered poltergeist activity in her bedroom, including a lamp which floated across the room. So serious were the manifestations that she was afraid on occasion to pray in her "apparition" room. Those who had worked with her were quoted in a major southern newspaper as saying that behind the scenes—away from the thousands who flocked to see her—this dubious visionary was so obsessed with recognition that when someone slighted her or otherwise caused anger, she "would threaten to call down angels to destroy them." Her mood swings were such that she threw tantrums and would spend hours crying alone in her basement. Without even knowing all of that, the bishop had publicly expressed "grave concerns."

Other deceptions were more refined and fooled even major theologians. It is always necessary to watch for evil masquerade and to turn again to *Matthew* 24. For right after Christ's warning about quakes and pestilence is the warning that *"many false prophets will rise up and deceive many. And because lawlessness will abound, the love of many will grow cold."* A few paragraphs later Jesus adds: *"Then if anyone says to you, 'Look, here is the Christ!' or 'There!' do not believe it. For false christs and false prophets will arise and show great signs and wonders, so as to deceive, if possible, even the elect."*

But there was no reason as yet to think this was true of places such as Zarvanystya or Hrushiw—they seemed more in line with *Joel* 2:28—and some interesting prophecies had already come out of Ukraine—true prophecy. One of the visions, reported by Josyp Terelya in 1987, included the image of eight men taking power from Gorbachev in a coup. "Under a Christian temple was a secret hiding place," said Terelya. "There were eight men there—eight rulers, all eight waxen yellow. They laughed horribly and bared their teeth. Gorbachev told me (in the vision) it wasn't he who was in charge of the state."

Terelya also predicted that in a short time, in a matter of a few years, the republic of Ukraine would be an independent country—a prophecy that, at the time, was only slightly more likely than Texas splitting from the United States.

"I saw certain lights that were probably angels," Terelya told me. "I can't understand how I knew they were angels. But this much I do know: Hrushiw was only a part—a big part, but only a part—of a larger outbreak of heavenly phenomena."

At Hoshiw it was claimed that a silhouette of the "Angel of Ukraine" was seen above an old monastery, a monastery that had suffered not only under the Communists, but also when the Nazis invaded. At a huge and majestic Orthodox monastery in Pochaiv, where a pillar of fire had been seen way back in the 12th century, witnesses again claimed to have seen strange fires and (according to one Orthodox official with whom I spoke, Vasyl Savich Darmogay), what looked like supernatural candlelight next to one of the buildings. Near Ternopil there were images in the clouds and in Pidkamin a tableau or "living picture" of the young Jesus appeared for three remarkable days on the side of another repressed church. Here too there was a large and inexplicable glow. Elsewhere, witnesses spotted strange pink and blue clouds or images of the Virgin. "All the Christian people were happy," noted one man with whom I spoke, Dybyna Pavlo. "All the Communists were angry."

But the KGB couldn't keep those long-oppressed believers—the Orthodox who had been persecuted, the crushed Catholics, and the haunted Baptists—from their Christian call. During an apparition of the Virgin Mary, Terelya recorded these prophetic images and words: "I see a large field in flames and upon it are many nations. There is not even time to dig graves. There is no water. The heavens and the air are on fire. I beg you to beseech the Eternal One to forgive you and accept you under His wing. In the past, God's plan of salvation was given to mankind through His prophets. Why don't you follow the path set by the Holy Father, the Eternal God? You can save the world by your prayers. How many warnings must mankind be given before it repents? The world continues on the road of self-will and hedonism. If Russia does not accept Christ the King, the entire world faces ruin.''

Terelya was told during the heavenly visitation that the spirit of anti-christ was sowing envy and dissension. Many lies were being proclaimed against the truth. The world was gorging itself on depravity. *"The people are falling into the hands of Satan,"* said the vision of Mary. *"They are blinded by unceasing idolatry. How many come as false messiahs and false prophets! So I warn you to be diligent and circumspect, for happy are those whose lives are blameless, who walk according to God's commandments.*

"But these are few, and everyone must be careful to use these symbols wisely in order not to fall into the trap of the Anti-Christ. Cast from your shrines any signs of Satan that have been forced upon you. The churches are weeping and perishing. Lead a pure and sinless life. The Kingdom of Heaven-on-Earth is at hand. But it will come only through repentance and penance. You can achieve the destruction of all the arms that have been arrayed by the unbelieving nations through prayer and fasting, through the action of all people who have accepted Christ. The Eternal God is calling out to you.''

Terelya was told that *"times are coming which are spoken of as the End Times"* and Mary mentioned *"the Kingdom of God on earth, which will last for a thousand years."* He saw a vast ocean. Half of it was quiet and pleasant, the waters very calm and transparent. The other half was dark and stormy. Lightning cut through the horizon and an awful noise rumbled over the ocean. After these flashes of lightning he saw an image of Lucifer. He appeared as a handsome, swarthy man in a dark suit. Everything was beautiful about him but his eyes were red. All of a sudden the ocean subsided and a crimson cross appeared over the water. A strange light covered the entire earth.

"Lucifer is losing strength," said the alleged Virgin. *"To maintain himself on the throne of darkness he began to portray himself as repentant, but this is not true. Lucifer is cunning and clever. He is preparing a great deception*

for all of God's creation, and especially for the people of God. For a short time a godless kingdom shall maintain itself from one end of the earth to the other. This kingdom shall be given birth by a lascivious woman. From her womb will come the spirit of godlessness. The godless spirits are the servants of anti-christ. They will begin to deny the existence of the human soul in order to destroy religion and morality. The anti-christs have strong reason to deny the immortality of the soul, because depriving man of the soul, they shall have an open and fertile field for the seed of disbelief."

Lightning flashed again and the clouds continued to roil. The ocean again subsided and a light covered the earth from end to end and at this time an awful noise extended over the face of the planet. From the ocean emerged an immense, fiery column which resembled a dragon. Its head was like a white light. He grew at a fast rate. "My mouth was dry and bitter," Terelya told me. "The voice of the woman continued: *'This is the beast, the servant of the Anti-Christ and himself an anti-christ.'*"

Terelya also noted an "immense earthquake" and a red sky. He had a vision of a Russian soldier with three large green rockets. He saw the destruction of a large concrete wall in Germany (a prophecy of the Berlin Wall). He also saw a map of Ukraine with many black and gray blotches. He saw Ukraine divided by an immense red river. He saw another persecution. But there was hope in the U.S., which held the scales of justice. While it had much evil, he was told, America also had many people who are "good and devout." He saw a white rider on a white horse arriving to slay the Red Dragon.

CHAPTER 31

The Black Beast

"Before Christ's Second Coming the Church must pass through a final trial that will shake the faith of many believers," says the new Catholic Catechism. "The persecution that accompanies her pilgrimage on earth will unveil the 'mystery of iniquity' in the form of a religious deception offering men an apparent solution to their problems at the price of apostasy from the truth. The supreme religious deception is that of the Anti-Christ, a pseudo-messianism by which man glorifies himself in place of God and of His Messiah come in the flesh."

The *spirit* of anti-christ precedes the *physical* Anti-Christ. The spiritual battle precedes the physical one. Chastisement occurs in spiritual form, through attack by demons, before it manifests in earthquakes or hurricanes. Severe and definitive condemnation of evil is forthcoming. The decisive moments draw near. The abomination of desolation is not just homosexuality and the occult, but also the errors of ministers and priests. Satan was sifting humanity like wheat and soon the chaff would be swept away by the winds of persecution. It is a persecution that will come from both outside and inside of Christianity. It is a persecution that will include bishops against bishops, minister against minister, modernists attempting to extinguish the traditionalists, prayer-warriors versus witchcraft, feminists turning to the goddess, the goddess really a mask for old Beelzebub, who seeks apostasy, a falling-away that will open the door, felt Father Stefano Gobbi, "for the appearance of the very person of the *Anti-Christ!*"

The separation process was already well underway. Angels were drawing their army from the little, the poor, the humble and weak. They were collecting watchmen and handmaidens, a great company of the humble to attack the stronghold manned by the proud. Satan would be outraged! His defeat—never could he have imagined this—would come at the hands of the smallest and humblest! The Prince of Pride would be defeated by humility!

That weakness the angels had long ago spotted, the Achille's heel of arrogance. They knew that pride is like air in a balloon; just the prick of a tiny pin defeats it. How that prick would hurt! On the verge of victory, Satan would fizzle into nothingness. It didn't take a prophet to know that. He is full of hot air. But until such time he would challenge every God-loving human. In a message stunningly similar to the later Medjugorje apparitions, Gobbi quoted his heavenly voice as telling him, *"This is the hour of Satan and of his great power. It is the hour of darkness! This is the hour when the abomination of desolation is truly entering into the holy temple of God."*

The coldness of hatred still lingered on the world's roadways. In fact it was colder than ever. The devil had seduced some of God's very own pastors, who had fallen into hidden apostasy. But even in the dead of winter—this most cruel winter—the hour of liberation drew all the closer, said Father Gobbi, the Italian priest who claimed to relay messages from Mary; and the buds of renewal were already appearing.

That is the fig tree. The Church is the fig tree. Soon it would flourish. Soon there would be a New Jerusalem, which must come down from Heaven, the heavenly Jerusalem, to transform the new heavens and the new earth. The Second Pentecost is coming like dew on the world and will transform the desert into a garden. Paradise will be joined to earth. Satan's power will be destroyed and he will be bound with all the wicked spirits and locked into Hell, no longer able to so harm the world. For now, as in cold weather, the tree was bent to the ground and covered with soil (as figs are covered in harsh weather), but little buds showed on the unseen and barren branches. While it was fun to decode the Bible, and convenient to base prophecy on world politics (such as Israel), it was the spiritual world—the spiritual fig and the spiritual temple—that prophets, projecting into an immaterial realm, saw in their visions. Yes, Israel is a great sign of the times, but Christianity is the ephemeral tree!

That was the spiritual dimension. Heavenly trees. Living waters. They went largely unseen. We saw them as fleeting signs—as flashes of light—but more than ever in the angels who arrived as the 1980s drew to a close and the war intensified. Gobbi said Michael stood at the head of the heavenly cohort *"which is now drawn up for battle. Gabriel is at your side to give each one of you the very invincible strength of God, and Raphael is healing you of the numerous wounds which you often bring upon yourselves in the great struggle in which you are engaged. Be ever aware of the angels of God who are at your side and invoke their help and protection often. They have great power to defend you and to rescue you from all the snares which Satan, my adversary and yours, sets for you."* Satan was attacking on the spiritual field with every kind of temptation, said Gobbi, and the angels, archangels, and all the heavenly cohorts *"are united with you in the terrible battle against the dragon and his followers. They are defending you against the snares of Satan and the many demons who have now been unleashed with furious and destructive frenzy upon every part of the world."* We were urged to entrust ourselves more fully to the angels. We were told to ascend the holy mountain. *"Walk in the light of their invisible but certain and precious presence. They pray for you, walk at your side, sustain you in your weariness, console you in your sorrow, keep guard over your repose, take you by the hand and lead you gently along the road."*

This is "the hour of the angelic power." The great battle which is now being waged, said Gobbi, is above all at the level of spirits, the wicked spirits against the angelic spirits. "You are being involved in this struggle which is being waged between Heaven and earth, between the angels and the demons, between Saint Michael the Archangel and Lucifer. To the angels of the Lord is entrusted the task of defending your person, the life of the Church, and the good of all humanity."

The angels were engaged, said Gobbi, to prepare God's great victory in the glorious reign of Jesus. Before the victory occurred, there would be the oft-mentioned tribulation. "Never as today have immorality, impurity, and obscenity been so continually propagandized, through the press and all the means of social communication," said Gobbi. "Above all, television has become the perverse instrument of a daily bombardment with obscene images, directed to corrupt the purity of the minds and the hearts of all. The places of entertainment—in particular the cinema and discotheques—have become places of public profanation of one's human and Christian dignity. This is the time when the Lord our God is being continually and publicly offended by sins of the flesh. Holy Scripture has already warned you that those who sin by means of the flesh find their just punishment in that same flesh. And so the time has come when the *angel of the first plague* is passing over the world, that it might be chastised according to the Will of God. The angel of the first plague cuts— into the flesh of those who have allowed themselves to be signed with the mark of the monster on the forehead and on the hand, and have adored his image—with a painful and malignant wound, which causes those who have been stricken by it to cry out in desperation."

Television was growing into another abomination of desolation. It made barren the minds and souls of a generation. It planted the seeds of every indiscretion. It beamed evil into living rooms like a great idol. It turned every home, every private sanctuary, into a little Babylon.

On September 18, 1988, at Lourdes, France, Gobbi announced the onset of "ten decisive years." It is a period of time, Mary supposedly told him, when *"there will come to completion that fullness of time which was pointed out to you by me, beginning with LaSalette all the way to my most recent and present apparitions."* The final secrets would be revealed during the purification of the earth—or what Gobbi, in a striking parallel to Wilkerson, referred to as "the travail of the new birth." A chastisement was being prepared, and in addition to apostasy, there would be the "overturnings of the order of nature," such as earthquakes, droughts, floods and other disasters. These went along with the signs in the stars, moon, and sun. "The miracle of the sun which took place at Fatima was a sign which I gave you to warn you that the times of these extraordinary phenomena which are taking place in the heavens have now arrived," he said Mary told him. It was the hour of great trial for America. Disasters would multiply. *"You have continued to walk along the way of rejection of God and of His law of Love. Sins of impurity have become ever more widespread, and immorality has spread like a sea which has submerged all things. Homosexuality, a sin of impurity which is against nature, has been justified. Recourse to the means of preventing life has become commonplace, while abortions—these killings of innocent children, that cry for vengeance before the face of God—have spread and are performed in every part of your homeland. The moment of divine justice and of great mercy has now arrived. You will know the hour of weakness and of poverty; the hour of suffering and defeat; the purifying hour of the great chastisement."*

In this period, sufferings would increase and the "mystery of iniquity" would become manifest. He would penetrate into the very interior of the Church and sit in the very temple of God, "while the little remnant which will remain faithful will be subjected to the greatest trials and persecutions." It remained unclear whether the Anti-Christ would materialize in human form or continue on in his spirit form, which was already pervasive. The Church was being persecuted not just from outside, but also from within. There were pastors who had struck compromises with the dragon. There was already a hidden but extensive persecution. Conservative Christians were treated with amusement or disrespect as radical Episcopalians ordained homosexuals and modernist Catholics tried to feminize the liturgy. The apostasy was threatening to break into the open. All was heading toward transformation. All was in preparation for that event, one day, perhaps soon, perhaps in the longer

term, when Jesus would return in glory. The Church would
know its greatest pain, but after that it would know its
greatest glory! "In the hour of the great trial," said Gobbi,
"paradise will be joined to earth, until the moment when
the luminous door will be opened, to cause to descend
upon the world the glorious presence of Christ."

The time remained hidden in the secrets of the Father.
No amount of decoding the Bible was going to crack that
secret. It was a secret even to the angels, but events leading
up to it already had started, in the way of spiritual warfare
that will culminate in victory for the small and humble
who with Christ will bring an era of peace.

"In the struggle between the woman clothed in the sun
and the red dragon, the angels have a most important part
to play," said Gobbi. "For this reason, you must let yourselves be guided by them with docility." The guardian
angels had to be invoked in an extraordinary communion
of prayer, with trust and serenity, he said, in the painful
hours of purification. How the scorpions stung! How they
bit! But what balm were the angels. "Indeed, in these
moments," said Gobbi, "Heaven and earth are united in
an extraordinary communion of prayer, of love, and of
actions, at the orders of your heavenly Leader." The Holy
Spirit had come as a great sign of mercy. "It is the hour
of the Holy Spirit Who, from the Father and by means of
the Son, is given to you ever more and more as a gift, as
a sign of the merciful love of God Who wants to save mankind. By the fire of the Spirit of Love, the work of the great
purification will be quickly accomplished. The Church
groans as it awaits His merciful work of purification."

There would be splendor after the end of the age. There
would be renewal. The time would come for a great
awakening. For now, man still faced a gigantic satanic rep-
tile, a creature that sought to undermine any coming
revival. "The red dragon is Marxist atheism, which has
now conquered the whole world, and which has induced
humanity to build a new civilization of its own without
God," said Gobbi. "In consequence, the world has become
a cold and barren desert immersed in the ice of hatred and
in the darkness of sin and impurity. The black beast is also
Masonry, which has infiltrated the Church and attacks it,

wounds it, and seeks by its subtle tactics to demolish it. Like a poisonous cloud, its spirit seeps in everywhere, to paralyze faith, extinguish apostolic ardor, and produce an even greater alienation from Jesus and His Gospel.''

The spirit of anti-christ had also been operative through rebellion like that of the French Revolution, which was incited in part by demonic Masonry. Masons belong to a large and secret organization and while it shows itself to the public as a social club, in its deeper recesses are old Egyptian rituals—old Babylonian idols—and that group known as the Illuminati who are connected with an extensive network of bankers, media moguls, and multi-national corporations. The plan for two centuries now—since the inception of Masonic Illuminati in 1776—has been to create a "new world order" with one world economy, one world government, and one world religion. They hope, at some point in the near or distant future, for an overturning of the Christian order, thus making way for worldwide pantheism and the Anti-Christ. Much has been written about how the Illumined Masons helped provoke the French Revolution through what was called the Jacobin Society. Voltaire and Robespierre were reportedly prominent Masons. So insidious is the group that George Washington warned at least twice about their influence in 1798. This may have been the cloud he saw coming to America from Europe. The Illumined Masons played a key role in establishing the Federal Reserve and the United Nations, the very land of which was donated by John D. Rockefeller, an enormously prominent and wealthy American with ties to the Rothschilds, a German banking clan that reputedly has deep roots in Masonry. They also influence world leaders through think-tanks such as the Trilateral Commission, the Council on Foreign Relations, and the Club of Rome. High-ranking government officials have long belonged to these groups but their participation is often a curious secret.

"The dragon manifests himself in the force of his power," warned Gobbi. "The black beast on the other hand acts in the shadow, keeps out of sight, and hides himself in such a way as to enter in everywhere. He has the claws of a bear and the mouth of a lion, because he works everywhere with cunning and with the means of social communication, that is to say, through propaganda. The seven heads indicate the various Masonic lodges, which act everywhere in a subtle and dangerous way. This black beast has ten horns and, on the horns, ten crowns, which are signs of dominion and royalty. Masonry rules and governs throughout the world by means of the ten horns. The horn, in the biblical world, has always been an instrument of amplification, a way of making one's voice better heard, a strong means of communication.''

In this period of history, said Gobbi, ''Freemasonry, assisted by its ecclesiastical form, will succeed in its great design: that of setting up an idol to put in the place of Christ and of His Church. A false christ and a false church.''

It was a tremendous approaching moment. Gobbi said the purification or chastisement had already begun. The hour had come, he preached, for the abomination of desolation. His reference to the bear and lion seemed connected to the prophecy of the four beasts in the Book of Daniel. In that prophecy Daniel saw a bear and a lion with eagle's wings. The lion is the symbol of Great Britain, and its eagle's wings can be seen as a symbol of the United States—which grew out of Great Britain and uses the eagle as an emblem.

The bear, of course, is Russia's symbol.

What the third beast, the leopard with four heads and wings, may represent is anyone's guess, but the fourth—the dreadful beast with ten horns—is what Gobbi alluded to in his message on Masonry.

That beast, says *Daniel 7:23, "shall be a fourth kingdom on earth, which shall be different from all other kingdoms, and shall devour the whole earth, trample it and break it in pieces."*

CHAPTER 32

Death of the Dragon

There is only one problem with the devil's plan, and that problem is Jesus. His victory is assured. The dragon would be defanged, the beast sunk back at sea. Come the angels! Come the cleansing fire of purification. As the catechism said, "The Church will enter the glory of the kingdom only through this final Passover, when she will follow her Lord in His death and Resurrection. The Kingdom will be fulfilled, then, not by a historic triumph of the Church through a progressive ascendancy, but only by God's victory over the final unleashing of evil, which will cause His Bride to come down from Heaven."

In select settings the Lord showed how swiftly He could break down a stronghold and rearrange nations. One such show of force was prophesied by Gobbi. In Vienna, on August 31, 1988, the priest quoted Mary as saying, *"With Austria and Germany, from here I bless the surrounding countries which are still under the yoke of a great slavery and today I announce that the moment of their liberation is close."*

That was a reference to Communist nations, and a wild one. At the time there may not have been a geopolitical expert in the world who would have ventured such a prediction. Maybe one day, but Communism had been

226

around the whole century. It wasn't going to go away overnight. The fall of Communism!

Yet a year later, Poland elected a non-Communist government and that sparked similar democratic movements in other East Bloc nations.

With astonishing speed Communists were shaken from power in Hungary, Bulgaria, East Germany, and Czechoslovakia. The Berlin Wall, symbol of the Iron Curtain, was removed (as Terelya too had foreseen) and dictators were purged. Approximately 3,000 new churches opened during a nine-month period in 1989, and Orthodox Eucharist was celebrated at Assumption Cathedral inside the Kremlin for the first time since 1918!

The miracles were taking place just as the Archangel Michael had prophesied to Terelya. And they immediately preceded the collapse of Communism. Shortly after Terelya's jailhouse vision, the hard-crusted Soviets, once obsessed with destroying any last vestige of theology, began lifting the religious oppression which, since the time of Lenin, had pervaded Russia. The Holy Spirit was at work; something new was afoot in the Kremlin. On January 7 and 8, 1985, U.S. Secretary of State George Schultz and Soviet Foreign Minister Andrei Gromyko suddenly found themselves at a negotiating table in Geneva discussing the reduction of nuclear arms—something many thought would never happen. Two months after *that*, on March 13, 1985, Mikhail Gorbachev had risen to power. He and Reagan would soon begin a series of summits that set the stage for an end to the Cold War—at least for the time being.

As the oppression lifted, so did the curtain on hidden religious secrets. At a place called Buchach, in Ukraine, I trudged through muddy fields and searched nearly door-to-door in 1991 until I found the almost legendary image of what looked like an apostle that had miraculously etched itself onto a pane of glass and had been hidden there for many years, away from the repressive Communists. A peasant had been working outside one Sunday when he noticed it on the window at his home in this region south of Ternopil. It was a detailed portrait of a man's head—as I recall bearded—and the feeling around it was tremendous. They claimed the glass had been melted and the pane remolded, but still the image reappeared. When the peasant woman who was keeping the image (it circulated secretly among a number of villagers) brought it from its hiding place and unwrapped it, I gawked in disbelief and wonderment, for the image looked like nothing I had ever seen, somewhat like an etching but not really like an etching or engraving or anything physical. It was just *there*. Townsfolk also saw miraculous signs at a nearby church which the KGB had used as a burial ground for executed priests and children.

The Lord was rearranging things, including entire countries, in preparation for a future awakening and denouement. It was part of the great descent, the solemn and yet joyful descent, of the angels. They are often responsible for miracles like those worked at Hrushiw and Buchach. They cause us to wonder at their character. As creatures of a spiritual nature, says John Paul II, angels have no body "even if, in particular circumstances, they reveal themselves under visible forms because of their mission for the good of mankind." Therefore, they are not subject to the laws of corruptibility which are common to the material world. "As creatures of a spiritual nature, the angels are endowed with intellect and free will, like man, but in a degree superior to him," said the pope. "The angels are, therefore, personal beings." As ambassadors of the living God, added the pontiff, they have special duties not only to individual humans "but also to entire nations" (*Daniel* 10:13-21).

The angels are given charge of us as we journey through the innumerable hazards of the world. Their miracles, their countenances, their unfathomable splendor in spirit form, may well exceed the extravagant descriptions in *Ezekiel* or *Daniel* (crystalline clothes, eyes with torches of fire, feet like burnished bronze, girded as in *Daniel* with the gold of Uphaz). The seraphim of Isaiah's visions had six wings but most early biblical allusions say nothing about wings, which may be a symbol of an angel's ability to move vast distances in a twinkling.

They are larger-than-life spirits woven into Christianity, Islam, and Judaism. Milton described them as flaming seraphs and medieval theologians believed angels spun the planets and moved the stars.

Although New Agers try to make angels into cream puffs—nearly cosmic pets—their business is often serious stuff. Their business is saving us from Satan. They love us too much to see us stray into Hell. From the first they have come to warn and, when necessary, to carry forth correction or punishment. It's another of their functions. To deny this—especially to ignore their connection to warnings and prophecy—is to deny one of their main biblical roles.

"Nowhere in the Old Testament is there a more significant use of angelic power in judgment against God's own people than when David defied God's command by numbering Israel," wrote Billy Graham. "God sent a pestilence among the Israelites and 70,000 died. He also sent a single angel to destroy the city of Jerusalem. David 'saw the angel of the Lord stand between the earth and Heaven, having a drawn sword in his hand stretched out over Jerusalem' (*1 Chronicles* 21:16)."

When Herod committed idolatry, giving glory to man instead of God, *"The angel of the Lord smote him"* (*Acts* 12:22).

So too did God warn the Egyptians that He would send plagues if the Pharaoh did not let His people go. When God was not obeyed, Egypt suffered lice, locusts, disease, hail, and darkness. God used nature to right the many wrongs. The storms devastated Egypt's trees and farmland.

In the Book of Numbers an angel is again seen with a sword (22:23) and in the Book of Judges there is an angel associated once more with fire (6:21). We also see that warnings are *conditional*. God often plans to chastise us but relents when He sees signs of improvement. Or He lessens what He planned. We see in *2 Samuel* 24:16 how He sent a plague that killed 70,000 from Dan to Beersheba but called off punishment when the angel was ready to destroy Jerusalem.

To think that angels are innocuous winged creatures who are meant to set atop a Christmas tree—to see them only as dimply, chubby, and babylike cherubim—is a misreading of Scripture, for their purpose, as much as anything, is to set us straight. This is not an act of heavenly venom. This is not an act of callousness. This is an act of mercy.

This is not an act of callousness or gloom and doom. This is an act of mercy. It is far better to save sinners through earthly chastisement than to present them with the greatest chastisement—Hell.

More than anything, the angels come to *prevent* such chastisement.

They fight to be at our sides. They fight against Satan's strongholds. In *Daniel* the angel was withstood for 21 days by the demonic principalities of Persia until Michael came to the rescue (10:13).

That Michael (or "Mika'il") has descended again in our times means not only that war is in progress but also that it is a time of reckoning. It is a time for self-evaluation. It is a lull before the potential storm. And God is using angels, as always He has used angels, to direct, inspire, and apprise us. The earthly developments are but a shadow of what's going on in the heavenlies. There is a war being fought, a spiritual war, and often the locutions of visionaries and pastors—the prophetic inspiration from worship services and Pentecostal revivals—signify events more in a spiritual than a physical realm. There were even signs in outer space. You may recall that at Medjugorje, peasants saw the word for peace—*MIR*—scrawled supernaturally in the sky. Five years after that the Soviets launched a new space station to replace the *Salyut*. The date was February 13, 1986, and the name of the new Soviet station was *"MIR."*

The sense of supernatural presence—that something was going on—even extended to tabloid writers who often manufacture articles. According to one such report, which was given greater currency when *Parade* magazine facetiously reprinted it on January 6, 1986, six Soviet cosmonauts witnessed what looked like a band of glowing angels in outer space while aboard the orbiting *"Salyut 7"* space station. Although there was no reason to believe that report (which first appeared in an especially outrageous supermarket tabloid), there were other reports, far less sensational but equally interesting, in credible periodicals, of strange goings-on up there. The observations in space seemed to possess a nearly mystical dimension. Other aerial phenomena, observed by astronauts and cosmonauts, have included mysterious flashes of light seen by Buzz

Aldrin during his first trip to the moon, and what became known as "chain lightning": lightning that seemed to begin over the West Coast of the United States but make its way across the nation to the East Coast in a way no lightning known to man does. While the flashes of light may have been the retina's response to sudden bursts of cosmic radiation, officials admit that some of the phenomena are beyond current understanding; and taking poetic license, knowing Satan fell like lightning, we may see it as a metaphor of the heavenly descent—and the warfare.

What, if anything, might be going on in space, there was little doubt something extraordinary, truly unusual, was happening back on earth. Many accounts I heard from hard-nosed types—cops, lawyers, doctors, psychologists. "There's a gal I know who's a very spiritual woman and has apparitions of an angel who suddenly appears next to her in an empty church when she's praying," said one highly respected priest. "He's garbed something like a monk, in a robe, and he tells her a lot of things about me, what I'm going to be doing. She gets information about me and is told to pray for me and all priests. I asked her, 'Will I ever see this person?' She said, 'Eventually, some time, you will.' I asked, 'What does he look like?' She said, 'He's very calm, somewhat swarthy complexion, very, very handsome. And very tall and husky, an appealing person who looks very human.'

"She said the angel has spent hours with her, talking to her and telling her to pray for priests. That's the main thing he does. She said, 'You know, he told me you're going to be in a certain church next Wednesday and there's going to be five priests on the altar with you, concelebrating the Mass.' I said, 'Well, he's wrong. It's not going to be Wednesday. It's going to be Tuesday.' She said, 'No, no. He said it's Wednesday.' I said, 'Well, I know my schedule, and it's going to be Tuesday.' I didn't know about this concelebration. She said five priests would be there and he—the angel—would also be there.

"Well, after the phone call, after she said this, I went and checked my schedule. I was certain she was wrong. But she was right: It was a Wednesday, not a Tuesday. So I went to the church that night for the charismatic Mass.

We had four priests concelebrating, not five. And I thought, well, this is where the revelation is wrong. After we began the Mass a fifth priest came on just a few minutes late. The chances of that happening were just astronomical. She had said her angel would be there and I was looking for someone of the angel's description. And way in the back of the church, in the last pew, there was someone who fit that description perfectly. I sort of glanced back there and when I looked up again he was completely gone—disappeared.''

I heard similar accounts from other Catholic mystics. Many experiences, as in past centuries, occur far from public view, in chapels and convents. Just before she went for her interview to become a nun, Sister Nadine Brown, a nationally known nun from Omaha, was on a lake in Minnesota with a young boy named Johnny whose family she knew. "He wanted to take me out on my last day and so we went out on a huge lake in a putt-putt boat," says Sister Nadine, who has had several angel encounters. "We couldn't get through this channel and there was a huge yacht coming down this narrow neck of a waterway. They were right there. But they couldn't see us. It was going to hit us—them in their large boat, us in this little one. Johnny was getting ready to jump while I called on the angels. I called on them! And right then a loud noise like the patrol people blew—a horn from somewhere—sounded and the boat just kind of swerved. I felt there was this huge male angel there, between this tiny little boat I was in, this little dinghy, and that huge yacht, just protecting us. I saw his gentle, smiling face. I've seen angels several times, but I see them mostly in prayer. I have lots of prayer strength with angels, particularly in spiritual warfare. So I've had a lot of experiences with St. Michael.''

When I asked Sister Nadine, who lectures around America on spiritual warfare, how Michael appears to her in prayer, she said he's "very gentle, very, very handsome—qualities that you would think of Jesus, and there's an authority about Michael. I wouldn't want to be against him. He's large and I have seen him once with wings, but basically I see him without them. I see him in the form of a man—masculine. Sometimes he's in white apparel, but other times he's in full armor, with his sword drawn. And I see him without the armor. He's very approachable. He comes *instantly*—very quickly. What I have witnessed is fire. I see them with fire. I don't know what I would compare it to. I've seen them full of fire, even inside themselves. And I've seen angels with their chariots on fire. It's fire that consumes the enemy and pushes the enemy back. The enemy will just disappear in the face of that.''

She and other nuns have seen them in church and felt them during exorcisms. Notable was the time that Sister Nadine was called to pray for a high priest of the occult—a satanist. During the deliverance she ''saw'' a huge coiling snake come out of him. The snake then took on the aura of Lucifer. Instantly she felt a second presence—that of Michael. She felt the Lord told her to now leave the matter in the hands of that most capable angel. ''It was a total deliverance,'' she says. ''The man became a religious.''

Another time, high in the Rockies, on a narrow path in a car with another nun, Sister Nadine grew worried when a carload of drunken men began following them. She called on the Lord and using the weather, He sent a mist or cloud that guarded them from view—coming between their car and the one behind them. It felt like a shield. ''We were going at a snail's pace,'' she says, ''protected and escorted by the angels.''

In California, Father John H. Hampsch, a psychological consultant and expert on mystical theology, as well as one of the nation's most well-known deliverance ministers, said he too has noticed the angelic presence, and has seen physical manifestations of Satan. ''I think Michael the Archangel, whom Isaiah called the archenemy of the devil, is highly operative today because the devil is so operative,'' says Hampsch, who also has served as an officer for the archdiocesan communications office in Los Angeles. ''The more the devil gets loosed the more God will let the good angels come to counteract him because there's a crescendo of activity these days in spiritual warfare. I get calls every day from people who suffer from demonic obsession. There's a tremendous explosion of spiritual warfare. I've been a priest 42 years. When I was a young priest

I never got phone calls telling me about poltergeist activities. I get these every day now. Demonic forces are obviously at work, in very obvious ways: people waking up with all kinds of slashes on their skin and beds jumping around and evil images appearing to them. I get that every day. I never did when I was a young priest. And there are sexual attacks: incubus and succubus. It's getting very common. I've seen people thrown across the room. I was involved in exorcisms in Rome and saw some things that make *The Exorcist* look like Mary Poppins. Those are heavy-duty exorcistic experiences. But it's not just one-sided. There's also good fighting against the evil. For that reason I think God is releasing many more angels.''

From Ajmer, in India, I received letters written by a priest named Robert Lewis who fought the fight on Satan's own turf: in a nation of many superstitions and idols. Yet even there the Holy Spirit was moving powerfully. Father Lewis told me he had performed ''hundreds'' of exorcisms, the people seeking his help from all over the subcontinent. There were cures and ''practically all the miracles written about in the Gospels.'' The people came despite the primitive nature of Hathikhera Post, where Father Lewis resides, a place where water and electricity arrived just five years ago. They came to see for themselves. They came to feel the peace. The pilgrims came when word spread of apparitions and healings. They came to a beacon of light, where Satan, the master of many fellow countrymen, was not allowed.

CHAPTER 33

The Heavenly Embrace

There were reports of supernatural events—Christian manifestations—in Syria. There were reports from Iraq, a town called Mozul (a mile or so from ancient Nineveh). There were reports from Australia and the Philippines and Argentina.

No, the Lord wasn't appearing on network news, nor was He manifesting in downtown Manhattan. It wasn't His style. He wasn't about to make an appearance at the Kremlin. He would not do a spot on *The Tonight Show*.

We were being nudged—tapped on the shoulder. It wasn't God's style to ram anything down our throats. He was giving signs according to denomination, in the outback and often impoverished zones of the world. In Ireland, in old areas with long histories of persecution, angels were seen at roadside grottos. I visited a place called Gortaneadin where pillars of light and otherworldly fog were reported. One witness, a girl named Rosemary O'Sullivan, saw a "teenage" cherub holding a tall lighted candle, an angel with blond hair and a knee-length white robe. He said he was her guardian and bore a likeness to Rosemary herself. To the north, in Bessbrook, was a young man named Mark Treanor who claimed to see his guardian angel on a nightly basis. Mark was also widely known for alleged visions of the Lord, Who he said came in a brilliant

light, "like opening a window shade in a dark room."
Another reputed visionary, Beulah Lynch, said that during
a vision of Christ, she was shown a globe with two angels
atop, facing each other. The angels, she was told, "are
touching the earth."

I often use the terms "reputed" or "alleged" because no
one can ever be sure of authenticity. We can only exercise
our best judgment. There are extremes that people fall into,
of over-belief and of over-skepticism. We can only take the
cases that seem most credible when compared to other
accepted cases or biblical precedents—which is why angels
are especially interesting. They are throughout the Bible.
"It's so difficult for us to handle something we know so
little about," says Father Michael Scanlan, the former
leader of Catholic charismatic revival. "Mystical
experiences are something we know very little about. It's
very easy to be misled. It's very easy to exaggerate. I do
believe a great deal of caution is needed."

Father Scanlan sets forth as key criteria the humility of
the seer (or for that matter anyone involved in the spiritual
movement) and of course personal fruits. Simply believing
oneself to be a master of discernment in itself shows a lack
of that humble spirit and always stands as a detriment.

But Scanlan, who had been to Medjugorje in 1983 (and
was harassed there, escorted out of the country by the
KGB), has no doubt that there is a major interlude of supernatural phenomena around the globe. To ignore it is to
ignore its frequency throughout history, especially as
recorded in the Bible. To ignore or demean it is to reject
Christ's own instruction to prophesy and watch for His
signs. We are told by Paul (*1 Corinthians* 14:39) to *earnestly* seek prophecy. It edifies the Church (*1 Corinthians*
14:4). As Scanlan says, prophecy is to be taken seriously
while keeping in mind that "you never understand before-
hand exactly what's going to happen." There is a danger,
he warns, in trying to use chronology. "The Scriptures and
saints speak of things in a way that is not really chronologi-
cal," he says. "You can't add up all the days of the years.
You can't plot out when this thing or that thing is going
to happen." Prophecy paints matters not so much in fine
detail as with "broadstrokes." It gives us the essence of

coming events—a general feeling—so that when events occur, says Scanlan, believers are not caught completely off-guard and God's plan can be better understood.

Often, prophecies are most valuable when viewed in *retrospect.*

Scanlan believes we are in the latter days or End Times but also sees the possibility that the End Times could take a long time to play out. He believes that a warning is "definitely" upon us, that "God is allowing some very strong things to happen to bring our attention to the seriousness of our times." The major battleground, he feels, will be the United States. "I think we're in for it if the civilization of personalism and love and submission to God does not start to triumph. We're in for some kind of crash." How a potential chastisement shapes up will depend, he says, on "how much we repent or change before the climax arrives." He refuses to try and detail the future "because I don't think that's how prophecy has worked in the past." He feels that when it comes to prophecy we should "take the main thrust from it, take it so you're not surprised if these things happen, but more important, do the things being asked of you."

In the mind of another prominent deliverance minister, Father Emile LaFranz, we are in a "most significant time." There is no problem spotting the forces of darkness in his own city of New Orleans, long a hotspot of voodoo, where occult altars and spooky murals are a part of the flavor on Bourbon Street. (During the 1990 Superbowl, a voodoo priest made a talisman for quarterback Joe Montana on national television.) "No doubt New Orleans from the beginning, because of its involvement with voodoo and the like, has been under special attack," says LaFranz. "But this is broadening more and more to almost every part of the country. I don't know if there's a place that we can say is not under some type of attack. I don't know of a place around the country where there aren't active covens and worshippers of Satan, even in small rural communities. What was once undercover is now coming into the open more and more."

The Holy Spirit is manifesting as a guarantee that we on God's side will win a magnificent victory. Father LaFranz quoted John Paul II as saying (before he was made pope) that mankind is in a "final confrontation" with the forces of evil. This confrontation is especially intense among those on the front line in the spiritual field, where Satan's technique is miscommunication and division, causing fellow prayer-warriors to misunderstand each other or develop unwarranted suspicions, or to judge each other—looking for the specks in others' eyes—without concentrating on the logs, the timber, in our own.

Worst of all is envy, which is a deep but largely unrecognized form of hatred.

Such jealousies and imagined transgressions split up congregations, worship centers, and prayer groups, leaving us naked in front of the enemy.

Most damaging are the rifts between Christian denominations, when what the times call for is finding common ground in Christ. So much energy is spent fighting each other or disagreeing on what amount to petty matters—picking on differences in the way various folks worship—that the devil is able to make inroads everywhere. The holier a person thinks he or she is—the more he strives for dominance or outward appearances—the more dangerous is such a person. There is no pride as loathsome as spiritual pride. When Christians enter into games of power or oneupmanship—as we are all prone to do now and again—it is an immediate sign of spiritual immaturity. The size of a prayer group is less important than how in touch with the Spirit each member has been.

The devil smiles when we judge people instead of loving them.

He smiles when we focus on negativity.

Who could claim to be without fault? That was Satan's boast. That remains his belief, that he is faultless and worthy of replacing God. Filled with hot air, he makes himself appear bigger than he actually is. Often he succeeds in intimidation. He wants to make us feel helpless when we are just the opposite. "Christians need to be conscious of the powers they have in Christ and realize they have the *authority*," says LaFranz. "It's not accepting that word and not accepting the authority we have that limits us." LaFranz has "no doubt" that angels are arriving in large

numbers because America has "lost its soul." In such a
climate of evil, LaFranz, an expert on the occult and a
priest for 35 years, urged that we be on the lookout for
demonic deception. He believes many mystical claims are
"problematic." There are researchers who insert the New
Age into their angel work, and the danger here is the sin
of idolatry. They mix angels with devas and elves. They
hardly ever mention demons. They make it seem like
there's nothing to worry about—that God doesn't judge us
and that we are already heavenly. They turn angels into
a cult. Angels are not toys. They are not servants at our
beck and call. They are not our pet parrots. Yet many are
those who treat them as such. "There is fluffy stuff with
no mention of Jesus in some books," complains one expert
on angels, Father Karl Chimiak of Maryland. "Those in the
New Age have a great devotion to angels, but what angels
are they in contact with?"

As always, we come back to Paul's warning in *2 Corinthians* that "Satan himself transforms into an angel of
light." I heard some "angelologists" quote occult
philosophers and treat angel pins like New Age crystals.
They do not want to be bothered with discernment. The
occultic approach is the Pollyanna approach: everything is
sunshine and thus not to worry—when in reality one of the
very reasons angels are coming is because of the darkness.

The "good news" is not angelology but Christ, and from
what I can tell, Jesus was no Pollyanna. He was very serious. He never told a joke. He constantly admonished. He
warned of tribulation. He died on a cross.

But He also resurrected, and we must follow Him to that
glory. Life is serious business and there is judgment. There
is special danger for those involved with sorcery, including
Eastern idols that can be traced back to Babylonia. In Sur-
abaja, Indonesia, was a woman known as Grandma Tan
who worshipped idols with great zeal until she "died" of
a heart attack. It was an NDE. She was ready for the ritual
of Buddhist mourning when a Christian began to pray over
her. Suddenly Grandma Tan opened her eyes, sat up, and
pointed to the Eastern idols. "Take that down!" she cried.
"Get rid of all objects of worhip in this house! From now
on this family worships only Jesus! I was in Hell, and He

came to me and told me He was the true God and my Savior. He brought me out of that terrible, dark place!''

Unlike many NDEs, which, as with New Age angelologists, mention suspiciously little about Hell, the Christian near-death experiences often contain not only a glimpse of the glorious afterlife but also the element of eternal judgment. Sister Shaw related the vision of that ten-year-old Chinese girl named Sen Ching who saw two roads in the afterlife: one wide and winding and easy to find, but burdened with mud, the second narrow and straight and paved with gold. At the place where the two roads issued, a heavenly person was sitting on a chair with a ''big book'' on a table that was bright and shiny. In it mankind's sins were recorded. Everyone, it seemed, had to pass before this judgment and then was assigned one of the roads.

The ''presence'' talked to Sen Ching about lies she had told during her life, mentioned her impatience, and also brought up disobedience to her parents. But she professed faith in Christ and was set upon the bright road.

Such a glimpse of the Radiance was also claimed by Zdenko ''Jim'' Singer, the Croatian man who'd had the experience with two mysterious strangers while in desperate financial straits in the park in Toronto. He had now graduated to the position of plant manager at the ink company, and his mystical experiences had also graduated.

Starting on May 28, 1989, Singer began falling into an ecstatic state during which he encountered what he claimed to be a supernatural light. ''I can only describe it as an enormous glow,'' he told me. ''It started as a rapid blend of colors that seemed to rotate or swirl for a moment, then explode into a huge, all-encompassing, and infinitely beautiful white glow. Human words are difficult. I felt something physically happening to me. It's so hard to describe in human terms. I felt a warmth, but I'm not talking about just a temperature warmth. I felt like a child or baby in the total care of a mother or father. Think of the most blissful state you've ever been in and multiply it by geometric proportions. There was an awesome feeling of well-being and peace. An awesome tranquility. It was physical and mental. I started feeling this tremendous calm. My wife Natalie and I had been lying in bed talking when it happened. It was the eve of our 19th wedding anniversary, and we were in bed talking over plans for our usual dinner of celebration. There had been nothing unusual leading up to the apparition. It had been an otherwise routine day in a routine year. Natalie and I are both immigrants from Croatia who had staked out a new life in Burlington, Ontario. Natalie worked in the rectory of the nearest church, St. Raphael's, as a housekeeper and cook, while I was plant manager for General Printing Ink, a division of Sun Chemical Limited. I was certainly not the type who had visions! I considered myself a no-nonsense administrator, and depending on my assignment and circumstances, I was in charge of between 35 and 300 employees. I was a hands-on, nuts-and-bolts type, managing materials, directing maintenance and transportation, interacting with customers across the continent. For me the only miracles were those created in the laboratory.

"From what I understand," he went on, "this is hardly the standard resumé of a visionary. And yet it happened to me. I was beginning to experience apparitions. It was the type of experience I had previously only read about and only half-heartedly believed. My state of 'ecstasy' or whatever you want to call it lasted several hours. My hands were raised, palms up as if in reverence. I'd like to stress one point: there is nothing I have ever seen on television or at the movies, nor in dreams, that remotely approaches the force and splendor of what I encountered in 1989, at the beginning of a series of profound spiritual messages. No special-effects wizard in Hollywood could hope to reproduce the radiance I saw, and the voice that came from it."

The experiences continued for a hundred straight days and included a splendid vision of Heaven—the afterlife. His wife stayed by his side, wondering at the incredible atmosphere of peace and the glow that seemed to surround her smiling husband.

"Our Lord just showed me these people standing there who seemed to be talking to each other and the background was like they were standing in front of an endless and beautiful body of water," said Singer of Heaven. "They were standing there in front of this water. I saw Natalie's mother. She looked to be about thirty, wearing a white tunic and peaceful—you should see the expressions on those faces! The contentment and satisfaction on their faces, the bliss, was just unbelievable. I'm not saying this is exactly what Heaven really looks like. I believe the Lord showed things in a way the human mind can understand. He also showed me my tiny little brother, an infant, and he was still an infant. I was a young boy when he died of jaundice at 6 or 7 months old. How would I know he was my brother? And yet I knew instantly! He was standing there staring at me, with great joy like someone across the street smiling in acknowledgment—no special words or greeting but an acknowledgment that was more precious and subtle.

"It was like the Lord was saying, 'Look what's awaiting anyone who wants to earn his way here,'" continued Singer. "Natalie's mother made a big impression. Perhaps it was psychological bias, why she made the strongest impression. Another reason was probably that she had suffered much and was beautiful and humble in suffering. I got the feeling—a tremendous feeling—of love and God being in terrible pain that He can't allow people who have cast themselves so far away from Him to come into His eternal presence. When we cast ourselves away from Him, we deny ourselves the privilege of being near to Him. It's not like God casts us away. We punish ourselves. He wants us with Him. He's calling us into His embrace."

Although Singer occasionally speaks to church groups, and assisted Father Svetozar Kraljevic, a priest from Medjugorje, and Vicka Ivankovic, one of the visionaries, on a tour of Canada, he is largely a "hidden visionary" whose phenomena are being actively followed by the local bishop. I can make no final discernment on Jim—that's the role of ecclesiastical authorities—but I had interviewed him on ten separate occasions, often from morning until evening, in tremendous detail, and had only found impressive consistency in those details. I also found a deep sense of sincerity and a continuing awe—years after the events occurred—at what he had experienced. He handled everything in a very humble and self-sacrificing manner, and the fruits in his family were palpable. Both of his daughters had won diocesan awards as outstanding Christian youth.

I was also interested in Singer because there had been true prophecies. In 1989 he was allegedly told by the Lord of a coming miracle. It involved an airplane. The way the Lord put it was that *"in America, on the fields of corn, many of My children will feel My presence and the granting of their prayers as they are saved from the airline disaster."* Shortly afterward, on July 18, 1989, United Flight 232, a DC-10 on the way from Denver to Chicago, lost engine power and began to descend in spirals.

The pilot aimed for an emergency landing at Sioux City, Iowa.

The 168-ton craft cartwheeled and broke into fragments that spewed across the runway—and into a cornfield.

Miraculously, many passengers survived, and *Life* magazine even ran a story about how much the passengers had prayed in those terrifying moments.

The headline was "Finding God On Flight 232."

There were other prophecies that came true, and still others that awaited fulfillment. Just before the war in the Persian Gulf, Jim was told that in a few days mankind would make a decision that would determine whether Satan would be allowed additional years of his particular aggression. Obviously, Satan has been allowed that additional time. Did the world make some kind of wrong decision? Singer didn't know if the End Times were really coming, and didn't see any final cataclysm, but he referred to "final times" (perhaps in reference to Satan's time) and he too saw a large regional war in the former Soviet territories. *"The disturbances which, in these times, will be brought to you by the heavens are intended to exile the malefactor from your souls,"* said the Lord. *"He seduces you with false emotions and beliefs. He is the infection which you, in My Love, shall eradicate."*

If man didn't repent, two new sexually transmitted diseases would be coming, diseases that would be "more vicious" than AIDS, Singer believed.

He referred to Satan as the "Shining Darkness."

"The Shining Darkness, that malefactor, is drawing your attention to the great evil which he threatens you with, the sort of catastrophe that your minds cannot begin to

imagine," said one message, *"while he, in the meantime, is multiplying his evils in other parts of the world."*

The Lord said the dragon with seven heads and ten horns now dwells on earth.

He specifically warned that there would be terrible events in Singer's "ancestral homeland," which referred to Croatia.

And indeed, not only Croatia but other parts of former Yugoslavia were soon embroiled in a horrendous civil conflict as Serbs attacked Croatians and Muslims, focusing upon the former Yugoslavian republic of Bosnia-Hercegovina—where the Virgin Mary, warning that peace was in a state of "crisis," had indicated coming events to the Croatian children in Medjugorje back in 1981. Medjugorje, where the warnings were issued, is right there in the war zone. I was there in 1989, and while there were always those ethnic animosities, no one really foresaw the intensity of such a conflict and certainly not the attendant atrocities as Serbs destroyed or heavily damaged hundreds of churches. I visited the city of Mostar during the conflict, touring Peter and Paul Church, which had been completely destroyed. Churches were the first target in many villages and bullet holes now scar antique altars and crucifixes.

Peasants were starved in besieged cities and women raped by the hundreds.

More than 300,000 deaths were recorded over the course of the next three years and I saw the sad death notices posted on telephone poles and watched as soldiers in camouflage gear now stood as a prominent feature in Medjugorje, once known for its supernatural tranquility.

Bosnians fled from their homeland, seeking safety in Croatian cities such as Zagreb, where 72,947 were housed.

It was the worst conflict on European soil since World War II, a terrible fulfillment of prophecy, beyond question a satanic war; no describing all the atrocities.

Yet the hour was coming when Satan's extended power—so virulent throughout our century—would meet the greater power of angels and would finally be broken.

CHAPTER 34

Gabriel's Trumpet

That's what Catholics were seeing in prophecy. Among Protestants there were different ways of stating the feeling of special times, but in general they were tapping into the same impulse. Words of knowledge flowed in such quantity that they were distributed in whole volumes. Evangelists like Pat Robertson minced few words in proclaiming a remarkable future on the horizon. In Jewish circles, the Lubavitcher sect of Hasidic Jews also saw special times.

The Lubavitchers were thought fanatical by some, prescient by others. Most Jewish leaders seemed highly skeptical of such beliefs, and a good number felt claims of the supernormal belonged in the realm of psychiatry. "I think every age appears to see itself as somehow unique and often more troubled than preceding ages," Rabbi Shel Schiffman, executive vice president of the Synagogue Council in New York, told me. "If you read accounts of people in different ages it seems to be a constant theme: people harking back to a less troubled time. Some people have tied this to the UFO phenomena and the question is: are these to be considered serious religious phenomena or is it an expression of the anxieties of the age?"

At Yeshiva University, Rabbi Shalom Carmy, who teaches philosophy and Jewish studies, saw it in sociological terms. "From the beginning of the century there have

245

been many Jews who've felt the time of Messiah is coming, partly because of the apocalyptic nature of the century: persecutions, the Holocaust, breakdown in morality, and so forth. All these things cause people to think that we are coming to a point of crisis that has to go one way or the other.''

Dr. Grosso, the skeptic I've quoted before, also went so far as to link some of the angel stories with channeling and UFOs, although he saw both largely as myths brought about by a sort of millennial hangup. ''It's fascinating how indestructible is this fantasy of total transformation,'' he says. ''That's the underlying hope: that there will be a complete renovation of the world, lions lying down with the lambs. The connection with the millennium is very direct. You read the Scriptures and they say that the End Time will be preceded or led by the arrival of the angelic hosts. So that's very much a part of the millennial imagery. As for angels, I think the angel epidemic is a tip of the iceberg of related phenomena like channeling. The angels are functionally equivalent. They work the same way, as tutelary spirits. They provide assistance. The UFO contactee movement, which flourished in the 1950s, during the atomic-bomb scares, had people in touch with big brothers from outer space and once again these beings are functionally very similar to angels and other types of tutelary or helping agencies of the supernatural order.''

That view was greatly at odds with academics such as Father Scanlan, who though cautious, believes very much in angelic intervention and invokes his own guardian each day. It was also contrary to scholars like historian Shimon Deutsch, a rabbi who says there indeed has been a swell of authentic mysticism (including a rash of healers in Israel) and points to miraculous cures which took place after blessings by the Lubavitcher leader and mystic Rebbe Menachem Mendel Schneerson before he died in 1994. Schneerson experienced visions and apparitions, according to Deutsch, and inspired massive rallies in Israel, Russia, France, Australia, India, and the United States—a global lighting of Hanukkah candles. The rebbe had said that the fall of Communism was a sign of the Messiah's coming, the direct symbol of pounding swords into ploughshares. Indeed, he even used the analogy of lions and lambs setting down together peacefully.

Even skeptics like Grosso are perplexed at certain of the signs. "Now and then you come across a story that is very puzzling—where a being appears mysteriously, helps, guides, inspires another human being, and then disappears in circumstances that are quite unexplainable. As for the hitchhikers, there are some cases that are pretty well-authenticated."

And the reports mushroomed as the 1990s opened the last decade of the millennium. There were hitchhiker stories from Massachusetts to California. The mystery had amassed tremendous momentum. I remain wary that many of them were simply reheated folklore, a continuation of what had started at the end of the 1800s, or that they were deceptive spirits. But many ministers and priests remain open to it—including some highly prominent deliverance ministers who are far more expert than I am in detecting just such demonism—and at any rate, it was so widespread that it has to be reported as part of the prophetic impulse.

And it crossed all religious lines.

Where before there had always been vague allusions to Christ coming "soon," now there was a new twist: the "hitchhikers" were telling drivers that the Archangel Gabriel was bringing the trumpet to his lips.

This seemed dramatic because the trumpet in *Revelation* is used by angels to announce purification (8:7).

Excitement was reportedly raised at the 700 Club, one of the nation's largest ministries, when a caller from Tennessee told the story of passing an old shabby-looking man walking along the highway. She felt she heard an inner voice tell her to pick him up. She really didn't want to but, listening to that "voice," dutifully pulled over and the man entered the car. He suddenly looked clean and neat. "You know, I don't usually pick up strangers," she told him frankly.

"But the Lord told you to pick me up," he casually stated.

I don't know what else was said. I know only that the story was making the rounds and had been punctuated by another hitchhiker prophecy. The man supposedly told her, "I have a message for you: Gabriel's trumpet is almost to his lips."

These stories were coming or soon *would* come from virtually every state. It was a truly baffling phenomenon. Surely many were fictive, changed slightly according to locale and storyteller. And I wondered: what was meant by "soon"? Roadside strangers had been mentioning apocalyptical events as coming "soon" for several *decades.* Jim Bramlett of Campus Crusade reported an incident that happened in Atlanta, while in Eureka, Missouri, was an eyewitness named Gary Ridings, 34, whom I located. Ridings, a craftsman, belongs to A Land of Praise Christian Church and claimed his experience occurred during 1993 while in his Ford pickup. "It was later in the evening, probably 10:30, and I was coming on Highway 270 towards Highway 44 and I guess somewhere in between 40 and Manchester Road there was a fellow walking down the highway. He wasn't really hitchhiking and I just pulled over for some reason, which is very strange because I would never do that.

"The man was just a regular guy with silverish, grayish hair, I'd say in his forties, maybe closer to fifty. I would say, an estimation, between 5'8" and 5'10" and I'd say 160-170 pounds. I thought this would be a good opportunity, this fellow, he's not hitchhiking but he probably needs a ride and I could share Jesus with this man.

"He didn't look like a rough-looking character at all. I thought maybe he had run out of gas or had car trouble. So, I felt pretty safe about the whole thing. He wasn't dressed up. I can't even remember what he was wearing to be honest with you. I think it may have been jeans. It was very casual. He was walking the same way I was driving. He kind of had a cheery type of face, reddish. I picked him up and he said, 'Thank you, thanks for the ride.' If I'm not mistaken, it was around the time of the flooding of the Mississippi in St. Louis. I think I commented on how disastrous it was. I said a lot of things to try to get him to say something and he really didn't say anything.

"So we started heading out 44 West towards 141, and in that area there are a lot of lights because there's a great big fireworks place, big tent on the left-hand side as you're going out west 44 and we just passed it, almost to 141, and this fellow said, 'The coming of the Lord is at hand.' And when I turned to the right side—he was on the right side and I had been looking to the left—he wasn't in the truck any longer. He was gone.

"I was still going on the highway—probably 55 to sixty miles an hour. He'd been in the truck maybe ten minutes. I was scared. I pulled off the road. More than anything for me, it may have been just a warning to know the time, to know the work that must be done and to change some things in my life. Maybe I haven't been fervent enough. It's one thing to witness and to share your words, it's another thing to live the words you share. I think it calls me to awaken unto righteousness, a greater walk with God. That's what I really think it's all about. It made Heaven seem much closer."

Another report had an older man on a highway leading to Las Vegas—a man who, as in previous cases, pronounced that Jesus is coming before he disappeared in the back seat. Whether or not the Nevada case was true, any real angel of warning could pick few better places than Las Vegas. In no other locale is materialism and sensuality so openly exhibited. There are casinos that display pagan gods or even advertise "the greatest occult show" on earth. There are exhibits glorifying a Roman emperor with laser-and-light shows casting images that look demonic. There are numerous strip joints and call-girl services, advertised on the roofs of taxis or in the yellow pages. There are chapels where couples can find instant marriage (one even has a drive-through window) and "science of the mind" churches.

If you win at the slots you can visit the local palmist or buy a crystal at Glitter Gulch Jewelry.

You can also find the emblem of the serpent at a major casino on Las Vegas Boulevard.

If the hitchhikers were angels of warning, they were picking their spots, and whether or not it was the Apocalypse, something was going to happen. There was too much of a prophetic pulse. There were too much phenomena—wherever it came from.

One day—perhaps "soon"—the other shoe would drop.

CHAPTER 35

The Old Man
Near Chattanooga

Most eyewitnesses were ordinary folks who lacked pretension. A good example was Vincent Tan. He is a chemist who now lives near Chattanooga, in a place called Collegedale. His birth name is Tan Ban Soon. He was born in Singapore and his parents were Buddhists. Tan, 30, had discovered Christianity while he was at a library reading a book on nuclear physics. Between the pages was an offer for a Bible course—just stuck there. He ordered the course and became a believer. Then in 1983 he immigrated to America.

On the night of March 25, 1993, Tan was working late in the laboratory, striving to complete a series of tests due the following day. He had moved his car close to the building because there'd been criminal activity in the area. Every once in a while he glanced through the window to check the vicinity of his car and the empty parking lot.

At about 1:30 a.m., Tan prepared to leave the private lab, where he did environmental and other kinds of analytical tests. He was looking out the door and ready to lock up when he happened to see a man standing next to his car on the passenger side.

"The first thing I did was I went back to my office and

prayed about it because I wasn't sure what was going on,''
says Tan. "I wasn't sure what he was up to. I prayed about
it and thought that I would use chi-sao (a form of martial
arts) if I had to. I didn't know how many people were out
there. And I thought it would be better if I had something
with me, and so I took a rod with me and stuck it behind
my back. I went out the door closest to the car and I opened
the door and I asked the man in a very casual, polite way,
'Hi. Can I help you?'

The man replied, "Hi, Vincent." Somehow, he knew
Tan's first name.

"Do I know you?" Tan asked.

"Not really." The man had been looking into the car.
He was dressed in jeans and a t-shirt, thirty to 35 years
old, with well-kept short hair.

"What is your name and who are you?" Tan asked.

Then the man said, "I have the name of the secondary
and primary school."

It was an allusion to the school Tan had attended, Saint
Gabriel primary and secondary school in Singapore.

The man continued. "You don't need to use chi-sao on
me."

"How do you know I was going to do chi-sao?" a
thoroughly befuddled Tan demanded.

"I know." Then he added cryptically, "And by the way,
mom is fine. You love the Lord very much, don't you?"
Vincent's mother had heart complications that were worry-
ing Tan but could not have been known to the stranger.
After Vincent responded to the question about loving the
Lord, the stranger said, "He loves you very much too."
Then in a different, more serious tone—an unforgettable
tone—the stranger referred to the Lord and said, "He's
coming very, very soon."

It was like the classic hitchhiker legend—but this time
in a lonely parking lot. The man asked for a cup of water.
Tan said sure and turned for a moment. When he glanced
back at the door he was gone. "Just like that. I never got
to see him. I never saw his face. It was dark. All I know
is that he was a male person. I never really got a chance
to look at him. I would say he was between 5'11" and 6'1".
He had a normal American voice, no accent, very normal,

except for the one instance when the man said, 'He is coming very, very soon.' There was a change in the tone of his voice, a change in urgency. The rest of the time he was pretty much casual.''

The next morning, back at work by 9:45, Tan wondered if it was a dream or really true. He was strongly compelled to share the experience with people. He prayed for a while and was able to remember the event more clearly. He was still trying to convince himself.

That night, Friday, 24 hours later, he had a dream. "I dreamt the whole scenario that happened, but this time I was looking down at the trees and it was like 3-D. I saw the man, his back only, and I saw myself standing at the door and heard my voice. I was looking at myself because I'd never seen myself before. I heard my voice say, 'Hi, can I help you?' I heard the whole conversation. At the end of the dream, when he asked for a cup of water, I turned around slightly and the door shut with a click and that was the end of the dream. I woke up. It was two or three in the morning.''

His pastor vouched for him, asking him to share the experience from the pulpit. As for his ill mother, she had undergone surgery and was recuperating nicely—a verdict announced by the doctors, Vincent later learned, around the same time that he was speaking with ''Gabriel.''

Had that been Tan's only experience, it would have been chalked up as just another strange encounter, one of thousands. But his second experience occurred two days before Christmas in 1993. And in many ways it was more astonishing. ''What happened was that I was coming home from visiting a friend, about three miles away from home, at about 11 o'clock at night, and I saw the truck on the roadside,'' says Tan, who also drove a truck. ''I wasn't sure I wanted to stop, because it was cold and I didn't know who was there. So I figured I'd just drive by and see if it was someone I should stop for. So I did. I drove by and saw this old man, about 75 years old, an old man dressed in like overalls. I stopped my truck and he was looking at something on his truck. It was a very old Ford truck, faded white and beat up, yellowed with a bit of rust. It was on Strandifer Gap Road in Collegedale, about 17 or 20 miles from Chattanooga. I felt sorry for him and asked if something was wrong."

The man said, "Yes, my battery is dead."

"Can I help you?" asked Tan.

"Yes, could you jump me with the jumper cables from your truck?"

The man was clean-shaven, 5'7" or 5'8", a little taller than Vincent and stout, like a rotund farmer. He weighed maybe 170 to 185. Full head of gray-white hair, short and neat. Normal nose. Long and pinched a bit at the end, but normal. Gray eyebrows.

Vincent didn't think he had jumper cables in his own truck. Usually the cables are in his second vehicle, a car back in his garage. He was ready to say no but then he suddenly remembered that he *did* have jumpers in the truck. What happened was that in October he was going somewhere else and a guy stopped him on the road and asked him for a hand—another dead battery. He'd told the man he had no jumper cables but that he would go get them if he wanted, although he was running late for an appointment. Instead, Vincent ended up praying and after prayer spotted a coat hanger on the ground, picked it up, broke it in two, put one end to the battery's positive end and the other to his own battery, used the other piece to somehow touch the two cars and ground them, and they were able to start the car. After Vincent left, he'd decided to buy cables for his truck.

"So I remembered I *did* have a jumper cable," Vincent told me. "I turned my truck around so our trucks were together and then I put his on because I had always hooked mine on first, but then I realized he was done, he had put it on already. I said, 'Well, we're almost ready. But I need to do something first.' And he said, 'I did it already.' And I said, 'Did what already?' And he said, 'I placed bricks by your tires already. That's what you wanted to do.'"

Tan always chocked the tires because the hand-brake was weak. But how did this guy know? Also unusual was how the man had been able to so quickly connect his end of the cable without a flashlight. It was very dark.

"I said, 'I guess we're ready.' Then he said, 'Can we wait

in your truck while it's charging?' I said sure, because it was cold out there.

"We went and sat in my truck and he said, 'Can we pray? God can work miracles, even start a car with coat hangers.'"

Again Tan was astonished. The man also knew about that time he had started another car with the hanger. "I was starting to realize this was somebody who was not natural. I told myself months before, with the other experience, that if I got another opportunity to meet a person like that, I would ask a lot of questions. But, you know, it was like he knew exactly what was going on in my mind and I couldn't ask any questions. It was as though my mouth was shut tight and all I could do was answer all that he asked me. So I just sat there and when he said, 'Can we pray?' I said, 'Sure.' This is what he prayed: 'Most holy and powerful God in Heaven, we know You are coming very, very soon. Help us now in Your own time and way, in Jesus's name. Amen.'"

So powerful was the prayer that it sent chills down Vincent.

"He asked me if I thought the Lord was coming soon. I said, 'Yes, I do.'

"The man said, 'He is coming very, very soon. And we need to be ready now and always.' He said, 'I'd like to share something with you. Can I use your Bible?'

"I said, 'Sure.'"

Tan had a King James Bible in his glove compartment. The man couldn't have known that either, but he immediately went for the compartment and took out the book. Then he said, "Do you read your Bible?"

"Yes. I try to read it every day."

"That's very good. It's unfortunate that many do not do that. Having Bible-study is like being in a big room with many candles that are lit."

This was yet another indication to Tan that the man was not a normal human because a week after Independence Day, Tan had had a dream in which he was looking in a very big room and in this room there were many candles but not all of them were lit. A week later he had the same dream again.

Although Tan's truck was dark, the old man turned right to the pages he wanted in the New Testament. Tan shined the flashlight. The stranger read two verses from *Matthew*, chapter 24:36 and 42: *"But of that day and hour no one knows, not even the angels of Heaven, but My Father only. . . Watch therefore, for you do not know what hour your Lord is coming."*

Then he turned to another book and it was *John*, 14:1-3, as Vincent held the light: *"Let not your heart be troubled; you believe also in Me. In My Father's house are many mansions; if it were not so, I would have told you. I go to prepare a place for you. And if I go and prepare a place for you, I will come again and receive you to Myself; that where I am, there you may be also."*

Last he had a verse from *Revelation* 3:11. He flipped right to it: *"Behold, I come quickly; hold that fast which thou hast, that no man take thy crown."*

While the man's eyes seemed normal, "there was something about his voice. He had a very strong voice. Very strong voice. Very powerful. And I cannot think of words to describe it. I wouldn't say it was low; it was very powerful, strong. He knows what he's saying and is very sure when he says something.

"After that he closed my Bible and put it back into the glove compartment.

"Then he said, 'The truck is ready.' So we got out and he went up to the truck and I asked him if he wanted me to follow him until he got home and he said, 'That won't be necessary but thank you very much. By the way, I left a small token of appreciation for you. It will be enough to fill up your car tomorrow with gas.'"

Somehow the stranger knew Tan also had a car.

"After he said that he'd left a small amount of money and drove off, I followed him because I was going the same way. I could just see his tail-lights. Not too close. I wasn't sure where he was going. I followed him for anywhere between a half a mile and a mile. We came to a really sharp curve, a large sharp curve that leads into Collegedale, and as soon as he made the sharp curve, he just disappeared. I thought, 'Well, I better catch up with him.' I thought trees were blocking my view. So I sped to catch up with him.

But he was just gone. And I didn't see any sign of the car. I thought I couldn't see him because of some trees. I had followed him a long while because he was going slow. Four to five minutes. I thought maybe he went down a side road. But I looked and looked and there was no side road."

So Tan went home and the next morning was going to tell a friend what he'd experienced. He wanted to go over and talk after an appointment and errands. He took his car to a service station to fill it up, but when he got there, he realized it didn't really need any gas, he hadn't been using it, but he figured he would fill it anyway. Tan pumped as much as he could. It would only go to $2.34.

"On the way home I was going to go to my friend's house and I realized I'd left something in my truck—a Christmas gift for my friend—so I went home, put my car in the garage, and was tidying up the truck when I found some money on the passenger seat. I counted it and there were two one-dollar bills, a quarter, a nickel, and four pennies—exactly $2.34."

A month later Tan was driving by the same area and noticed there was no vegetation where he'd lost sight of the man.

"I realized there were no trees where he disappeared. I realized he had disappeared in front of my eyes."

CHAPTER 36

Mightiest Warriors

The two incidents intensified Tan's prayer life as did such experiences in other places. I continued to collect signs and wonders. One was from the Most Reverend M. Pearse Lacey, Auxiliary Bishop Emeritus of Toronto. He told me about a recent surgery and its curious aftermath. It was on his shoulder, a six-inch incision.

"For some strange reason the wound only partially healed, leaving a hole the size of a quarter and half an inch deep and continuously draining," says Bishop Lacey. "The bandages were changed three times daily. I left for Betania (the shrine in Venezuela) with my sister and some 95 pilgrims and a small bag of bandages. The doctor's parting remarks were that perhaps we would have to do a skin graft when I returned. I did not go to the shrine specifically for a cure, though I believe that was in the back of my mind. While there I was prayed over by Maria Esperanza, and I rubbed some of the miraculous waters of Betania on my shoulder. Within a couple days the wound dried up and healed completely. I returned to the surgeon only a few weeks ago. He was greatly curious and he examined the area closely and admitted that in operating he had observed the possibility of another cancer. His examination, however, revealed no evidence of anything cancerous. He found a healthy mature healing."

In May of 1994, when the missionary Gwen Shaw returned from a trip to Asia, she reported a miracle that had taken place in Nepal nearly two years before. "On September 7, 1992, at 5 p.m., a big cross-shaped cloud appeared in the sky over Taksen village in central Nepal," she reported. "It then changed from a cloud into a fire. Suddenly, the image of the Lord appeared on the flaming cross. The whole village watched it for two hours. They fell on their knees, crying and weeping and all were converted to Jesus Christ. I believe this is just the beginning of many wonderful things that will take place in these last days as the sign of the Son of Man will appear in Heaven (*Matthew* 24:30). Jesus said that these things would happen just before the angels gather His elect from the four winds, from one end of Heaven to the other."

In Los Angeles, Dominic Berardino, one of the area's major charismatic leaders, said his people were experiencing visions of a great protective force. These were subjective visions but they were similar to many other reports. "There was a lady from Arizona who wrote me a letter two years ago after she got back from our large charismatic convention in the Anaheim convention center," Berardino says. "There was an *incredible* closing liturgy with Cardinal Roger Mahony, and she said standing behind the cardinal center stage, she saw an incredibly large angel who stood higher than the whole arena and that was more than fifty feet to the roof. Then there were larger angels around the whole place because we had filled the auditorium, and she said outside she saw warring angels that made a full circle around the outside of the arena and were keeping out black, fallen angels. There was this tall angel, maybe it was a principality or a power—whatever classification you want to give them in the hierarchy—standing behind the cardinal. There was such a sense of presence. Everyone felt that. And six months later, other people shared that they had seen similar things."

Such protection was certainly needed, for it is known that satanists and witches gather to throw curses upon charismatics, according to Berardino. They even have photographs of Christian leaders to use during their rituals. That's a problem in a metropolitan region that has a good share, probably ten percent, of the nation's 30,000 to 40,000 witches. Add to that the increasing decadence of the film industry, which not too long before had come out with the blasphemous *Last Temptation of Christ* (released by a film conglomerate whose headquarters were appropriately nicknamed "Black Tower"), and it was no surprise that on June 28, 1992, a 7.4 quake struck Southern California, causing the earth to actually drop several feet in the Yucca Valley (the capital of methamphetamine production).

The region was also plagued by mudslides, riots, and brushfires fanned by the scorching Santa Ana winds (which *The New York Times* described as "weather worthy of Satan").

I heard a similar angel story—a story of angels in the midst of decadence—when I was speaking in the Washington D.C. area in 1993 at the same time that homosexuals were converging there for a huge gay-rights rally. Just before the Christian dinner I was attending, one of the homosexuals staying in the same hotel walked mystified toward the tables at the entrance to our banquet room, seeming very confused. When someone asked if they could help him, he said he just wanted to know what was going on; he thought he had seen an angel down the corridor!

He probably did. By the early 1990s, their presence had become monumental. *Time* and *Newsweek* ran cover stories on angels, and there were specials on network TV. A poll showed that 69 percent of Americans believed in them. I heard from folks who saw an angelic apparition gently touching the forehead of a sick young man or arriving in human form to bolster the morale of an ailing ministry. I heard from a non-denominational worshiper in Indiana who saw a light like Singer's light, one that got brighter and brighter in his bedroom until he could sense the Lord. I spoke to a woman in Alabama who claimed to hear angelic music at night, and to hear their swishing movements. I met with Father Joseph Whalen, a Connecticut priest who has recorded dozens of miracles related to the intercession of the Archangel Raphael. In Minnesota, Leo Murphy, the former mayor of a town called Eagan, was praying with his wife in a chapel at St. John Neumann

Church when to their astonishment, they saw a sizable young man prostrate on the floor facing the tabernacle. He was kneeling down and then lowering the upper part of his body so that his elbows and stomach were on the floor.

"The first thing that flashed through my mind was Sister Lucia, one of the three children who Our Lady appeared to at Fatima—her description of the angel prostrating before the communion host," said Murphy. "Angels always prostrate before Christ in His tabernacle just as the man was doing. After prostrating himself for some time, he would straighten the upper part of his body while remaining kneeling with hands folded, praying intently, facing the tabernacle. He kept repeating this up-down movement until he sat down in the chair closest to the tabernacle."

The man stared at Murphy and his wife in a rather unusual way and when they finished praying, he rushed over to them. "He did not walk or run like we do, but rather seemed (nearly) to levitate across the floor," claimed Murphy. "He immediately greeted us and shook our hands as he came next to us. My wife commented that his hand was hot, much warmer than a normal human." He spoke *to* them more than *with* them; he made statements of fact and did not respond to what Murphy and his wife said.

The man expressed dismay that since Vatican II the Catholic Mass had become more of a social gathering than a worship service.

As usual, the stranger disappeared after leaving the chapel.

I received reports of angels coming in consolation. I received reports of them in times of desperate, even terrifying need. In Houston was Becky McGinnis, who in 1990 had given birth after a very long and painful pregnancy. Frightened about losing the baby, she had put the infant under the protection of the Archangel Michael and began to devote herself to a prayer chaplet invoking his aid. At the same time, her four-year-old daughter was having nightmares on nearly a nightly basis—so scared she often slept with her parents. They live in a four-townhouse complex and shared a wall with another, rather mysterious townhouse.

One night after dinner they were asked if they would allow the people who lived behind them—a peculiar bunch—to hook into one of the McGinnis' outlets. The strange neighbors had apparently lost their electricity. A cord was plugged into an outlet just outside the McGinnis' townhouse, on the patio.

"This went on for a couple nights," said Becky. "Then I awoke one night to such terror. There was nothing to be seen outside from our bedroom window upstairs, but fear was all around me, almost physical. I crawled back into bed, pulled the sheet over my head, and began to pray the prayer to the Archangel Michael, written by Pope Leo XIII. *St. Michael the Archangel, defend us in the battle. Be our safeguard against the wickedness and snares of the devil. May God rebuke him, we humbly pray, and do thou, oh prince of the heavenly host, by the power of God cast away Satan and all the evil spirits who prowl about the world for the ruin of souls. Amen.* I must have said it twenty or thirty times, like a litany, until I fell into a deep sleep. When I awoke again it was morning."

After breakfast Becky looked onto the patio and saw ropes strung from one wall to the other, draped over the outside wall. "Someone had tried to get onto the patio! I ran outside and sure enough, a small work table outside was pushed up to that outside wall where the ropes were dangling. I had jelly legs and a sick stomach when I went back into the house. Our patio door had been broken several months earlier and we had no lock on it for protection. I was unknotting the ropes when I heard someone at the door, knocking. It was the lady from behind us and she was a little upset. She said, 'There was no need to threaten my husband last night. He only wanted to flip the fuse box to turn back on the electricity.' I told her I had looked out but had not seen anyone and my husband had slept through the whole night. She explained that her husband was on top of the fence when he heard a man's voice in his ear. It said, 'Unless you want a shotgun down your throat, get off that patio NOW!'"

The neighbor had flown off the fence, deciding he didn't need electricity after all. Who it was who chased him away remained a mystery.

By the next weekend the apartment behind the McGinnises was vacant, as if those weird neighbors had fled from there. It turned out that they were reputed pornographers and the room next to their daughter's bedroom—the one sharing the same wall—was where they had been taping their escapades.

"And that explained her nightmares," said Becky. "Their equipment and movies were confiscated by the police. Within days of their hasty departure, the Mafia was knocking on the door searching for the people and their movies. In an apartment in another building was something even more shocking. The upstairs closets were packed with stolen merchandise. In the downstairs bedroom, walls were painted black and an image of Satan came out of the black wall. It had been a shrine to Satan and the bathroom was a drug lab. The patio was a jungle of marijuana."

While it certainly seemed that an angel had prevented something sinister from occurring that frightening night, Mrs. McGinnis was careful to remind people that it is not the angels we go to first but always Christ and His Blood. We plead His Blood in such circumstances. We plead His Blood and say: *Praise You, Jesus, You are our Strength and Love. Praise You, Jesus, You are the Name above all names. Praise You Jesus, You are Emmanuel, God with us. Praise You, Jesus, You are King of kings. Praise You, Jesus, You are the Holy One of Israel. Praise You, Jesus, You are our defense. Praise You, Jesus, You are the Everlasting One and the Mighty Warrior.*

In Finneytown, Ohio, two young girls were walking through a wooded area when they were confronted by a couple of teenage males who wanted to violate them. As the boys began carrying out their intentions, a large man holding a shotgun suddenly came out of the woods. The teenagers fled in terror, releasing the girls, who insisted to their parents that they had been saved by an angel.

In Mexico City, a lawyer named Rocio Sanchez de Yzar went to the bank to remove something from her safety-deposit box shortly before the bank was set to close. This story was told to me by the Most Reverend Donald W. Montrose, bishop of Stockton, California. "As she was preparing to replace her box, the door of the vault snapped shut," said Bishop Montrose. "She was alone inside the vault. At first she didn't worry because she was sure someone would remember that she was in the vault. No one came. She could not open the vault from the inside. After a time, she took off her shoe and knocked on the vault door. No one came to her rescue.

"She sat down and began to think. It was Friday afternoon and nobody would return to work until the following Monday.

"After a while she noticed it was becoming harder to breathe. 'Am I going to die in here?' she thought.

"By this time she was praying earnestly. By now an hour had passed. She thought of her guardian angel and began to pray to him.

"Suddenly, on its own, the door of the vault snapped open. She was nearly in a faint. No one was in the bank except a uniformed guard. He came to her rescue and called an ambulance."

There were many stories of roadside rescues, of cars suddenly appearing out of nowhere to come to someone's aid, or to lead them through danger. There were angels who helped pedestrians cross dangerous roads. And there were always the intriguing hospital stories. One woman who was being operated on for a brain tumor recounted the great sweetness and comfort of an anesthesiologist—but later learned that there was no such person on the hospital staff. In Arizona, Arlene Gillman told a similar story. "In September, 1993, I had my third surgery on my leg within two and a half years," said Arlene, who lives in Mesa. "While praying to Jesus, I said, 'I don't mind going through the surgery again, Lord, but it's the little things.' Not enough sleep at night and those dreadful blood tests taken every morning around 4 a.m. My veins are very hard to find and sometimes they don't give enough blood to fill a tube." Back in intensive care after the surgery, Arlene had her experience. "On the first night a young man in his early twenties came into my room for a blood draw. I said to him, 'Oh, no, not another blood test.' And he said, 'Just a pinch.' Well, I never felt the prick or the needle break through the skin. All I felt was the needle on my arm. He had a fair complexion and nice, short, light-brown hair, well-groomed. As I watched him leaving my room he disappeared when he got to the doorway.''

In Palm Coast, Florida, a friend of mine named Barbara Stephens lost her wedding ring while she was cleaning rest rooms at a church before an annual celebration of the Medjugorje anniversary.

Two days after she lost it, while in the dining room, she heard a "plop" on the carpet in the family room and thought it was a palmetto, one of the huge bugs for which Florida is famous.

She figured it came through a ceiling vent, which had happened in the past.

But when she went to look, it was her missing ring, right there on the area rug in the middle of the room.

CHAPTER 37

God In A Cave

No one was ever in any more danger than Dave Gant of
Bryant, Alabama. Owner of a logging company, Gant was
also a scuba diver who liked to go "spelunking," that is,
diving in underwater caves. On Saturday, August 15, 1992,
at around 10 p.m. Gant and two other divers took a boat
to the north of what is known as Nickajack Cave. The cave
had been fenced off by the Tennessee Valley Authority and
so they tied their boat to the fence, readied their gear, and
dove down under the fence and into the cavity.

It was in a mountain at a reservoir and they were looking
to spear catfish. They started in and about 150 yards back
there was a channel some thirty yards wide that opened
into different crevices and caverns. The water led to a back
"room" that was filled with bats. The only way in was
through the water. They went down and came back up four
times. The next time they dove, it was just Dave and his
friend Scott. They were down for about 12 minutes at a
depth of around forty feet.

"When we went to go up, we came to solid rock," says
Gant. "That's something that's happened to us before, but
we always just swam under a ledge. All you have to do
is make a circle and you'll find your way out. That's what
we did. We made a circle, back to the wall, on the roof
of the rock, back to the same place we started. We went

to make a bigger circle and ran into another wall."

They realized they were lost. They were in trouble. They couldn't find their way back to the surface. They had apparently gone into another cavern. Scott had a compass and knew the mouth of the cave was to the north, so he descended to the bottom to level his compass.

Dave checked Scott's air gauge. He had 800 pounds—only good for about 12 minutes. Dave had 3,000, which would last about half an hour. Gant motioned to Scott that he was heading back to the top. He'd look for air.

There was little to see. They had lights, but they were only good for about eight feet. After that it was just fading colors and murkiness. When Gant went back down he couldn't find Scott. He had kicked up too much silt. Where he expected to see Scott's light it was total blackness.

Scott had followed his compass and gotten out of the cavern just in time. When he surfaced there literally was not another breath left in his tanks.

David Gant wasn't so lucky. He had more air, but he was still lost—totally disoriented. "If it wasn't for my bubbles going up, I wouldn't have known what up or down was," he recalls. "I didn't have any idea which way was out."

After twenty minutes Gant began to breathe slower in an attempt to conserve his diminishing air supply. All he could see were "honeycombs" and passages too narrow to get through. At 10:30 p.m. he spotted air and thought for a moment that he was back in the original cave. But when he popped his head into the air his head hit a roof of rock. It was just an air pocket about 18 inches in height and 25 yards long. In the center was a stalactite—a cylinder of lime shaped like a football and coming to within an inch of the water. Gant swam to it and held onto the rock for the next hour. His head was all that was out of the water. He remained there with the help of inflation gear, holding the rock like a straphanger. All he could think about was Scott, wondering if his friend was alive. "I had been thinking of how it was going to be to take that last breath of air," he says.

Fish swam by, including gar, making startling splashes. On three sides was slick limestone rock. Hours passed with excruciating slowness. At about 2:30 a.m., still trapped in the underwater cavern, it occurred to Gant that the way out might be under the air pocket. He put his mask back on and decided to take a quick look despite his low air volume. He dove for about three minutes but ran into nothing more than rock wall or passages that were again too narrow.

There was nothing. There was no perceivable way out. At 4:30 a.m. he tried the other side, to no avail.

More time passed. Minutes seemed like hours. Hours seemed like centuries. Around 9 a.m.—after 11 hours in the cave—Gant heard what sounded like bubbles. They were coming up from the bottom. He figured it was a team of rescue divers and went down as fast as he could to intercept them.

The floor of the cavern was a pile of boulders and the bubbles were coming from them.

There were no rescuers.

"That's when I really lost hope," he says. "It was like someone pulled the life out of me."

He surfaced again and held onto the stalactite. "I just gave up on life then." He was fatigued. The water was 64 degrees. It was already a miracle he wasn't suffering from hypothermia. He'd been expecting rescue divers to pop up at any time, but none had. It was just him and the darkness and all the water, along with the saving grace of the stalactite.

"I was just hanging on that stalactite feeling sorry for myself. This was now Sunday. It was getting up towards dinnertime. There were hundreds of prayers going up for this old boy. There were churches that their whole service was holding hands praying for me. I'd been there 14 hours and had never said the first prayers. I'm ashamed of that. I was depending on *me*.

"About twelve o'clock the Lord put a conviction on me. He let me see myself for what I was, and the kind of life I'd been living. I'm ashamed of it, but my nickname had been 'Dirty Dave.'"

A Baptist, Gant hadn't been a real churchgoer since the age of 15. But suddenly he began to pray. And the Lord responded—in a huge way. "The first thing He did was save my soul. He came into my life and saved me. I know what 'saved' means. I know what it feels like. I felt Him three times, one right after the other. The Lord knew what was in my heart, he knew I was sincere, and there wasn't anything between me and Him. Not *anything*. I done gave up on life. I was looking for the afterlife.

"I asked the Lord to come into my life to save my soul, and he did it, just like that. It felt like a big invisible hand, three different times, went straight in my chest all the way to my toes and pulled out pure evil—pure evil. Three different times, one after the other. After the first time I didn't think I could feel any better. I felt so clean. After the second time I felt just that much cleaner, and after the third time it's a wonder that cave didn't cave in, I was shouting so loud, echoing in that cavern, just praising the Lord for what He just did for me."

He was still hanging onto the stalactite. He considered it the "hand of God." He felt the Lord's presence in it. Then Dave's hand let go and he felt the Lord lay him on his back in the water and "baptize" him. When he came back into the air pocket he was brimming with the Spirit. "I never felt so clean and so alive, so happy in my life! I was just praying to the Lord to take me."

He was then startled by a voice. It was like a conversation between his heart and brain. God was in his heart. "The Lord told me to get my family ready to meet Him," says Gant. "Then He said, *'Go tell the whole world that I'll be back for my children before the year 2000.'* I didn't add a word to it or take a word from it. That's exactly what He told me to say."

There was only one problem: How was Gant to tell *anyone.* He was ready to die in that cavern. Yet, somehow he knew his situation would be taken care of.

"I'd always heard about visions but didn't know what one was," says Gant. "Until Sunday. This is shortly after 12 noon. The Lord gave me a vision. It was like a conscious dream. It wasn't played out on the wall, it wasn't like a movie projector on the wall. It's just exactly like a dream. The Lord let me see myself in my black wet suit in the daylight hours. He let me see Mapleview Park (near the reservoir) and what appeared to be hundreds of people all over it, everywhere—just like it was. He let me see myself get out of the boat and tell everyone that the Lord saved my soul.''

The next five hours passed like 15 minutes. Gant felt like a dead battery being charged. His light was nearly dead, but nothing fazed him. Suddenly he saw a strange fog directly in front, where he hadn't tried to find an escape route, believing it was a wall. The fog was slightly luminous, just light enough to see, about 12 feet wide and eight to 12 inches high over the water. Inside were what looked like four oblong objects. They and the fog were slowly moving away. The fog left his sight but still reflected back slightly into the water.

Then the cavern was dark again.

After twenty hours the air pocket was thinning and it was getting hard to breathe. The TVA was lowering the water to try and flush his body out—everyone figured him for dead—and the wider space thinned the air pocket.

But suddenly there was a roaring sound and pockets of air began to arrive, replenishing the air pocket for 15 minutes.

At 5:30 p.m. he heard more sounds, and this time it was a pair of divers—a rescue team. They called to each other. They were all giddy with disbelief. And Gant headed towards them. The way out was the same way Gant saw the luminous fog leave.

No one expected to find him alive, not to mention ''feeling like a million dollars.''

As they left the cave, he saw the many people watching from a platform, and about a quarter mile from there, Mapleview Park was filled with hundreds of onlookers and well-wishers, just as the Lord had promised him.

CHAPTER 38

Time Is Short

Like Gant, the world needs its evil purged or we too will find ourselves in the dark, with water up to the neck and little room in which to breathe. That's the essential message, especially from Medjugorje, where the Virgin Mary, in apparitions that have been indicated as credible by everyone from David DuPlessis to John Paul II, urged us on February 25, 1992, to draw close to God "so He may protect you and guard you from every evil."

"Satan is strong and wants to sweep away the plan of peace and joy, and make you think that my Son is not strong in his decisions," Mary also said on August 25, 1991. *"Therefore, I call all of you, dear children, to pray and to fast still more firmly. I invite you to renunciation for nine days, so that with your help everything I wanted to realize through the secrets I began at Fatima may be fulfilled. I call you, dear children, to grasp the importance of my coming and the seriousness of the situation."*

She has come as Queen of the Angels to advise us that we have entered a period of warning, a period that precedes the change of era, a period that is indeed very serious. Since 1989, when the quake struck San Francisco, America has been a nation under judgment. And not just in California. "For the last year, it seems, the Northeastern United States has lurched from one abnormal weather event to another," said a baffled William K. Steven in *The New York Times* during 1993. "First came the coolest summer in decades. Then one of the worst northeasters on record lashed the Atlantic seaboard in late fall. December and January were unusually mild. Successive snowfalls surprised the region in February, and hard on their heels last week came yet another damaging northeaster. And while all this was going on, the Far West was enduring monumental snows and drenching winter rains that reversed a 10-year pattern of drought."

Worldwide there had been eight "catastrophic windstorms" in the 1960s, then 14 in the 1970s and double that during the 1980s. In 1992, a record 1,297 tornadoes stormed the United States and there were brushfires in California that caused $1.7 billion in insured damage, comparable in monetary terms to the great Chicago fire more than a century previously. There have been floodings of the Rhine, windstorms in England and France, flooding from Chicago to Italy. Mudslides haunted Asia and South America, while a volcano erupted in a huge way in the Philippines.

As before, the signs in nature often coincide with major events in the societal domain. A particularly interesting sequence occurred in April of 1992, as pro-life demonstrations began in Buffalo at the same time that an important case concerning abortion in Pennsylvania went to the U.S. Supreme Court.

It was just then that a 6.3 quake hit California near a town called Joshua Tree and a few days later, on April 25 and 26, at the screeching height of the nationally-televised abortion battle in Buffalo, that three more tremors struck near Ferndale—the eighth largest seismic disturbance in California history.

By the end of the pro-life protests, which dominated the national media and spelled a defeat for pro-lifers (who failed to rouse the public and close the clinics), Los Angeles was up in flames.

Rioters and looters took to the streets in the aftermath of the Rodney King verdict.

A little taste of brimstone.

LA in flames!

Then, on "gay pride day" in 1992, a day before presidential candidate Bill Clinton gave an abortion-rights speech in Little Rock and the Supreme Court upheld a woman's "right" to abortion, the most powerful quake to hit California in forty years rumbled out of the high desert east of Los Angeles. The tremors shattered glass, set fires, and opened huge cracks in mountain roads. So powerful was *this* jolt that it sloshed swimming pools in Idaho and rocked houseboats on Lake Union in Seattle.

Gay-rights activists had to brave the tremors to attend their parade.

That was followed by a series of peculiar storms, peculiar in the number of them that were deemed "storms of the century." In August of 1992, just a month after the quake, South Dade County in Florida was hit by Hurricane Andrew, which left 250,000 homeless and caused an estimated $18 to $30 billion in damage. At its peak Andrew's winds approached 180 miles an hour and caused *the costliest disaster in American history.*

The next month, a hurricane named Iniki hit Hawaii, causing $1.6 billion in insured damages. Iniki was the fourth costliest in history and Hawaii's own "storm of the century."

In December, a "northeaster" ravaged the East Coast with waves that reached heights of thirty feet and destroyed hundreds of homes from Maine to Virginia. Scuba divers in New York had to rescue motorists along the East Side highway, while on Fire Island (famous as a wealthy homosexual resort) expensive homes were actually washed out to sea.

Those tempests were closely followed in March of 1993 by a great blizzard that swept from Florida to Maine, releasing more rain, sleet, hail, and snow than any storm since 1888.

You guessed it: the National Weather Service declared it "the single biggest storm of the century."

But that was hardly the end of it. Months later a colossal flood hit the Midwest as relentless rain turned the Mississippi into an inland sea. The flood, described by one meteorologist as almost of "biblical proportions," became the *second* greatest disaster in American history, destroying or damaging 56,000 homes and inundating an area comparable in size to the state of Indiana.

"The Year of the Killer Weather," said a cover headline in *Life*. "Why Has Nature Gone Mad?"

While not every tremor or storm could be declared a sign from Heaven, there clearly was an increase in intensity. Of the ten most costly catastrophes in American history, five had occurred since 1989 and the top four most costly disasters of all time—Andrew, Hugo, the San Francisco quake, and the Mississippi—were recorded in the short five-year period between 1989 and 1993.

Then came 1994 and the earthquake that shook Los Angeles.

The time was 4:31 a.m. and the date January 17, a Richter 6.6 that rumbled for ten terrifying seconds just north of LA, collapsing freeway interchanges, bursting gas lines that spewed eerie flames, and jarring virtually everyone in America's second-largest city awake. No wonder mystics like Duduman, not far away in Fullerton, saw flaming swords and trumpeting seraphs. No wonder there was even a minister who claimed to be in touch with the angels of Sodom! The quake put a number of network shows off the air and damaged the sets of "Murphy Brown" and "N.Y. P.D. Blue," striking at the heart of America's entertainment business. "It was one hell of a wake-up call," said Steve Bornfeld in *The New York Post*. "As if being whacked by a vengeful god, the Ritz-Carlton Huntington Hotel here—housing about 100 TV columnists from around the country—shook, rattled, and rolled yesterday morning thanks to the violent earthquake that rocked Southern California."

The homes of actors like Jack Nicholson and Warren Beatty were damaged. The trophy room at the estate of Michael Jackson's parents was shaken into disarray. In home after home, the first thing to fall seemed to be the television set. A young upwardly mobile film-industry couple died tragically as their million-dollar house tumbled down a hill, and when President Bill Clinton visited the disaster zone, he and top aides were rocked by two massive aftershocks, one measuring more than five on the Richter and causing light fixtures to sway precariously over the president's nervous head.

There were collapsed roads and electrical outages. There was eerie silence on the normally jammed freeways. About 100,000 businesses were damaged, causing an insurance crisis. The quake's epicenter—the area in which it sought to inflict the greatest damage—was in Northridge, which along with two nearby towns is the porn capital of the world. The triangle formed by Northridge and the communities of Chatsworth and Canoga Park contains nearly 70 companies that produce 80 to 90 percent of the X-rated videos made every year in the United States. Newsmen said an office owned by VCA Pictures, the industry's giant, was "totaled" and that virtually every porn company suffered some kind of destruction. "I'm telling you," said one agent, "it's enough to give you an attack of religion."

But God was speaking to more than just pornographers. By the very next day, much of the Northeast and parts of the Midwest were reeling under an assault of winter weather that in some ways was more severe than the Blizzard of '93. The attack lasted much of the week. For three days in a row, a state of emergency was declared for Kentucky as freezing rain, heavy snow, and subzero temperatures closed all four interstate highways that crisscross the state. "This is the absolute worst situation we've ever had to face as a result of a winter storm," noted James M. Everett, executive director of Kentucky's Disaster and Emergency Services.

The storm would not let up. Businesses and government agencies were closed up and down the East Coast—including federal agencies in Washington. The state of Colorado, digging out from three feet of snow, reported 160 avalanches. There were also avalanche warnings in the state of Washington; 17 inches of snow in Boston; and for New York, the coldest temperatures in half a century.

It was 22 below zero in Pittsburgh and zero even in places such as Nashville.

The unusual mass of frigid air was one of 15 storms that would hit the New York area that winter, while in pricey Malibu, California, a fierce rain unleashed flows of mud that buried cars on a coastal highway. Hills stripped of grass by previous wildfires turned into muck that in some cases flowed three-feet deep on the scenic highway. The torrent of earth poured into a dozen beachfront homes and sandbags had to be used to save lavish houses. The soupy mud smashed through doors and ran like a waterfall off the decks of the stilt-perched homes in the celebrity-packed community 25 miles west of Los Angeles, said one report. ("There was this huge bank of mud coming toward me. The things you see in the movies, it was happening to me," added Vera Smith after a mudslide engulfed her Mercedes.)

The severe weather, coupled with the quake, slowed the music industry and caused a bit of soul-searching. "Fires, floods, and storms in Southern California in 1993 led to 26 deaths and $1.3 billion in damages," noted *The New York Times.* "And the 1992 riots touched off by the acquittal of four police officers in the beating of a black motorist caused more than fifty deaths and $1 billion in property losses. Add to those disasters the scores of lives lost and the billions of dollars of damage from the eathquake in the San Francisco area and the Oakland Hills firestorm, all within the last five years, and Californians cannot be blamed for feeling they are living in apocalyptic times."

In yet another "coincidence," the New Testament reading at Catholic Masses on January 23, 1994—the very first Sunday after the LA quake—was from *1 Corinthians* 7:29-31 *("I tell you, brothers, the time is short")* while the Old Testament reading that same Sunday was about Jonah's warning to Nineveh.

There was also apocalyptic fever in the African nation of Rwanda, where the seers at Kibeho had been given terrifying visions of anarchy, foreseeing war, a "river of blood," and so many dead—in many cases missing their heads—that there was nowhere to bury them.

By the spring of 1994—a decade after the vision— Rwanda was plunged into just such a holocaust. The small central African country collapsed into anarchy on April 6, 1994, after President Juvénal Habyarimana, a member of the majority Hutus, was killed in a suspicious air crash. His death came on the eve of fulfilling a peace accord between the Hutu-dominated government and the minority Tutsis. Upon Habyarimana's death, militant Hutus began massacring Tutsis such that, within 14 weeks, an estimated 500,000 were killed—more dead than in three years of fighting in Bosnia-Hercegovina and a more rapid pace than the killing of Jews by the Nazis.

Just as the Virgin had predicted, the bodies were beyond real count and many were decapitated with machetes. Mass graves were dug, but there were so many corpses that as many as 10,000 were thrown into the Kagera River, bobbing toward Lake Victoria.

On May 18, 1994, a subhead in *The New York Times* read "Blood in the River."

Blood even flowed down church aisles.

Several priests were buried alive and in a single 24-hour period 250,000 fatigued or blood-soaked refugees streamed across the border to Tanzania, running for their lives.

Soon, in what was widely described as the greatest such tragedy in a generation, the count of refugees became 2.2 million. "This is the beginning of the final days," fretted a resident of Goma, Zaire, where many of the refugees fled. "This is the apocalypse," he was quoted as saying on the cover of *Time*.

Cholera swept through the refugees, while at night the volcano of Nyirogongo, overlooking the camp, glowed ominously.

CHAPTER 39

The Spirit of Anti-Christ

Slowly, in the gradual and forceful way in which He works, the Spirit of warning is moving across the world. More than that, He is warning us so that greater disturbances can be avoided. What some call the period of mercy has nearly run out and we are now at the threshold of a cleansing that will continue to gain momentum if we persist in our circumstance.

We approach the end of a special period, the end of modernism and perhaps also the end of the first Pentecost. We await a new Pentecost. We await a world more in tune with the Lord. We await a return to human goodness. At Medjugorje, the Virgin Mary said her appearances there would be her last on earth, and considering that her manifestations have been reported since the first century A.D., we may take that to mean that we approach a major and glorious resolution.

The Bible's prophecies, especially those in *Matthew* 24 and *Revelation*, are living documents that continually repeat themselves. In every age they repeat certain aspects of the prophecy. Only parts have been realized; the entire predictions have never been completely fulfilled. Some eras are known for their famines, others for their war and spiritual hostilities. Some are infamous for their plagues, schisms, or persecutions. Several periods have been known for their false prophets. With each passing era, the repetition of signs, the ongoing cycle, comes nearer to completion. The signs enter a larger cycle, with increasing fulfillment. Wars are greater in number. So are famines and quakes. We see the onset of classical plague. We see more false prophets.

If matters grind on as they are currently grinding on, if we see a continuing rise and then a tremendous surge in major tremors, plagues, and war—the kind of huge battles, truly momentous battles, forecast by so many seers—then the alarm must be rung. Someday the regional happenings we are now seeing, those storms and brushfires, may evolve into increasingly large storms, mudslides, and drought—increasingly frequent quakes—until, one day, they are punctuated by a mega-event that will finally get our attention, a disruption in the ocean or immense winds or some form of rumbling or "fire" from the sky, as the many seers have long warned about. Such events are not unknown to man and are not unknown to our specific continent. It was only 1,000 years ago that a tidal wave covered what is now the Seattle metropolitan area. More recently, on September 1, 1992, an offshore quake sent tsunamis or tidal waves crashing along a 200-mile stretch of Nicaragua's coast, with waves as high as 30 feet, leaving 13,000 homeless.

These pre-signs are sneak previews of what larger regional disturbances may come.

Our era is fascinating because we have come closer to fulfillment of all the elements in *Matthew* 24 than most previous epochs. If current trends continue, we will come closer still. Only in our era has the Gospel been preached—nearly—to all the nations. Only in our era has there been the military technology to turn a third of the waters into wormwood. Only in our era can we cause actual fire to rain from the sky (if not from a downpour of meteorites). Only in our generation has there been such a public influx of the supernatural. Only in our era have our worldly institutions moved in such a sophisticated fashion—using the high-tech of scientism—to move *against* that same supernatural element, institutionalizing apostasy and secular humanism. Only in our generation

have they sought to institutionalize the slaughter of inno-
cents, which we should recall as having occurred during
momentous moments in the lives of Christ and Moses.
Even in Nineveh, abortion was against the law! Although
it is not yet as progressive as in Nineveh or Babylon, where
government authorities constructed public idols, only in
our time has the occult—our abominations of desolation—
become so refined and taken so many sophisticated forms.
Add to that all the supernatural phenomena and the *"signs
in the sun, in the moon, and in the stars; and on earth
distress of nations"* set forth in *Luke* 21:25 as an addendum
to *Matthew* 24, and you have an interesting scenario.

As I write, reports come to my desk of "fragrant oil" falling upon a Christian center in Florida and the same oil ooz-
ing from holy statues in Catholic circles. There are reports
of Mary appearing in dozens of nations while Christ, set
back and awaiting His major manifestation, appears along
the Turkish border in southeastern Bulgaria to Muslim
mullabs. In Arkansas, a woman claims that while driving
from Branson to Lead Hill on June 5, 1994, she saw a supernatural rainbow. She felt the Lord was telling her it
represented a "final outpouring" of the Holy Spirit before
our wickedness is forcefully purged. "So many different
colors, and the biggest I had ever seen," she said. "It
wasn't an ordinary rainbow. I knew at once I was in the
presence of the Lord, so I got out of the truck. I was caught
up with the Lord and saw a round circle appear in the sky.
A ray of light came down through it and touched the earth.
Sparkles of light danced from one end of the rainbow to
the other. It reached the end of the rainbow and then the
sparkles of light began to dance back to the other end of
the rainbow again. It came to the end and danced around.
Then the lights and the ray went back into the circle and
it closed."

While we cannot confirm the many similar accounts, and
should never base our faith on them, it is preposterous to
think that all such signs are fabrication or mass hysteria.
If but a fraction of the phenomena you have just read are
true, we are in an unusual time indeed, one that grants us
hints of what will come as future supernatural signs, just
as battles and tremors are indicators or pre-signs of larger

such events in the coming years or decades. Identical phenomena arrive from Catholics, especially at Med- jugorje. I myself saw signs in the sun, moon, and stars above that incredible village during four visits. I saw the sun throw off terrific colors. I saw it pulse. I saw it send rays of light to the earth, rays that formed a perfect cross. I watched with other pilgrims as a star split into three smaller stars that turned blue, red, and white, squiggling downward through the sky before forming back into a nor- mal star. I saw what looked like tiny meteorites—said to be angels—whiz past Podbrdo hill seconds before an appa- rition. I saw them with my own eyes. I saw manifestations in the moon and on August 15, 1990, I saw an inexplicable light over St. James Church that resembled a dove. I watched it from different angles in broad daylight for at least 15 minutes.

I also saw the "distress of nations" in Bosnia's horrific combat. This is another clue. This is another indication or pre-warning—before the arrival of larger warnings. This is a preview of potential coming events just as the storms and quakes and viruses are precursors or forerunners of natural mayhem that will come if we don't get our act together.

They are the beginning—only the beginning—of warning.

The sky there and around the world, the spiritual sky, the sky in the heavenlies—seen as fire by the world's many visionaries—is the fire, the red light and the glow, of purification. It is not God's vengeance so much as our rejection—and thus the withdrawal—of His protective and bonding grace. God's power is greater than all forces of nature, and when it recedes, when it is rejected and with- drawn, we encounter chaos in nature, in society, and most importantly, in our hearts.

We are more prone to quakes. We are more prone to crime and riots. We are prone to warfare. We are also more susceptible to demonic attack. A spiritual chastisement already is in progress. The spirit of anti-christ, long- prophesied, is now prominent in the world. It has always been around but it is prevalent over the U.S. as it hasn't been before. There is no telling how long it will continue to mushroom. If, in my opinion, this evil is broken during the current decade, then the long-awaited Anti-Christ—the actual personage of evil—will be postponed for another era. The prophecies in *Matthew* will begin a new cycle. On the other hand, if the evil episode we are currently experiencing continues to worsen, there may well be those alive who one day will live under the Anti-Christ's direct and nefarious influence. There is a great evil developing, a new evil, according to one prophecy to which I adhere, an evil "not currently known to man. It will arrive almost imperceptibly, with few people noticing the depth of its evil, for it will appear to have beneficial and convenient aspects. It is an evil comparable to abortion—that is to say, that even if evils as great and widespread as abortion were to be eliminated, this is enough of an evil that it will present mankind with an enormous challenge."

Such evil is allowed by God as a merciful test, a second chance that, depending on our response, will lessen or increase the coming chastisements. I was fascinated that in the above prophecy, given under reliable circumstances in December of 1990, it was forecast that in the autumn of 1994 mankind would face one such test, a decision that would determine the length and breadth of coming purifications. As I write, the world community is set to gather in Cairo under the auspices of the U.N. to make a decision on the worldwide promotion of birth control and abortion. Hopefully, the world will make the proper decision.

If abortion and other abominations of desolation are allowed to continue, we will move into a more direct period of warning and then into the period of judgment. This is why the trumpet sounds. This is what is meant by the mystical impulse. A voice like a trumpet sounded with Christ's appearance in *Revelation* (1:10), and it was Gabriel—so often mentioned by the mysterious strangers, so prominent in the current rash of angel stories—who first explained the abomination of desolation to Daniel and who also sounded a trumpet back then, telling Daniel that *"seventy weeks are determined for your people and for your holy city, to finish the transgressions, to make an end of sins, to make reconciliation for iniquity, to bring in ever-*

lasting righteousness, to seal up vision and prophecy, and to anoint the Most Holy."

This is the real message behind the otherwise unfathomable appearances of strangers who mention that the trumpet is being drawn to Gabriel's lips. Along with Michael, Gabriel is one of the angels before God, the angel of annunciation, mercy, and revelation, the only angel, along with Michael, mentioned in all versions of the Old Testament, believed by Mohammedans to have dictated the *Koran* and in Jewish legend to be the angel who dealt destruction to sinful cities of the plain, including Sodom and Gomorrah.

He comes now with the Heavenly host to indicate mercy and purification. Neither he nor the other angels come to give us sensationalistic and ridiculous prophecies. And that's what we are often faced with: implausible predictions from questionable sources. According to the September 9, 1994 *Los Angeles Times* news service, one such prophecy in current circulation is that elderly Nazis hiding beneath the South Pole are plotting to take over the world with the help of space aliens! Another popular forecast is that a monster quake is about to make Phoenix a seaport, split the continent, and cough up Atlantis. Yet another doomsday scenario informs us that earth is ready to pass through a galactic "photon belt." As the newspaper indicated, one early Church father fell into the same trap, analyzing the dimensions of Noah's Ark and calculating that the world would end in A.D. 500. Other students of doomsday and The End included Joseph Goebbels and the occultist Nostradamus. They are not exactly the kind of men Christians should be linked with. We must be careful of the company we keep. We must walk a tightrope between authentic prophetic impulse and wild imaginings. Events most likely will evolve over time and often in very mundane fashion.

It is my belief that in many cases such purification or chastisements will differ according to region and in some cases will not be immediately noticeable for what they really are. It is the watchmen who will see. It is the prophets who will pronounce. Prophecy is not always set in concrete, but this much can be said: the winds of the Holy Spirit are blowing and if we prove worthy they will scatter the great evil before it manifests further as the spirit of anti-christ.

Of special concern is the way nations are handing over their militaries and economies to global powers. Any movement for one world government, especially one with military force and designs on a global religion (using the ecology) must be confronted and stopped. Many are the prominent visionaries who warn of globalism. On September 18, 1992, the Ukrainian activist Josyp Terelya received this alleged message from the Virgin Mary: *"The Lord often uses the word 'dragon,' the name that God has given to the devil. And the words 'beast' and 'false prophets,' these are the forces which the devil—the deceiver—uses for his evil purposes. The word 'beast' is a sign that you are to understand as symbolizing the visible organizing of Satan on earth, which today dominates many nations on earth and is composed of three evil spirits: false religions, politics, and commerce. And the 'false prophets' are that part of Satan's world organization which masks itself in Christianity, that advertises itself everywhere and has the voice of nations to speak out of a dead head."*

In Omaha, Sister Nadine Brown, the intercessory nun who had a number of angelic encounters, told me about the most extraordinary one, an account of needing a coffee pot one day and heading to a shopping area about ten minutes from her religious community. "I'd never been there before, but I thought, I don't have much time, I'll just dash down there," Sister Nadine says. "About three o'clock in the afternoon on a weekday I pulled in. I don't notice people much, so it was interesting that when I pulled in I saw one of the most handsome young men I had ever seen in my entire life. It reminded me of how Scripture describes David when he was a shepherd boy. I'd say he was in his twenties. Anyway, I parked the car. He was somewhere in front of me in the parking lot. I got out of the car and had to go to the back of my car because that's the direction I was going to that particular store. I got out of my car and turned to walk to the back of my car and there he was. There he was! I didn't process it at the time, but I had just seen him clear across the parking lot. Now here he was, face to face with me."

According to Sister Nadine, the man directed her toward *Daniel* 7:23-24—the same message that tied into Gobbi's warning about the "black beast." She believes that it pertained to a global body of politics that would come against America, England, and France, a new world empire about to rise, unique in that it would be run by a committee after the three nations are subdued by an eventual world dictator. When, after a few abbreviated minutes, she came out of the store, she tried to find the man but naturally could not.

Many are the biblical interpreters who go further. There are a good number of prophets who believe the Anti-Christ himself is now alive, perhaps a young man. We take great pains not to become paranoid, and we acknowledge that there is a trickster out there; that however heavenly a revelation seems, it must **always** be held at a distance and tested before we accept it into our hearts. We pray to the Holy Spirit for constant discernment. We make sure that the titillation of visions doesn't replace praise and prayer, and we spend twice as much time with the Bible as with any other books, including this one. We keep our hearts open to the subtle voice of God, praying and fasting instead of treading onto dangerous supernatural territory. We keep in mind that dramatic pronouncements, whether about Christ or the Anti-Christ, can be more in the spiritual realm than the worldly one. We keep in mind too, that important events are often prophesied far in advance, as it has taken now 150 years for many of the reputed and astonishing prophecies from LaSalette to unfold. We heard of the Anti-Christ back at the very beginning of our era from holy mystics such as Jeanne le Royer in the 18th century, or going further back, to Dionysus of Luxembourg, who died in 1682 and who reminds us that, while we must be careful about paranoia, we should always be equally careful about the rise of the great evil. "After the birth of Anti-Christ the people of the world will be very wicked and godless," said Dionysus. "People of real virtue will be very scarce. Pastors in many places will neglect the service of God... Even the religious will crave for worldly things."

In the first-century *Didache* is this additional warning: *"In the last days false prophets and corrupters shall be multiplied and the sheep shall be turned into wolves and love into hate. When their iniquity shall have increased they shall hate each other and persecute and betray; and then shall appear the deceiver of the world as the Son of God. And he shall do signs and wonders and the earth shall be given into his hands and he shall do evil such as has not been done through the ages. Then shall all created men come to the fire of judgment and 'many shall be scandalized' and perish. He however who shall have persevered in his faith shall be saved from the accursed one."*

The lying wonders will continue to increase and of late have moved steadily in this direction. I believe that if the evil is not overcome by the end of our decade—a time-frame consistent with seers such as Gobbi as well as many evangelicals—then the abomination of desolation may well begin a final thrust towards his takeover of the temple. I am concerned that the 1990s will serve as a major entrance to new forms of evil. I fear a repetition of the 1960s. It does not escape my attention that Woodstock has returned, nor does it escape my notice that it is heaped with occultism. As *The New York Post* reported on August 16, 1994, one of the key musicians "doesn't go to rock festivals like Woodstock just because he enjoys entertaining large, muddy crowds. Rock shows, says (this musician), are where he sees UFOs. He saw some at the first Woodstock and some more at last weekend's festival."

These are not just weird acid trips. These are often real psychospiritual indicators. There is voodoo in our music. There is voodoo in many aspects of our culture. There are demonic images interwoven with what our children watch on MTV and there are cartoon characters who advocate rebellion or subtly feed our youngest the first precepts of New Age philosophy. There are educators who care less about education than about fulfilling a political agenda and there are children who are dispensed condoms and taught that sodomy is a viable "lifestyle." There's a child killed by gunshot in the U.S. every two hours. There are celebrities and government leaders who cannot shake scandal— who are even accused of molestation or murder. There is nudity now even in prime-time and in mainstream newspapers. There are debates about genetic engineering, frozen embryos, euthanasia, and fetal-tissue research.

These are issues that serve as a prelude, and as a doorway, to the great evil. I believe with all my heart that this great evil will be broken by the Lord. If we don't help Heaven break it, then the Lord will dispel it through the more painful avenue of chastisements. His angels are poised. The archangels are poised. They await the command. They touch the earth at all four corners and beseech us to observe the signs from Heaven. I have not attempted to come up with a specific date, knowing the history of specific predictions and how they can become problematic.

During 1994, there was great excitement that something major would happen on June 9, a date several seers had received in "revelation." Most of it started with Pastor John Hinkle of Christ Church in Los Angeles, a good and humble man who claimed to have heard a voice say that on June 9 the Lord would "rip the evil out of this world." He interpreted this message as meaning that millions would be touched and that the world would be "totally changed" on that day. He expected everyone in the world to see God's intervention and glory. He didn't know exactly what that would mean, but he expected a "supernatural manifestation, a sign, a miracle." Obviously, there was no cosmic sign or miracle that day, no event that caused millions of sudden conversions. In Arvada, Colorado, David Griffis, assistant director at Youth With A Mission, also claimed to have been given the June 9 date and suspected it had to do with an earthquake. He expected commerce to come to a halt and the earth to be covered with smoke—obviously, some kind of monumental calamity. "A day of darkness is coming that no man can stand," Griffis quoted the Lord as saying. "He will cry to be consumed, but it will not be so. The earth will move and the sky will be dark. All will hide from Me, but My glory will be revealed."

While the dramatic aspects of their prophecies failed to materialize—indicating the danger of public interpretation—there was a powerful and highly unusual earthquake at 00:33:16 hours Greenwich Mean Time on June 9 (an earthquake nearly 400 miles below ground, felt from

Bolivia to Canada) and there is no saying what transpired in the heavens. Similar messages come to us in tremendous volume. They buzz over fax machines and through the mail or take the form of locutionists who now populate every diocese and ministry. When they get too specific, they often become inaccurate. They are not blueprints. They are rough road maps. They are picking up on a prophetic impulse just as first-century Christians picked up the spiritual undercurrent, as did Gregory the Great when Rome was under siege, and the 18th-century seers as modernism and humanism swept across the planet.

This part of Hinkle's prophecy I can accept, the word supposedly from the Lord to more closely review *Matthew* 13, which in verse 41 says, *"The Son of Man will send out His angels, and they will gather out of His Kingdom all things that offend, and those who practice lawlessness, and will cast them into the furnace of fire."*

For the faithful, there will be a glorious light one day in the future—on a date that no one can predict—as God steps in to show His Love. Hinkle claimed to have had a vision of that manifestation, "this great glorious light" that is "awesome" and "beyond description." He saw that glory "coming over the whole world and as it came over the world, it changed everything that it touched. I saw two men fighting and they were just going at it. His glory moved across it and instantly they stopped fighting and started dancing and singing and praising God. The glory of God is about to be revealed, so awesome the world can't even imagine. He told me one time—and it's in Scripture—that 'the mind of man cannot conceive My glory.' That's what is going to happen. There was a glorious, glorious light, a great shaft of glorious light, kind of golden white, scintillating like diamonds—indescribable."

CHAPTER 40

When Heaven
Touches the Earth

Based on all I've seen and heard, I have my own little "prophecy."

I believe matters may shape up like this: regional events, battles, and disasters will be sent to break down the pretenses of our technological society over the next few years and perhaps several decades. We will hear, for example, of something like a dam bursting in one country, with unusual loss of life, or a major typhoon in another—not just a major storm but a monstrous one. These events will grow or lessen based upon our response. When, in whatever period it occurs, the Lord seeks His major action, many inventions of mankind will be dismantled and there will be more of a peasant attitude and way of life everywhere. The world will not end but will significantly change. During the period of change will come an event as a great warning—more a fear of fire than fire itself, or some other global alarm. There may also be strange loud rumblings and possibly an event that involves a great roiling of the ocean. At some point there is also a war on the horizon, if not Armageddon, then perhaps a miniature armageddon; our era's own "armageddon" as there have been mini-armageddons before.

Storms, tremors, food shortages, and societal unrest, along with viral mutations that cause virulent disease, will increase in various places during this time of trial and purification, and perhaps major effects will be seen in several of the larger cities. I must admit that I doubt America will remain a superpower unless it quickly changes its current course. (I am surprised at how many seers envision not only a decline but sometimes even its destruction—whether internally, in a moral and economic meltdown, or by way of foreign enemies.) The global event which I mentioned as a worldwide "alarm" may be an astronomical scare of some sort, and if so, perhaps there was another preview or precursor in Shoemaker-Levy, the comet that we watched hit Jupiter: not something that kills us but rather serves as a wake-up call. I note that the comet began to hit Jupiter on July 16, the feast of Our Lady of Mount Carmel, which was how the Virgin allegedly appeared to the youngsters in Garabandal, Spain—the visionaries who, among other future glimpses, claimed in the 1960s to have seen a coming event that will be "like two stars...that crash and make a lot of noise, and a lot of light...but they don't fall. It's not going to hurt us but we're going to see it and, in that moment, we're going to see our consciences."

The Lord will do whatever He has to do to break down our pretense and our Godless society.

If we respond, He won't have to do as much.

If we pray—but most importantly, if we convert non-believers—many coming events can be greatly lessened.

In my opinion the Anti-Christ, whenever he does come, will have tremendous influence—a man of influence, not actual raw political power. We note that Karl Marx was one of the most powerful men of the last two hundred years, yet ruled no formal government. Perhaps few will notice his influence until afterwards. He will not have blatant visibility until his plan is accomplished. That is to say, he will not rule, control, and be tremendously obvious at the peak of his influence. He will be like a super-Marx, his power more immediate, his spirit fouling the temple.

Whether such events are in the near or more distant future is difficult to predict because God's time table is not only different than ours but also fluid. It contours through time according to human response. There is flexibility. There is patience. God will allow only that which He absolutely *must* allow. Will we finally see fulfillment of *Matthew* 24? To do so, for that prophecy to complete itself in our time, we would have to experience much greater tribulation than we have so far, as well as see the sun darken, the stars "fall" from Heaven, and the moon without light. The pre-signs of such an event have probably not yet occurred. I don't know if they will in the near future. But I believe that many incredible events will occur between now and the year 2040, events that will bring our era closer to fulfillment before beginning a new cycle. In that sense, and on a spiritual plane, they will indeed be apocalyptical. If not the Second Coming, we will witness some kind of a major manifestation of Christ's glory and power. There will be an awakening that will be much greater than previous such "awakenings." The Lord will in some way be heard and felt in an unusual infusion of grace—heard from east to west and north to south, and perhaps in the not-too-distant future.

Often, I wonder about private revelation. Often, I believe that personal prophecies go too far. Often, I question certain reported phenomena. Yet, there is something about this one, the source of which must remain anonymous, that caught my attention. It is supposedly from the Lord and was given on December 3, 1990: *"I will come not as a man of flesh, but like My mother, who already nurses Me and holds Me in her arms, as a light and power. I will manifest Myself in a series of supernatural events similar to the apparitions but much more powerful. In other words, My 'second coming' will be different than My first, and like My first, it will be spectacular to many but also unknown initially to many, or disbelieved. Yet truly I tell you, the arrogance of the world will have been broken, and so many more than normal will believe. I will come in towering light. My mother held me in her arms at Medjugorje, as an infant. I will come as she has come, in light. Know this about the world: I would not appear on television, nor ride a car, nor travel in an airplane. Would I come in such a manner? Would I live in such a world? You think of the changes in very simple ways, without realizing the fundamental mistakes of mankind. The very artifice of your societies is false and against the accordance of God's Will. This artifice shall not last. Your very conceptions of happiness and comforts are of a great evil and falsity. They will not stand. My greatest nemesis is science, even more so than mass media. The science that alters life, the science which creates a counterfeit heaven, the science that toys with the womb and genes, the science that has filled the air with the power of the enemy, the science which creates chemical witchcraft and fouls the earth, the science which seeks to create life but cannot in actuality even sustain it, the science which has denied God."*

This pretense will not stand. Soon, in my opinion, the arrogance of the world will be broken, and many more than normal will believe and praise Jesus. That is why the Spirit and His archangels are touching the earth. They are ushering in the necessary changes and guiding us into God's ultimately victorious battalion. They shield us from Satan's rampage. They execute God's commands on cities and nations. They rescue His lambs. Their presence is commensurate with the need. For every demon there are at least two angels. They are powerful in their tranquil strength, they are sweet in the grace, they are at our sides in every circumstance and will never abandon us no matter how situations seem.

They stand at the four corners of the globe to usher in a great new era, a brightness brighter than previous enlightenments. For after the purification comes the Glory of God and reverence for Him in a new way. We will then truly see the touch of Heaven, and we will conduct life with Him constantly on our minds, in unison with the Holy Spirit, watching for His every signal and feeling Him in our hearts as we orient our existence to our Creator and form our lives into a constant service of worship.

We will learn the key to Heaven: love of our brothers and, most importantly, love of God.

What glory awaits us! What challenges! The joining of Heaven and earth means just that: life here more like it is in Heaven—as opposed to the way it is now, slogging in the worldly mud. Who could not look forward to this!

Heaven will touch the earth and humanity will go about life with far more consciousness of the interaction with those angels in the Spirit. We will move in the Spirit as we haven't for centuries, perhaps since ancient times, perhaps as never.

"Such extraordinary events shall take place that the most incredulous shall be forced to say, 'The finger of God is there,' " said one of the 18th-century seers, Sister Marianne Gaultier. "Oh power of God! There shall be a terrible night during which no one shall be able to sleep. These trials shall not last long because no one could endure them. When all shall appear lost, all will be saved. It is then that dispatches shall arrive, announcing good news. It is then that the Prince shall reign, Whom people will seek that before did not esteem Him. The triumph of religion shall be so great that one has never seen its equal."

The same comes from a recent word of knowledge: "Yea, and the glory of God shall be seen over vast areas of these states. For I will come, and the judgment and the glory will come together, saith the Lord."

Another visionary saw a streak of lightning tear across the heavens and the sky part and shafts of heavenly light streaming down through the opening—piercing the gloom of earth and illuminating it with a wonderful radiance.

"Through the aperture I saw descending, first the pierced feet, then the garments white as snow, then the extended hands, then the beautiful face and head of Jesus Christ, My Lord," said another seer. "He was surrounded by an innumerable company of angels. In fact, quick as a flash of lightning the entire heavens were filled with seraphic heavenly hosts, cherubim and seraphim, angels and archangels, surrounding the Christ of God."

Infirmities of the spirit will be cleared away, along with worldly rubble. We are entering a different era. It will take time for the world to be disinfected and healed. But in the end it will be a different planet. It will be God's planet. It will again be seen as His creation. When the archangels descend, it is a special time, and just as lower-ranking angels arrived in full force earlier, so now come these higher spirits—Michael, Gabriel, Raphael. They and the other archangels raise their trumpets. They unsheathe their swords. They hold the cosmic hourglass. They are poised to eliminate a great demonic disturbance and they will not fail. Their victory is declared by the Blood of Christ.

Mighty is His army, mighty in majesty, mighty in the anointing. Great glory! Sound the trumpet of Gabriel! The blanket of darkness will indeed be parted by God's light and the satanic night will turn to the dawn of His new morning.

Notes

Chapter One: One of those who has written poignant angel accounts is Joan Wester Anderson, author of *Where Angels Walk,* published by Ballantine Books. I first met Joan during a taping of the *Joan Rivers Show* in New York and she subsequently helped me with contacts in angelology. The Graham quote comes from his book *Angels: God's Secret Agents,* which is probably the bestselling book on angels (Tyndale House, 1971). The Robertson quote is from a pamphlet called, "Angels, Demons, and the End Times," published by the Christian Broadcasting Network in Virginia Beach, Virginia, 23463. The Scanlan quote comes from a personal interview. The figure of 69 percent comes from *Time*, December 27, 1993.

Chapter Two: For the main part I use the King James and New American Bibles. As a reference I also use *Mysteries of the Bible,* published by *Reader's Digest* in 1988. Mainly it was the Cro Magnon who represented supernatural forces and invoked them in their hunting, as is evidenced in cave art, perhaps including the horses in France's Pech Merle Cave, which seems to involve an invocation. See *The Emergence of Cro-Magnon Man,* by Tom Prideaux and the editors of Time-Life Books. The burial customs of Neanderthals, indicating reverence for the spirit, are covered in many books, including *Origins* by Richard Leakey (who, incidently, told me he is an atheist). One such cave is at Shanidar, in the Zagros highlands of Iraq. Much of the caveman ritualism seemed shamanistic and perhaps represented an early form of witchcraft. See the *Zondervan Pictorial Encyclopedia of the Bible* for "theophany." One wonders if Abraham, in *Genesis* 18, encountered a theophany of Christ. Graham believes it was a pre-incarnation theophany, for one of the three mysterious men identified Himself as "the Lord." An "innumerable company" can be found in *Hebrews* 12:22. Rembrandt did *The Holy Family and Angels,* while Michelangelo's name was signed to a sculpting called *Kneeling Angel.* The Graham quote comes from the book referenced above. Christopher Columbus and his crew sang Christian hymns on the way over and delighted in teaching them to the pagan Indians. One of his ships was called the "Santa Maria." As for the founding of America, John Adams, our first Vice President, and a key player in proclaiming the Declaration of Independence, rejoiced on July 3, 1776, that the Declaration "ought to be commemorated as the day of deliverance by solemn acts of devotion to God." I take this from *Letters in American History,* edited by H. Jack Lang (Harmony Books). Others saw the new nation of America as in mystical union with Christianity. Our founding fathers often referred to the Creator.

Chapter 3: See *Acts* for the Sadducees. The *Atlantic* article ran in 1978 and included experiments at Maimonides, Mind Science Foundation (MSF) in San Antonio, and several other parapsychological laboratories. I myself tried my hand during several informal tests and seemed able to interact with the machines. The machines were pioneered by a German physicist named Helmut Schmidt, whom I met at MSF. It is a hallmark of good research and bad discernment. The place I have mentioned my conversion previously is *Prayer of the Warrior* (it was printed by Faith Publishing, 1-800-576-6477). There were many other occurrences I didn't have the time to detail. I also investigated a severely haunted house in Binghamton where the room became so cold (in the middle of summer) that we needed jackets or sweaters. In the Chelsea section of Manhattan I was called to help at a severe haunting of a townhouse where they said a bedroom window kept opening and closing of its own volition. The moment I entered the room the window cracked. Part of my conversion story is available on an audio tape called "The Final Hour" that can be ordered by writing The Mary Foundation, P.O. Box 614, Lakewood, Ohio 44107. The tape is free, although donations are gratefully accepted. It is also detailed to a certain extent on a video of the same title ("The Final Hour"), available through Signs of the Times, 109 Executive Drive, Suite D, Sterling, Virginia 20166. The dream I refer to is in *Prayer of the Warrior*. The toxic-waste books I wrote were *Laying Waste: The Poisoning of America by Toxic Chemicals* (Pantheon) and *The Toxic Cloud* (HarperCollins). I had intended, originally, to include the fire experience in *Prayer of the Warrior*, but for some reason decided against it. I understand why now. It belongs in this volume. The fire was awful. There are few things that violate you as much as seeing all your belongings sullied and destroyed. The dense soot was black as coal and coated all the upstairs walls. It especially hurt to see the damage it did to a couple of special prayer books and bibles. But it was also a purifying experience. In life, I was quickly discovering, the difficult trials, the most intense of sufferings, are what bring us to higher spiritual evolution. They are what forge us like glistening steel—if we keep our faith and move ahead with persistence. The Lord refines us, says *Isaiah*, in *"the furnace of affliction"* (48:10). While it seemed like we'd lost everything, God replaced what we owned with newer and nicer clothes, carpeting, and furniture. And soon, members of my family moved toward deeper spiritual conversion. I've never regretted that it happened. It taught us how ephemeral material things are. I don't mention it, but about a week before the fire, I also had a dream in which I saw the second floor full of smoke. I watched the fire develop. Because of that dream I knew, in running back upstairs when it actually happened, how the smoke would move and how much time I had. I had also made inquiries a few days before the fire about a night-deposit box at Marine Midland Bank for my important papers, but never had followed through on it! As it happened, the book I was working on turned out to be my last secular project. I had been tiring of that scene for several years, and on a subconscious level, the folks in the secular world, in the "mainstream" media, were growing a bit antagonistic, or at least disaffected, with me. There was something that seemed to bother them. There was an unspoken spiritual clash. I'm sure they didn't even know what was happening. But my dealings with magazine and newspaper editors, as well as with the "logical" and disbelieving college professors with whom I dealt (while lecturing on the university circuit), were starting to leave me cold. They felt the same way. I believe they could "read" my new spirit on a subconscious level. I wanted to do something for the Lord and not too long after the fire I moved into what I was increasingly interested in doing, Christian reportage, specifically religious charisms.

Chapter 4: See *Mysteries of the Bible* for tongue phenomenon, page 352, from which I draw. The account of Thaddaeus is drawn from *The Shroud of Turin* by Ian Wilson (Image Books). For Gnostics and the early Church, see also *The Christian World,* edited by Geoffrey Barraclough (Harry N. Abrams, Inc.). The influence of Rome can be seen in Ninian Smart's *The Religious Experience of Mankind* (Charles Scribner's Sons), page 356. Other parts I take from Clifford Hill's *Prophecy Past and Present* (Servant Publications). Anthony of the Desert I found in Yves Dupont's *Catholic Prophecy* (TAN Books and Publishers, Inc.), originally taken from *Voice of Fatima,* January 23, 1968. The account of Constantine I draw from an excellent booklet on Michael, "'Neath St. Michael's Shield," available through the Daughters of St. Paul. The Chairopta and Colossae mention is from *St. Michael and the Angels,* compiled by TAN Books and Publishers, Inc. in Rockford, Illinois. For Halley's Comet and the "sword," see *The Return of Halley's Comet* by Patrick Moore and John Mason. Some on Gregory the Great is from *Encyclopedia Americana,* along with Robert Payne's *The Mystical Centuries.* See *Last Days Madness* by Gary DeMar for past prophecies of End Times, including Luther's comment, the sacking of Rome, the bubonic plague, and the sword-shaped star. For Francis of Assisi see the spiritual classic *The Little Flowers of St. Francis*, by Raphael Brown (Doubleday). I also draw from

Payne's book the description of the Michael fast. The information about false mystics comes largely from A. Poulain's *The Graces of Interior Prayer.* There was also a saint in the 12th century who announced Anti-Christ. The best book on Teresa of Avila is *The Life of Teresa of Jesus,* an autobiography (Image Books). For Luther see *Young Man Luther* by Erik H. Erikson, and *Luther and the Reformation,* by V.H.H. Green.

Chapters 5 & 6: Some of the prophecies come from Edward Connor's *Prophecy for Today* (TAN Books and Publishers, Inc.) Aquinas was in *Summa I,* 113:4. Bokenkotter wrote *A Concise History of the Catholic Church* (Image Books). The account of Washington has appeared in a number of Catholic and Protestant newsletters, quoting the *National Tribune.* I found the actual item through interlibrary loan. Gaultier comes from *Catholic Prophecy.* Nietzsche died mentally ill (demon-possessed?), though you won't hear much of that from philosophy professors. The "sword" quote came from Marx's "The Player" (see Richard Wurmbrand's *Marx and Satan* (Crossway Books). The information on Adventists, Jehovah's Witnesses, and American revivalists, including dispensationalists, comes from Smart's *The Religious Experience of Mankind;* Barraclough's *The Christian World;* Gary DeMar's *Last Days Madness;* William Martin's *A Prophet With Honor* (from which comes his quote); John Noe's *The Apocalypse Conspiracy;* as well as various religious encyclopedias and dictionaries. Let me note that with LaSallete the message is controversial, with some arguing that it was recorded many years after it was given and that the visionary, Melanie Matthieu, had read apocalyptic literature. The apparition occurred in 1846 but the message was not published until 1879. There were also a number of versions circulating, which worried authorities. At one point the Sacred Congregation of the Holy Office in Rome reportedly ordered the faithful to abstain from reading various versions of the message or "secret." The apparition itself, however, was approved by the Church. As for another matter, I understand that Plymouth Brethren are now lukewarm to many charisms. Some background came from a series of tapes, "The Second Coming," by Rev. Stephen Barham, Ph.D., available by calling 214-783-0910.

Chapter 7: The Graham quote comes from *Angels*, previously mentioned. For Knock see *A Woman Clothed With the Sun,* edited by John J. Delaney, from which comes the Purcell quote. See *Witness* and *The Final Hour* (Faith Publishing) for more on Hrushiw. Many details of Hrushiw come from my interviews with the controversial Terelya, my own trip there, and also from sources such as the *Lviv Pravda, Leninska Molod* and *The Moscow News.* Newspapers such as *Leninska Molod* described the episode at Hrushiw as an "illusion of light." The newspaper *Free Ukraine* seemed equally uneasy. Hrushiw was the subject of a front-page article in *The New York Times* on October 13, 1987—ironically, an anniversary day celebrating similar apparitions at Fatima, Portugal. On October 22, 1987, Terelya appeared before the Congressional Commission on Security and Cooperation in Europe. In attendance were political luminaries such as Louise Slaughter and Alfonse D'Amato. Terelya discussed the Hrushiw phenomena with congressmen, especially Chris Smith of Virginia. While imprisoned Terelya was written up by columnist Jack Anderson and also in the *Boston Globe.* The eminent historian Robert Conquest said Soviet anti-peasant and anti-Ukraine operations cost 14.5 million lives. Perhaps 25 to 50 million people from the republics of the U.S.S.R. were killed during the reign of Communists during this century, one of history's great and less appreciated holocausts. Said one expert with whom I spoke, Lubomyr Hajda of Harvard, "In terms of absolute data, the Ukrainian numbers are probably higher than any other mass atrocity we're familiar with. It's not proportionately as high as what happened to the Jews—whose entire European population was nearly exterminated—and we don't have a good reckoning from China, but the Ukrainian experience has certainly been one of the most horrific of this century." I used *The Omni Space Almanac* by Neil McAleer for some facts about *Salyut* and also consulted with the Soviet space agency representative in the U.S. The information on flashing lights came from *Spacefarers of the '80s and '90s,* by Alcestis R. Oberg, Columbia University Press, 1985. At times, cosmonauts or astronauts have felt they were able to "see" car headlights and then individual automobiles down below—from what I know, an optical impossibility.

But said Chris Faranetta, an American spokesman for the
Soviet space program, NPO Energia, "Things do happen.
It's a frontier." William Walsh's book is *Our Lady of
Fátima* published by Image Books. For the angels on the
field during World War Two, see *Time,* December 27,
1993. For Pio see Ruffin's excellent *Padre Pio: The True
Story,* published by Our Sunday Visitor in Huntington,
Indiana. See also *Send Me Your Guardian Angel,* by Father
Alessio Parente, and *Padre Pio, The Stigmatist,* by Rev.
Charles Mortimer Carty. I also employ Gary Cartwright's
Galveston, published by Antheneum. For China see *Hong
Kong* by Jan Morris. There was also a huge quake in Val-
paraiso, Chile, in 1906. As for Galveston, the question
arises: did pagan and cannibalistic practices among certain
Indians curse the terrain, attracting future demons? Galveston had once been inhabited by the extraordinarily
vicious and promiscuous Karankawas. Some dispute the
reports, but others believe these Indians did a ritual in
which they peeled skin off still-living Toyal tribesman and
devoured their fat while the women danced about shaking
human bones and fingernails. There were also pirates on
Galveston Island, and they too left spiritual baggage. Later
to Galveston came a war hero, who was described as
"devilishly handsome." In Hong Kong, meanwhile, it was
not unusual for a worshipper to revere 78 gods. Childless
women begged for fertility at a phallic boulder called Yan
Yuen. Before its quake, by the way, San Francisco boasted
3,117 establishments licensed to serve liquor and 2,000 or
more illegal pubs. It should have taken the hint: there had
been 465 tremors between 1850 and 1906, including one
in 1865 that caused a well-known and frightened senator
to flee a Portsmouth Square bordello, clad only in his long
johns. For current events I often use *Chronology of World
History,* by G.S.P. Freeman-Grenville, and *Chronicle of the
20th Century,* Chronicle Publications in Mount Kisco, N.Y.
I also employ, to a lesser extent, references such as *Who
Was When?* by Miriam Allen DeFord and Joan S. Jackson;
and *The Timetables of History,* by Bernard Grun.

Chapter 8: Earthquake data is from the National Earthquake
Center in Golden, Colorado, as well as almanacs. See
Divine Mercy in My Soul, the diary of Sister Faustina, pub-

lished by Marian Helpers, Stockbridge, Mass. 01263. Sister Faustina has been beatified. Some of the information on Ukraine comes from "Report to Congress: U.S. Commission on Ukrainian Famine—1988." See also *The Black Deeds of the Kremlin—A White Book.*

Chapters 9 & 10: The Vanishing Hitchhiker was published by W. W. Norton. The Tyler quote is from his book *There's An Angel on Your Shoulder.* Joan Wester Anderson's book seems like an anointed effort. See Hope McDonald's *When Angels Appear* for Brazil story. The encyclopedia of UFOs is published by Avon. I have collected information on UFOs since junior high school and investigated several reports when I was a newspaper reporter, including two near Lake Ontario, which seemed like a hotspot. It is also old Indian territory. One of them was like a light that seemed to start out as a dot and then bloom into a larger light behind farm houses in the town of Porter, as I recall. Another was a seemingly mechanical device spotted by two couples out one Friday night double-dating in Youngstown, New York. It was hovering over electrical lines. I do not discount the possibility that other planets have life and are visiting us. The possibility that some UFOs are mechanical has been indicated at places where debris has allegedly been found, such as Roswell, New Mexico. Underline the word "allegedly." There are huge questions of credibility in most of these cases. There were also wild rumors that the bodies of humanoids were kept at the Pentagon or at an air force base. I keep an open mind but try to be a bit scrutinizing. (UFO hoaxes are legendary.) The Barney and Betty Hill case I first read about in *Reader's Digest* and then the John G. Fuller book *The Interrupted Journey. Life* magazine also once did a spread on UFOs over Ann Arbor, Michigan. One of the first books I read was Major Donald E. Keyhoe's *Flying Saucers, Serious Business.* See also a book by Frank Edwards called *Stranger Than Science.*

Chapter 11: The societal stats were sent to me by Bennett's office at the Heritage Foundation, 214 Massachusetts Ave. N.W., Washington, D.C. 20002. It's called *"The Index of Leading Cultural Indicators."* For satanism in Nebraska see *The Franklin Cover-Up* by John DeCamp, available by writing AWT, Inc., P.O. Box 85461, Lincoln, Nebraska, 68501. For UFO phenomena and cattle mutilations see *Unmasking the Enemy,* an excellent study by Nelson S. Pacheco and Tommy R. Blann, distributed by Bendan Press, P.O. Box 16085, Arlington, Virginia, 2215-1085. By the way, one California contactee, Orfeo Angelucci, prophesied in 1955 that if man didn't shape up there would be a major cataclysm in 1986. Conchita Gonzalez and her recollections are available in Joseph A. Pelletier's *Our Lady Comes to Garabandal,* published by Assumption Publication in 1971 and available through certain Catholic bookstores. See also *The Apparitions of Garabandal* by F. Sanchez-Ventura Y Pascual, and *Our Lady at Garabandal* by Judith M. Albright. A scholarly treatment of apparitions such as those at Garabandal is available in *Encountering Mary* by Sandra L. Zimdars-Swartz (Princeton University Press). I spoke to three of the alleged visionaries via phone for *The Final Hour.* For Zeitun, see "Our Lady of Light," available by writing Pearl Zaki, 23 Eggers Street, E. Brunswick, N.J. 08816. Meanwhile, Johnston's booklet on Zeitun, *When Millions Saw Mary,* was published by Augustine Publishing in Devon, United Kingdom.

Chapters 12 & 13: The information from Zdenko "Jim" Singer comes from personal interviews with him during July of 1992 and also several subsequent meetings. I spent approximately 80 hours in formal interview and several hours at other times speaking with him at his home, at functions, or on the phone. Mr. Singer also appeared with me on March 17, 1994, on the "Sally Jessy Raphael Show." I also interviewed by phone Mr. Mattox and Mr. Habini. Father Abbott sent me his angel story as a personal report. The New Hebrides account is from Tyler's *There's An Angel on Your Shoulder,* although I first saw this account in nearly identical form in Graham's book *Angels,* though Graham identified the preacher as John G. Paton. I drew the John Paul II quote from George Huber's *My Angel Will Go Before You,* along with the Huber quote. The Terelya account can be read in greater detail in *Witness* (Faith Publishing Company).

Chapter 14: Terelya was a very controversial figure, with a fiery temper and a strong preoccupation with politics. He was also immersed in Ukraine's tendency toward rumor and folklore. At times he could be very confusing, showing the intermingling of spiritual forces. But beneath that was a loving, suffering soul and tremendous courage. His mysticism was fascinating and often legitimate, when it was left pure, without his interpretations. One of his claims, to have spotted Raoul Wallenberg in 1970, contradicts the recent memoir of Stalinist henchman Pavel Sudoplatov, but Sudoplatov's credibility has been widely challenged. Nonetheless, I continue to use discretion with Terelya's various claims as well as his mysticism, for I have occasionally felt an intermingling of spirits. The visions, taken often as composites, are in the book *Witness.* The Terelya visions referred to here occurred not only during the 1972 episode but also in 1970 and then in 1987. For flying saucers in the Soviet Union, see *UFOs From Behind The Iron Curtain,* by Ion Hobana and Julien Weverbergh. Once more, I take certain information from *UFO Encyclopedia* and other similar information from a reservoir of books too numerous to list, going back to childhood. It was said there had been poltergeist activity in a hotel room or rooms used during filming of *Close Encounter Of the Third Kind,* but this is not currently possible to confirm. At Roswell, they tried to claim that a disc had left wreckage that was thin and foil-like, yet exceedingly strong; also, a material that seemed like balsa wood but would not burn. This was in New Mexico in July 1947 and there are whole books about it, including *UFO Crash At Roswell,* by Kevin D. Randle and Donald R. Schmitt. I also consulted Jacques Vallee's *Revelations: Alien Contact and Human Deception.* On June 26, 1994, *The New York Times Magazine* wrote about a secret air base in Nevada, known as "Area 51," and rumors that scientists there were "'reverse engineering' one of the nine captured alien saucers housed there to learn exactly how its extraterrestrial power worked." *The Times* indicated the problems with such a seemingly outlandish claim, but added that the descriptions were "enticingly elaborate" and that the main claimant had pay documents showing he had worked at the base. The weirdest claim was that extraterrestrials controlled or at least communicated with Uri Geller, leaving him mechanical-sounding messages on a tape recorder. Geller had supposedly seen a UFO as a child. Again: deception? When I interviewed Geller in Manhattan in 1976, a very strange thing happened: a little rock that resembled a piece of a meteorite literally flew into the room and crashed onto his wood chess board, seemingly materializing out of nowhere. I believe it was poltergeist phenomena—not from Spectra or the Planet Hoova. UFOs often appear at "energy spots" so identified by dowsers, and they tend to mirror earth technology, or at least the futuristic imaginings of the day, appearing even with propellers during the airship wave of the 1890s (when this was the technology mankind could understand) and then later developing other capabilities, including far greater speeds and digital readouts, that our own air craft were developing—which indicated mimicry and deception. Those who promoted contact with extraterrestrials often had a New-Age edge, wearing pentagram-like pendants or other symbols of the occult. You can find ads for voodoo in the UFO magazines. They were sometimes sighted in areas where there had been cattle mutilations, the reports of which may have gone back to the 1890s. There were also the continued implications of reproductive manipulation and succubi or incubi. One investigator in the United Kingdom, Paul Devereux, linked UFO sightings with the occurrence of earthquakes. Proportionately, they also seemed linked to time, perhaps occurring with special activity at 3 a.m.—a time that, reversing the 3 p.m. on Good Friday, is considered by occultists who gather around that time for rituals as the "devil's hour." Clearly, the UFOs and their creatures were polymorphic: they could appear however they wanted to appear, changing from men to monsters. Some seemed Nordic. Some were the proverbial "little green men." Most were a sullen and unpleasant gray. Admitted one reputed UFO "investigator," Bill Cook, "the Grays could well be the demonic angels." He added that communications from these "entities" provided "much on the occult side. They claimed they had a lot to do with our religion. They spoke about witchcraft and cults on earth." One of the more credible and skeptical researchers, Dr. Jacques Vallee, a former principal investigator on Department of Defense computer networking projects, said there were 923 UFO landing reports by 1969 and since then, they have grown way beyond this early catalogue. "Therefore," he said in 1991, "the number of close encounters we need to explain is probably of the order of 50,000." His quote is taken from *Revelations*. By 1991 more than 600 people claiming to have been abducted had been interviewed by amateur and professional investigators, according to Vallee. By the way, he came to believe the UFO phenomenon went beyond simple parallels to fairies and angels. Walton's UFO, meanwhile, had looked like a large gold object at treetop level. Six others also witnessed the light, but only Travis was supposedly taken by the craft and subjected to a horrid experience with demon-looking creatures. The event was eventually made into a major movie called *Fire in the Sky*. There are huge questions about this event and its credibility. Arizona, I should point out, has more than its fair share of Indian burial mounds.

Chapters 15 & 16: The issue of *Christianity Today* was April 5, 1993, and the article was entitled "Rumors of Angels." Ann's angel account was printed in *Time* December 27, 1993. The girl falling down a ravine in Arizona was in *Ladies Home Journal*, December, 1992. See *The World and Work of the Holy Angels* by Father Robert J. Fox for the Pius XII remark. The Thomas and Basil quotes are from W. Doyle Gilligan's *Devotion to The Holy Angels*. See also Angelyn Ray's *Angels Ascending and Descending*, Father Pascal P. Parente's *Beyond Space*, and Gwen Shaw's Bible study on angels, entitled *Our Ministering Angels*. The California quake was February 9, 1971, and registered 6.6. Betty Malz's book was published by Chosen Books (a division of Baker Books) and is one of the few that properly balance angelic experiences with those of demons. She can be written at P.O. Box 564. Crystal Beach, Florida 34681. The Graham quotes are again from *Angels*.

Chapter 17: God's power is the umbrella power and it is over electromagnetism, gravity, nuclear forces, and all other natural energies. I saw the results of toxic contamination especially while researching *Laying Waste* and *The Toxic Cloud*. The Abraham account is always a bit confusing: two angels or three, with one seeming to *speak* for or take on the appearance of the Lord? Or was this a preincarnation appearance of Jesus, a theophany, as Billy Graham maintains? Or was the term "Lord" used in a way we don't understand? The information on Babylon and Nineveh can be found in the following: *Everyday Life in Babylon and Assyria,* by George Contenau (St. Martin's 1954); *Babylon Is Everywhere,* by Wolf Schneider (McGraw-Hill); *Babylon* by James G. Macqueen (Praeger 1965); *Nineveh and Its Remains,* by Austen Henry Layard (Praeger 1969); *Great Cities of the Ancient World,* by L. Sprague de Camp (Doubleday 1972); and *Mysteries of the Bible,* cited previously.

Chapters 18 & 19: The Hill quote comes from his erudite book, *Prophecy Past and Present,* published by Servant Publications, P.O. Box 8617, Ann Arbor, Michigan, 48107. I interviewed Sister Gwen Shaw, and draw the main quote from the interview. The quote on her healing and the other visions she reported come from her book *Unconditional Surrender,* distributed by End-Time Handmaidens, P.O. Box 447, Jasper, Arkansas 72641. Wilkerson's prophetic book *The Vision* was published by Spire Books. One quote is a composite. Wilkerson believed during the 1970s that "in the next decade, South America will become a powder keg, exploding in all directions"and in 1973 predicted that one-third of the United States would be declared a disaster area in the near future. The war he foresaw would cost 37 times as many lives as World War II. Hal Lindsay's major work was *The Late Great Planet Earth.* The DeMar quote is from *Last Days Madness* (Wolgemuth & Hyatt Publishers). I interviewed Ann Shields and was sent the Rome prophecies by a friend from the Albany area. The Duduman quotes come from his book, *Through the Fire Without Burning,* published in 1991 by Virginia Boldea Hand of Help Inc., P.O. Box 3494, Fullerton, California, 92634.

Chapters 20 & 21: The Akita quotes come from the excellent book *Akita* by Teiji Yasuda and made available in English by John Haffert and the 101 Foundation in Asbury, New Jersey 08802-0151. The account of the commissions comes from the 101 newsletter, volume 6, number 1. See *Our Lady of Fatima* by William Thomas Walsh for the best Fatima account. For the Ratzinger quotes see *The Ratzinger*

Report, by Vittorio Messori, available through Ignatius Press—another excellent book. The Gobbi quotes come from a book of his messages, *To the Priests, Our Lady's Beloved Sons,* available through the Marian Movement of Priests, P.O. Box 8, St. Francis, Maine, 04774-0008. Billy Graham's quote is from another of his books, *The Holy Spirit,* published by Word Publishers. The Terelya quotes are slightly abbreviated. Some of the Medjugorje messages are composite for reasons of simple facilitation.

Chapters 22, 23, & 24: I met five of the visionaries but only interviewed the three named Mirjana, Jacov, and Vicka in formal settings. The father of the seer Marija was the one who told me he saw an apparition of Jesus on Podbrdo hill back in the early days. The quote from Mirjana about God's love and the quote from Ivanka come from *Queen of the Cosmos* and *The Visions of the Children,* by Jan Connell. The pamphlet written by the Daughters of St. Paul is *'Neath St. Michael's Shield,* which I have cited above. Other material comes from personal interviews. I visited the cave of the archangel in 1991 and found it to be one of the most powerful places I have ever prayed at. It is only half an hour from San Giovanni Rotundo. Some of the NDEs indeed seemed like supernatural experiences, especially when the NDEers described the light as crystal clear, which reminded me of the angelic appearance to Lucia and her cousins in 1917; or, they saw deceased loved ones on a lush and meticulously kept pasture—as Sister Sasagawa saw a spirit in 1969 on a beautiful field. Betty Eadie's book was published by Gold Leaf Press. She also saw that the angels knew everyone by name, watched our every more, and arrived by the hordes when they were called. Every single person, in the sight of Heaven, is precious and carefully watched over. Although Betty stayed away from particulars, she hinted, both in her book and our conversation, that she had been left with a sense of urgency about what is now transpiring on earth and what will come in the future. But she showed no fear. "Fear is like walking in mud up to your neck," she said, when we spoke by phone, adding that mankind is now in a period of "rest" and spiritual awakening. "This is the time to awaken," she emphasized. "We all have our part and should be intensely busy at it."

Some claimed her book was at odds with doctrine about the Trinity and had New Age or Mormon elements. There were many NDEs that troubled me. I interviewed one man who I felt was the victim of demonic deception, as always there is deception in spiritual phenomena. It was not only the New Age approach to some of them—with no Godly judgment—but also the similarity they bore to UFO "abductions." I recall one such abductee who had claimed in 1974 that she was taken over a "crystal city"—like the crystal buildings certain NDEers mentioned—and heard "the voice of God." She also saw beings who, far from heavenly, resembled reptiles. Many UFO abductees and NDEers return, notes researcher Nelson Pacheco, "with a psychospiritual transformation that causes them to proselytize in the name of ecology and universal love. Although both of these are important and noble concepts, there is a subtle underlying assumption that is not often noted. This is the assumption that traditional belief systems are bankrupt and that mankind's salvation will come from 'space brothers' and 'beings of light' that come in the name of ecology and universal brotherhood—even if their methods are repulsive (e.g. UFO abductions and negative NDEs) or free of moral concerns (such as the unconditionally loving beings of light)." Moreover, certain NDE researchers have wandered off into occult areas such as spirit communication, reincarnation, and out-of-body experiences. Pacheco's information is in his book *Unmasking the Enemy,* cited previously. I recommend this book highly for those interested in diabolical deception. I interviewed my first and only NDEers in 1975 while a newspaper reporter. However, I have casually met a number of people who have shared such experiences since, including a monk at Gethsemani Trappist Monastery in Kentucky.

Chapter 25: That at least a number of UFO sightings were lying satanic wonders—fallen angels—seemed confirmed by the fact that one UFO contactee referred to his "extraterrestrial" as "Semjase," which seemed awfully similar to the name "Semyaza," a fallen angel and worker of darkness according to Mideast literature. ("One of our concerns," said this spaceman, "is aimed at your religions and the detrimental effect they have on the development of the human spirit.'') In the Dead Sea scrolls is an awful vision received by Amram, father of Moses, of an entity—Melkiresha, the "ruler of darkness"—who was remarkably similar to "aliens" described by UFO abductees such as Betty Hill. In the 15th century a French calendar known as the *Kalendrier des Bergiers* depicted devils piercing their victims' abdomens with what looked like long needles, resembling the "medical examination" given to Hill aboard a "flying saucer." As for Kibeho, this comes from a translation circulated by a devoted Mariologist named John Haffert. Because they are translations, I have brushed up some of the syntax and, as with Medjugorje, used composite quotes. I interviewed Jim Bramlett and also quoted a newsletter he sent me. The Otis quotes are from his book, *The Last of the Giants,* published by Chosen Books and a solid effort at research. His organization, The Sentinel Group, can be reached at P.O. Box 6334, Lynnwood, Washington, 98036. For references on biblical prophecy see *Armageddon, Oil and the Middle East Crisis* by John F. Walvoord, as well as his *Major Bible Prophecies.* See too, Grant Jeffrey's *Armageddon, Appointment With Destiny* and *Apocalypse.*

Chapter 26: The information on the *Jesus* film project, as well as the quote from Eshelman, come from his book, *I Just Saw Jesus,* available through The Jesus Film Project, Campus Crusade for Christ, P.O. Box 7690, Laguna Niguel, California, 92607-7690. By the way, Bradshaw was one who wasn't convinced there was an increase in supernatural reports from Africa. He saw things more in psychological terms and as a case of better reporting. The Chavda quotes on the sorcerer's tree are from his book *Only Love Can Make a Miracle,* published by Servant Publications, P.O. Box 8617, Ann Arbor, Michigan 48107. The Derstine quote is from *Fire Over Israel,* published by Treasure House in Shippensburg, Pennsylvania. The pamphlet explaining feasts is "God's Festivals and Holy Days," published by the Worldwide Church of God, original texts in first five chapters by Herbert W. Armstrong.

Chapter 27: Strieber's account is taken from *Angels and Aliens,* by Keith Thompson (who also provides information on the French calendar) and from a reading years ago of

Strieber's book *Communion,* a book I did not choose to allow to remain in my apartment. Elsewhere: Duduman's book of prophecy is now published by Virginia Boldea, Hand of Help, P.O. Box 3494, Fullerton, California 92634. As for AIDS, New York State had 2,479 cases in 1985 compared with 8,210 nationally, and 3,768 in 1986 compared with 13,147 nationally. The vast majority of cases were in New York City. By 1993 it was suspected that 200,000 or more in New York City were infected with HIV.

Chapters 28 & 29: The McIlhenny information on homosexuality is from his book *When the Wicked Seize a City,* published by Huntington House, P.O. Box 53788, Lafayette, Louisiana, 70505, or calling 1-800-749-4009. I highly recommend McIlhenry's book. Wilkerson's quotes are from his newsletter or his book, *The Vision.* The newsletter is issued by World Challenge, P.O. Box 260, Lindale, Texas, 75771. For more on paganism in Christianity, see Donna Steichen's well-researched book, *Ungodly Rage,* published by Ignatius. Sister Gwen Shaw's publication is *End-Times Handmaidens Magazine* and is available by writing P.O. Box 447, Jasper, Arkansas, 72641.

Chapters 30, 31, 32 & 33: I visited Betania in 1991. For more about Terelya, see the book *Witness,* published by Faith Publishing Company, 1-800-576-6477 or P.O. Box 237 Milford, Ohio, 45150. I had a number of experiences around Terelya and when first I was traveling to see a woman who was connected to him—a meeting that set up our project—I nearly crashed into a car passing to my right but the accident was prevented when a force gripped the steering wheel and against my own strength—which was steering right—veered the car leftward and out of danger. I had not seen the passing automobile. The Gobbi quotes come again from previously cited *To the Priests, Our Lady's Beloved Sons.* For Masonry see *En Route to Global Occupation,* by Gary H. Kah (Huntington House) and Pat Robertson's *The New World Order.* While 110 died in the crash foreseen by Singer, a phenomenal 186 lived. For Singer's messages from the Lord, contact the Ave Maria Centre of Peace, P.O. Box 489, Station U, Toronto, Canada M8Z 5Y8. Certain details on Tan were provided by Jim Bramlett.

Chapters 34, 35, 36, 37 & 38: The July 26, 1994, issue of *The New York Times Magazine* had a horrendous photo of bondage, as an example of lewdness in the mainstream media. Some of the information on the Buffalo abortion chronology came from John McTernan's article in *End-Time Handmaidens Magazine,* February 1994 issue, P.O. Box 447, Jasper, Arkansas 72641.

Chapters 39 & 40: Much is taken from news clips from *The New York Times, The New York Post, USA Today,* and AP and Reuters. Raphael is also one of the angels mentioned but not in all versions of the Bible. His appearance is in the Book of Tobit. My information on Gabriel comes largely from the extensive and useful reference book *A Dictionary of Angels* by Gustav Davidson (Free Press, 1967). As for the Gospel "nearly" being preached to all nations, when I spoke to Dr. David Barrett, who works at the headquarters of the Southern Baptist Foreign Mission Board in Richmond, Virginia, and is widely acknowledged as a foremost expert on missions and Church growth. He calculated that 1.5 billion of the world 5.7 or so billion have still not been evangelized, especially in Central Asia and Arab nations. That is roughly 3,000 of the 12,000 different peoples or "linguistic groups" in the world who have not yet been reached. The largest concentration is from Morocco to Mongolia, Kazakhstan to Indonesia. In the parlance of missionaries this general area, which includes India and many former republics of the Soviet Union, is known as the "10/40 Window" (because of its latitudes) and stretches to Japan, North Korea, and China's outlying provinces. According to Barrett, 95 percent of the world's unreached people are in this target area. There are still about fifty nations where it is not possible to reside and preach. While at the historical pace it may take a long time to reach the remaining fifth of the world's population, it has been a strange century, concedes Barrett, and broadcasting is one example of an evangelical "surprise."